The Utes
a forgotten people

The Utes
a forgotten people

Wilson Rockwell

WESTERN REFLECTIONS PUBLISHING COMPANY®

Montrose, CO

Library of Congress Publication Data
Rockwell, Wilson
The Utes: A Forgotten People
Includes Index

Library of Congress Catalog Card Number 98-060766

ISBN 13: 978-1-890437-23-7
ISBN 10: 1-890437-23-9

Third Edition
Printed in the United States of America

Cover design: Marti Ottinger

Western Reflections Publishing Company®
219 Main Street
Montrose, CO 81401
www.westernreflectionspub.com

To my wife, Enid Rockwell

TABLE OF CONTENTS

TABLE OF ILLUSTRATIONS

BACKGROUND

When the first white pioneers entered what is now the state of Colorado, they found three principal Indian tribes living in the territory. These were the Arapahoes and Cheyennes, who inhabited the plains region of the Eastern Slope of Colorado, and the Utahs, or Utes, who lived west of the Continental Divide.

The Utes were the oldest residents of Colorado with the Arapahoes and Cheyennes following in the order named.[1] Other so-called plains Indians who resided in Colorado Territory or visited the region to hunt were the Kiowas, Comanches, Sioux and Pawnees. All of these tribes, like the Arapahoes and Cheyennes, were deadly enemies of the Utes.

The Utes were generally on friendly terms with their Indian neighbors to the west and northwest—namely, the Snakes, Shoshoni, Bannocks and Piutes. To the south in the present state of New Mexico lived the Navajos and Apaches, who were unfriendly except for the Jicarilla Apaches with whom the Utes occasionally intermarried.[2]

The Utes were short, hardy, and muscular with a tendency toward portliness around middle age. They were so dark skinned that the other tribes referred to them as the "black Indians." They belonged to the Shoshonean speaking peoples, which included the Piute, Shoshoni, the Hopi of Arizona, and certain California tribes.

The tribe was divided into a loose confederation of seven bands. In the extreme southwestern part of Colorado lived the Southern Utes, who numbered about 1000 Indians.[3] They consisted of three bands—the Weeminuche band, the Mouache band and the Capote band.

North of the Southern Utes in the west central portion of the state dwelt the Tabeguache (pronounced Tabewatch) or Uncompahgre band, which comprised around 3000 people.[4]

In northwestern Colorado roamed the Northern Utes, who were divided into three bands which became known as the Grand River, Yampa, and Uintah bands. Numerically speaking, the Northern Utes were probably a little larger than the Tabeguache band.[5] The seven bands never exceeded 10,000.[6] Today the total number is only around 3000 due to depopulation of the seven bands by sickness and epidemics after their confinement to reservations and disruption of their natural way of life.

The seven bands were not limited to the Western Slope of Colorado, which was their principal habitat; but they wandered to some extent throughout all of the mountainous areas of the state, as well as northeastern Utah, northwestern New Mexico and northeastern Arizona.

They were an isolated, peaceful tribe so far as the white race was concerned. Consequently, unlike the war-like plains Indians, historians have neglected the Utes and know little about them except for the several treaties which they made with the federal government.

FOOTNOTES

[1]Leroy R. and Ann W. Hafen, *Colorado*, p. 52.

[2]Frank Hall, *History of the State of Colorado*, Vol. 4, p. 59.

[3]Ralph Linton, *Acculturation in Seven American Indian Tribes*, p. 126.

[4]Ernest Ingersoll, *Knocking Around the Rockies*, p. 88.

[5]Estimates as to the population of the various bands differ quite extensively. Frank S. Byers, son of the first permanent settler in Grand County, wrote, for example, that when the whites first came into the Colorado Territory there were about 1000 Tabeguache

Utes and 1500 Northern Utes. *Rocky Mountain News,* Denver, Colo., June 26, 1923.

[6]Albert N. McCall, "An Outline of Ute Indian Culture," *The Ute Indians of Southwestern Colorado,* p. 97.

EARLY HISTORY AND DEVELOPMENT

Prior to 1640 when the Utes first began to come in contact with the Spaniards of New Mexico, the seven bands were broken up into small family units for the greater portion of the year. Economic restrictions prevented them from gathering in bands or large groups for any length of time since it took a big area at that period to support a few people. The Utes had no horses, no knowledge of farming, and their crude weapons were made entirely of stone. The struggle for survival was, consequently, a hard one, and each family unit was given plenty of room to provide for itself a meager livelihood.

Each family usually followed a known circuit during the different seasons of the year so that no others of the band infringed upon its right to a certain hunting ground or berry patch which had been established by long usage. Each unit of the band was so familiar with the various locations of other families that when a medicine man was needed, there was no difficulty in finding him; and when danger threatened from the Kiowas, Cheyennes, Arapahoes, or other tribes of the plains, messengers were sent to all camps in the locality urging fellow tribesmen to gather temporarily in order to defend themselves. Defensive leadership at this early time was casual and temporary.[1]

Occasionally a family unit was no larger than a man and his wife who preferred to live alone, but, more generally, a couple lived with the parents of either spouse who most needed their aid and with whom they were most congenial. Those in control of the family unit were the older relatives, and since each household usually had some member of the grandparental generation, Ute children showed more respect to their older relatives than to their parents.

Late in the fall the various family groups moved out of the mountains to open sheltered areas for the winter months.[2] The Southern Utes wintered in the extreme southwestern part of Colorado and in northwestern New Mexico and northeastern Arizona. The Tabeguache or Uncompahgre band spent the winters along the Uncompahgre and Gunnison rivers between the present towns of Montrose and Grand Junction, and the Northern Utes sought similar protection along the White, Green and Colorado rivers. In so migrating the Utes followed the southward movement of deer and antelope, which provided them with meat and hides during their winter's hibernation.

In the early spring members of each of the seven bands assembled for the Bear Dance, the most ancient and typical dance of the Ute Indians. Then, after a short period of social contact and festivities during which many marriages took place, the families departed on their separate ways to their spring and summer hunting grounds.

Between 1630 and 1640 the Utes began coming in contact with the Spaniards, who were settling to the south of them in the present state of New Mexico.[3] Early Spanish relations with the Utes were peaceful. Trading flourished, the Utes exchanging meat and hides for agricultural products. A new item of trade was the horse. Often the price of a horse was too high in meat and hides; so the Utes started trading their children for horses. The Spaniards usually trained these Indian children to be sheep and cow herders at which they became very proficient.[4]

The introduction of the horse gave the Utes their first opportunity to more successfully hunt buffalo in the plains country of the Eastern Slope of Colorado. The buffalo soon became their chief economic resource, providing tepee covers, blankets, sinew thread, bowstrings, horn glue, skin bags, moccasins, and meat in greater quantities than the Utes had ever known. The horse also permitted them to make hasty withdrawals from dangerous enemy country and provided the means for transporting supplies back to central camp sites.

Where formerly the Utes scattered out thinly over the land in order to assure each family sufficient territory for an adequate supply of food and other necessities, the coming of the horse made it possible for the various family units to gather in large numbers under powerful chiefs or war leaders.

The bands still spent their summers in the mountains of western Colorado and the San Luis Valley, but now they did not linger long for the fall antelope and deer drives. They hastily completed these hunts and then continued on for buffalo in the plains country, where they now found their chief source of livelihood.

On these buffalo hunts they came in frequent contact with the hostile Arapahoes, Kiowas, Cheyennes, Sioux, and Comanches, who were rich in horses. The horse, which had first been obtained in peaceful trade with the Spaniards, was now sought in enemy territory. From a peaceful, withdrawn society of small family units, the newly consolidated Utes became warlike and aggressive.

The fall buffalo hunts under the authority of a band leader were usually preceded by two scouts. Once in the plains country, a hunting party was often changed to a raiding expedition or war party as opportunity offered. When camps of plains Indians were sighted, warriors were sent to cut the picketed horses from the center of the enemy villages and drive away as many as possible.

By 1675 when the Spanish governor Otermin first entered into the treaties with the Utes,[5] the transformation of their economic and social life was completed. From small family groupings dominated by the older and more experienced relatives in each camp, the Utes were consolidated into larger bands under the control of powerful war leaders. In place of the family hunting and foraging unit, a new cooperative group emerged where food was shared and where the buffalo hunt as a communal enterprise gradually overshadowed the earlier temporary gatherings for antelope, deer, and rabbit drives. The rare expeditions on foot of these small family groups to the plains in search of buffalo disappeared altogether and were replaced by the equestrian hunting party, a function of the band.

Whereas the social life of each band as a whole had taken place for only a short time in March when the various families gathered together for the Bear Dance, social activities became a year-around procedure, made possible by the centralized population.

Organized buffalo hunts and horse raids in enemy territory became the chief objectives of the seven bands since the centralized populations needed a uniform food supply and horses, which made a steady yield of buffalo meat possible.[6]

While not supplanting the authority of older relatives within the family circle, the band leaders or chiefs directed communal enterprises such as camp movements, hunts, raids, war parties and dances.

The authority of the band leaders did not extend beyond communal activities. In all affairs respecting individuals, the family group continued as the controlling unit. In thievery, for example, the matter was called to the attention of an older relative of the culprit, who took disciplinarian action against the thief and returned the stolen property.[7] In adultery, the families concerned had to work out the problem among them selves; and even in more serious crimes, like murder, it was left to the family to punish the criminal.

From 1630 to 1700 the seven bands of the Ute confederation enjoyed a comparatively peaceful period of consolidation and transformation from family units to warlike bands. During the 1700's the expanding Ute tribe engaged in many successful wars with the plains Indians. This century marked the zenith of Ute strength and glory.[8]

Scouts always preceded a returning war party to notify the camp of success or failure. Then, anyone wishing to welcome back the warriors rode out to praise those bringing home the loot. The returning braves usually reciprocated by handing out presents to those who came to greet them.

At the scalp dance, which took place the next afternoon, more gifts were bestowed. Warriors already well supplied with meat and horses often kept only the scalps that they had taken, giving their loot to other members of the band who were in need.

Consequently, warfare became a means of benefiting the entire tribe. Where formerly war had been merely a defense of one's kin in widely scattered family camps, now it became an important means of subsistence for the band. Gift led to return gift, and enemy horses, clothing, pipes, arrows, bows, and camp equipment were, as a general rule, distributed evenly throughout the band.

The women played an important part in this warfare. During raids in enemy territory, they kept the camp equipment in readines for a fast withdrawal. During fights in home territory, the older women, armed and wearing headdresses, followed the men into battle in order to scalp and obtain clothing and other loot from the bodies of the fallen enemy. Scalps taken in this manner were sewn on the shirts of male relatives, while other equipment was distributed at victory celebrations.

Squaws who participated in such raids took part in the parades around the band's camp, following the warriors who rode horseback. The Lame Dance, for women only, sprang up to symbolize in its peculiar step the difficulty of carrying back home the great weight of loot.

FOOTNOTES

[1]Ralph Linton, *Acculturation In Seven American Indian Tribes,* pp. 125-127.

[2]*Ibid.,* p. 124.

[3]*Ibid.,* p. 157.

[4]*Ibid.,* p. 159

[5]*Ibid.,* p. 156.

[6]*Ibid.,* p. 163.

[7]*Ibid.,* p. 169.

[8]*Ibid.,* pp. 172-173.

LEGENDS

For centuries the radioactive springs at the present site of Hot Sulphur Springs in Grand County belonged to the Utes. The only practical place of entry to Grand County from the east was over what is now known as Arapaho Pass. The Utes put up miles of stone earthworks here to keep the plains Indians from crossing over into their territory.

Ancient Ute forts have also been found a short distance southeast of the present town of Granby, situated ten miles east of Hot Sulphur Springs, and on Williams Fork about twelve miles southwest of the springs.[1]

The fortification near Granby was built of stone with log uprights, and the walls were still well preserved as late as 1939 when a collector of arrowheads tore them down. High rocky bluffs, forming a natural barrier, served as one side of the fort.[2]

According to Ute Indian folklore and records learned from such leading Northern Ute chiefs as Douglass, Yarmony, and Washington, most of the great Indian battles in Grand County were fought in the early eighteen hundreds. Consequently, it is assumed that the Ute forts in this area were constructed about this period.

The Utes have a legend concerning Hot Sulphur Springs. They claim that long before the coming of the white men a party of Ute Indians, consisting of an elderly chief and a group of young warriors, camped by the springs. The younger men wanted to cross over the divide to obtain scalps, horses, and plunder from the plains Indians. However, the wise old chief advised against it, saying that they were too few in number to successfully oppose their warlike enemies of the plains.

However, youth had its way, and the next morning the younger Utes started off on their mission of conquest. As they left, the older man said that he would await them at the springs. He built a camp fire in a little gulch on Mount Bross a short distance away and waited for the return of his comrades. But the young warriors never came back, and the old chief grieved himself to death. From this time on according to the Utes, the sorrowing chief's old camp fire has warmed the springs and given the water healing properties.[3]

The Utes made many pilgrimages to Hot Sulphur Springs in quest of health. At one time Chief Ouray, who was suffering from an acute attack of rheumatism, made the journey over from his home on the Uncompahgre near present Montrose. He rode on a litter swung between two horses in tandem fashion. After bathing in the warm water he was able to mount a horse and ride home.

About twenty miles northeast of Hot Sulphur Springs is Grand Lake, source of the Colorado River. White pioneers seldom saw a Ute Indian in this area since the Utes had a superstitious fear of this lake, based on another legend.

One summer day, according to this legend, a group of Utes were camped on the shores of Grand Lake. While they were performing their routine tasks, a band of Arapahoe and Cheyenne Indians, who had been raiding North Park (Jackson County), crossed Willow Creek Pass into Middle Park and made a surprise attack.[4] The Ute scouts, stationed on what is now known as Lookout Point, failed to see the approaching enemy, and the Utes were caught completely by surprise.

The men barely had time to get their women and children on a large raft before the fighting was in full progress. The women, using poles, pushed the raft into the middle of the lake out of harm's way.

While the battle raged, one of those strong, freakish winds which occasionally hits Grand Lake suddenly came roaring down the valley and caused great waves to rise on the lake. The raft capsized and everyone on it perished in the turbulent, icy water. The hard-pressed Utes eventually won the fight, but the warriors left alive were bereft of their families.

After that tragic occurrence, the Utes avoided Grand Lake, believing it to be haunted by the spirits of the men, women, and children who died there at that time.

The Arapahoes do not recall this Ute legend, but they tell of another battle fought near the lake in more recent times.[5]

A large number of Araphoes once camped several miles above Grand Lake on a hunting expedition. One of them met a white trapper in the vicinity, who told him that some Utes had set up their tepees beside the lake.

The trapper agreed to lead the plains Indians down to attack the Utes. The fight started in what is now known as Sagebrush Flats. The Utes, taken by surprise, retreated southward to the low ridge which borders the north side of the lake. They were driven along this ridge and on up the slope of Echo Mountain (now called Shadow Mountain).

The Ute fatalities were small. One man was killed at the foot of Echo Mountain, and two squaws and a baby met death part way up. The papoose was discovered hanging in a tree, his mother apparently having become too exhausted to carry him farther. The Arapahoes had no way of caring for the child; so they killed him.[6]

The Arapahoes also had a legendary fear of Grand Lake. During an unusually cold winter the lake was completely frozen over except for a small pool of water in the center. In visiting the region the Arapahoes noticed the tracks of many buffalo on the snow which covered the ice. The hoof prints of one were much larger than the others, and it seemed to come from the middle of the lake and return there. The Indians, therefore, concluded that some gigantic, supernatural buffalo lived in the lake. Because of this tradition, the Arapahoes often referred to Grand Lake as the "Spirit Lake."

About fifty miles east of Durango in Archuleta County lies Pagosa Hot Springs. "Pagosha" is a Ute word meaning "healing waters."

For a long time the Navajos contested the Utes' claim to
Pagosa Springs, and many skirmishes took place there. In 1866
the dispute culminated in a terrific struggle between the rival
tribes. The two sides were so evenly matched that the battle
became stalemated.

Finally, the war leaders held a conference and agreed that,
rather than annihilate all their warriors, each tribe should
select a representative to settle the matter in personal combat.
The Navajos chose from their number such a giant of a man
that the Utes had difficulty in finding a volunteer to go up
against him. But after long deliberation Colonel Albert
Pfeiffer, a white man who had been adopted into the Ute
tribe, offered to champion the Ute's cause provided that each
contestant go into combat stark naked and armed only with a
bowie knife.

The Navajo accepted these conditions, and the two men
stripped down. As the combatants cautiously approached one
another, the chances of the slight, wiry white man looked small
indeed against his massive opponent.

Just before the two champions reached each other, Pfeiffer
suddenly hurled his bowie knife into the Navajo's chest. Aston-
ishment replacing confidence on the big Indian's face, the giant
toppled forward and died at his victim's feet.

The Navajos, certain of victory, were taken aback at this unexpected turn of events, but, true to their agreement, they retired from the field of battle and never again contested the
Ute's right to Pagosa Springs.[7]

Albert Henry Pfeiffer, who won the springs for the Utes, was
born in Scotland in 1822.. He came to the United States when
he was twenty-two. He worked his way westward to Santa Fe,
New Mexico, where he was appointed captain of the mounted
militia in 1859. His wife, a Spanish girl, was killed by the
Indians four years later. Pfeiffer was a life-long friend of Kit
Carson and served several years in his regiment in the Navajo
country. In 1865 he was promoted to a lieutenant colonel for
meritorious service. After serving a brief time as assistant Indian agent in New Mexico, he staked out a ranch near Granger,

Colorado. The Utes liked him so well that they adopted him into their tribe, giving him the name of "Tata"[8] Pfeiffer.

FOOTNOTES

[1]"Early State History to be Portrayed by Indians in Pageant of Progress," *Rocky Mountain News,* Denver, June 26, 1923.

[2]Charles H., Leckenby, *The Tread of Pioneers.*

[3]*Rocky Mountain News, op. cit.*

[4]Mary Lyons Cairns, *The Pioneers,* pp. 25-27.

[5]*Ibid.,* pp. 75-77.

[6]Some believe that this battle is the Arapahoe version of the Ute legend since there are some parallels. However, mention of the white trapper in the Arapahoe account places the fight at a more recent date than the battle told about by the Utes.

[7]Josie M. Crum, "The Winning of the Spring," *Pioneers of the San Juan, Vol. I,* p. 130.

[8]Ute word for "father," according to Wilson Johnson, a member of the Ute tribe at the Uintah and Ouray Reservation.

DANCES

The Utes were great lovers of dancing. They danced just before and immediately after moving to a new camp ground. Dances preceeded and followed war raids. Each spring they staged their festive Bear Dance, and in June they held their most popular dance of all—the Sun Dance.

The Bear Dance[1] is the most ancient and typical of the Ute dances.[2] Among the drawings made by forgotten peoples on the bluffs and in the standstone caves along the south side of the Uinta Mountains in Utah are many portrayals of the Bear Dance in ancient times. Some of the petroglyphs show a bear dancing with a man drawn in the manner of the early Ute artist. Others portray a bear dancing with the square shouldered man of the Fremont period. Still others depict a bear dancing with a round-bodied man, a culture that was contemporary with the Pueblo-cliffhouse era.

The Ute myth concerning the origin of the Bear Dance has the usual beginning of a man going to sleep and having a dream. This man dreamed that if he went to a certain place in the mountains he would see a bear. It was in the spring of the year when the snow was melting, and the bears were just starting to awaken from their winter hibernation. The Ute went to the spot he had dreamed about, and there he discovered a bear shuffling forward and backward in a form of dance. The bear taught the Indian how to do this dance and how to sing for it.

Then he told the Ute to return to his people and teach them how to do the Bear Dance.

So, every spring from time immemorial when the bears start emerging from their winter sleep, each of the seven bands of the Ute tribe dances the Bear Dance, which has no significance other than being a festive occasion. Unlike most of the Ute dances, it is held only once a year.

The dance takes place in a large circular space, surrounded by upright poles between which willows or tree branches are woven horizontally. The entrance is on the east side of the enclosure while on the west side a large hole, or bear den, is dug about five feet long, two feet wide, and two feet deep. Over this hole is placed a resonator, which was formerly a large shallow basket. In recent times, however, a piece of zinc is more often used.

Five or six Ute musicians squat around this resonator, and each places the end of a long, slightly curved notched stick, known as a morache, on it. Another much shorter stick or a bone is used to rub over the notches of the morache, producing a very rapid reverberation. The musicians sing as they saw back and forth on their moraches.

The dancers, dressed in their best finery, assemble in the enclosure, the women gathering on the south side while the men congregate on the north side.

When the dance starts, the squaws walk over to where the men are grouped and select their partners by waving or pointing toward whomever they wish to dance with. Two bashful young girls, for example, often walk hand-in-hand up to two boys who are sitting together and motion to them. The men completely ignore the women and continue on with their conversation as if nothing was happening. After designating their choice of partners the women line up in the middle of the lodge and join hands.

As soon as the music and chanting begin, the men walk up to the squaws who have chosen them and also grasp hands. The two lines, which face each other, start moving forward and backward in time to the music. The dance step consists of two bold steps forward and three mincing steps backward. Thus, as the men go forward, the women retreat, and as the women advance the men retreat.

The Bear Dance lasts for three days and three nights. Occasionally the couples take hold of each others' arms and sway their bodies for a few minutes in rhythm without going forward or backward. Then, they again join hands with the members of their line and continue the step.

On the final day of the dance novelties are sometimes introduced, such as a man disguising himself as a bear and chasing some squaw around the lines of dancers. If any onlooker laughs at the antics of either, the man dressed as a bear runs ferociously toward the new victim and pretends to scratch him.

If anyone falls from exhaustion or a misstep during the marathon, the music stops and a medicine man treats the dancer. Placing the lower end of a morache, which he borrows from one of the singers, against the fallen figure, the medicine man saws rapidly up and down on it with the rubbing stick or bone. He begins at the dancer's feet and keeps repeating the process until the head is reached. Then he points the morache toward the sky and rubs the smaller stick upward over it as if brushing away into the air the evil spirit which has collected on the morache. Sometimes several of these treatments are necessary before the prostrate figure regains his wind and is ready to go on with the dance.

The dance procedure changes on the last day. The line of women stop the retreating step and start pushing their partners backward. When the squaws finally succeed in pushing all of the men across the enclosure up to the north wall, the dance is over.

It is timed so that it ends at high noon of the third day, and the dance is followed by a big feast for the remainder of the afternoon.

The Lame Dance originated when the Utes consolidated into well organized bands and started making raids on the plains Indians for horses and loot. It is danced only by women after the return of a war party to camp and symbolizes the difficulty of carrying the heavy burden of loot.[3] In the early days it was not uncommon for as many as a hundred women to take part in the dance.

Two parallel lines were formed by the dancers about thirty feet apart, the dancers of each line standing one behind the other and facing toward the west. Standing in front of the women and facing them were the drummers, usually four in number, and behind the drummers was a line of men singers.[4]

The squaws danced forward, dragging their right feet as though carrying a heavy load. Upon nearing the four drummers, the leaders of each line turned and shuffled toward each other until they nearly met. They then moved away from the drummers and danced side by side in the opposite direction from which they started, the other dancers following them and forming another double line.

The Scalp Dance originated at about the same time as the Lame Dance. A returned war party usually started off the celebration by parading around the camp on the morning after their arrival. In this parade the warriors, mounted on horses, carried the scalps on poles or fastened to their bridles. All wore their best attire, and it was customary for some of the horsemen to have women riding behind. The two leaders of the parade rode at the head of the procession and accompanied their songs by pounding on hand drums.

The Scalp Dance began in the late afternoon and came to a close right after dark. The singers and drummers stood in a line facing the east, the drummers occupying the center of the line. Two circles of women dancers, one circle being within the other, stood in front of the musicians. The inner circle moved with the sun (counter clockwise) while the outer circle danced in the opposite direction (clockwise). Each circle had a leader, who wore a feather war bonnet. The women carried scalps, but only the leader of the inner circle, who was the wife of a chief, was permitted to carry a scalp on a pole.[5]

The body of a wounded or dead warrior was often placed in the center of the dancing circle, and his wounds were washed while certain songs were sung.

When the Scalp Dance was concluded, the scalps were usually

taken to the chief of the band, who attached them to the tops of the tall poles of his tepee.

The Dragging Feet Dance, danced by both men and women, was a social dance held after a Scalp Dance. The dancers moved sideways with the sun, one foot being advanced sideways and the other lifted and placed beside it.[6]

The Deer or Tea Dance was an old social dance of the Utes. In this dance the men joined the squaws in a version of "ring-around-a-rosie." Unlike the Bear Dance, which occurred only once a year, the Utes had many Deer Dances.[7]

Both sexes participated in the Double Dance, which also was started in ancient times. It resembled the Bear Dance in that the dancers stood in two lines facing each other. Men and women did not alternate in these lines but stood in any convenient order. During the old days these lines were often thirty or forty feet long. The dance step consisted of the two lines alternately advancing and retreating about four steps so that while one line went forward the other stepped backward.[8]

Men and women both took part in the old Iron Line Dance, standing alternately in a dancing circle. The movement of this dance was sideways toward the sun, the dancers passing one foot either over or behind the other flat on the ground. All of the participants sang, and some of the men beat on hand drums in accompaniment to the songs.[9]

Like the Scalp Dance, the War Dance was a victory dance of the Utes. Before the celebration, the men rubbed colored dirt, mixed with grease, on their bodies, while the women placed the scalp tropies on the ends of sticks. Several braves pounded on a drum and sang as the squaws daced back and forth in a line, waving the scalps in the air. At the same time the warriors jumped around in a circle, waving their war clubs. These war clubs were big rocks attached to the end of cords and resembled a hammer in the hammer-throw of a modern track meet.[10]

A dance which emerged with the gradual development of the band was the Round Dance to combat the spread of disease. The men, women, and children who participated danced sideways in a circle, moving clockwise. The medicine men, who stood in the center, sang and fanned the dancers as they passed with a wand made of eagle tail-feathers. The left side and then the right side of the dancers was fanned from head to foot. This treatment was designed to ward off sickness and to bring health and vigor to the dancers. Between songs a medicine man made a talk about coming illness and his attempts to drive it away.[11]

In recent times the Sun Dance has become the most popular dance of the Ute Indians and has tended to cause the abandonment of all other dances except the Bear Dance.

The Sun Dance was introduced to the Utes about 1902 by their former enemies, the Arapahoes.[12] It is usually held in June of each year at the full moon. The Utes believe that those who participate will be cured of any ailment they might have.

In preparation for the event the Sun Dance pole is cut. The fallen tree is stripped of bark and branches except for a short branch near the top to which some willows, a buffalo skull, a colored cloth, or other symbol is fastened. The sacred pole is then carried to the camp and placed upright in a hole. A shelter is built around it, consisting of twelve smaller forked poles with a long pole extending from each of the smaller poles to the Sun Dance pole.[13] A wall of brush about four feet high is then piled up between the twelve poles with the entrance on the east side. A large drum, which furnishes music for the occasion, is placed on the left side of the opening.

About ten or twelve dancers, with their nearly naked bodies painted in various designs, enter the lodge in the early evening to start the proceedings. Each dancer has a small brush booth built along the outer edge of the lodge which affords him privacy when he is not dancing.[14] The dance lasts four days and nights during which time the dancers stay in the lodge and abstain from food and water.

When the drumming and singing begin, the dancers, wearing nothing but breech clouts, step out from their booths and start hopping slowly toward the Sun Dance pole. As they progress, each dancer shakes rawhide rattles in both hands and blows on an eagle-bone whistle, to which is attached a white eagle plume.

Upon reaching the Sun Dance pole, the dancers hop slowly

backwards, always keeping their eyes riveted on the fork of the pole and shaking their rattles and blowing their whistles.

When they arrive at the entrance to their booths, the music ends with a high shrill note and the dancers get a few minutes rest. Before long one of them emerges from his booth and the singers and drummers again start the music. The various participants dance whenever they so desire and do not all dance at the same time. As the night progresses, bonfires are built to keep the enclosure warm.

FOOTNOTES

[1]Frances Densmore, *Northern Ute Music*, p. 56.

[2]J. Monaghan, *Moffat County Interviews*, Book I, 1933-34, C.W.A. Workers, pamphlet 356, Doc. 1-73 incl., pp. 96-99. In possession of State Historical Society of Colorado.

[3]Ralph Linton, *Acculturation in Seven American Indian Tribes*, p. 166.

[4]Densmore, *op cit.*, p. 105.

[5]*Ibid.*, pp. 152-156.

[6]*Ibid.*, p. 112.

[7]Monaghan, *op. cit.*, pp. 74-83.

[8]Densmore, *op. cit.*, p. 118.

[9]*Ibid.*, p. 119.

[10]Monaghan, *op. cit.*, pp. 74-83.

[11]Linton, *op. cit.*, p. 192.

[12]Densmore, *op. cit.*, pp. 79-80.

[13]Monaghan, *op. cit.*, pp. 96-99.

[14]Helen Sloan Daniels, "Sun Dancing by Moonlight," *The Ute Indians of Southwestern Colo.*, pp. 113-116.

CLOTHING, EQUIPMENT AND SHELTER

The Utes originally lived in tepees, covered at first with elk hide and then later with buffalo hides when they became available. Thatched dwellings, made by placing brush over a frame of poles and known as wickiups, were also commonly used during the summer.[1]

After 1868 when the Utes were placed on reservations, their tepees were made primarily of cotton cloth furnished by the government.[2] They were conical in shape and held up by poles meeting at the top, where the hide or cloth was fixed so as to make a flue in order to furnish a proper draft. A flap of hide or an old blanket on one side of the lodge was used to close a small opening which served as a door.

The cloth or hide which made up the tepee covering soon became discolored by smoke, the darker coloring being near the "flue" at the top and lighter gradations extending downward to the base. In addition to this natural and not unpleasing discoloration, tepees were often painted in bright colors about the doorways and around the base.

The ordinary dress of the men consisted of shirts or robes, leggings, breech-clouts, and moccasins. When on a war raid they wore nothing but breech-clouts and moccasins. They wore no head gear except for special dances or ceremonies at which times they donned elaborate feathered headdresses. They delighted in painting their bodies and faces. Their war paint was black and yellow.[3]

The women usually attired themselves in moccasins, leggings, and belted leather gowns which extended below the knees. The older women's dresses were often patched and black with grease or dirt. However, the younger women and the wives of the chiefs usually kept their clothing clean, white, and handsome.[4] Although the men wore no headdress except for special occasions, the women wore basket caps for everyday wear.

Clothing was made by the women from the dressed skins of buffalo cows, deer, antelope, elk, and mountain sheep. Sinew thread was used for sewing, and the hides were tanned and smoked so that they would not shrink and would soften after becoming wet.

Before the introduction of beads by the white traders, the moccasins, shirts, leggings, and dresses used in festivities were often fringed and tied with hair or small tanned skins, decorated with paint. Sometimes these garments were embroidered with porcupine quills dyed in brilliant colors.[5]

A favorite type of decoration for the women both in early and modern times was row after row of elk teeth couched upon the shoulder yoke and sleeves of the dresses. Intricate patterns of beads were also used to decorate their costumes after this type of ornament became known to them.

The summer moccasins of the Utes were made out of buffalo hide with the hair on the inside.[6]

The Utes never cut their hair but wore it bound up in two braids which hung on their chests. They were not prone to have whiskers and never shaved, although they occasionally plucked out the hairs on their faces.

Infants were carried in a cradle board, shaped much like a gravestone with sides tapering toward the bottom. A curved willow branch awning was placed above the baby's head to protect it from the sun. A beaded yoke or collar was fastened under its chin. On the left side of this collar and also attached to the cradle board was a heavily beaded, diamond shaped

Ute Indian drawings on split rock in Shavano Valley near Montrose. *Photo courtouresy Walker Art Studios.*

Ute picture rock at Shavano Valley about ten miles from Montrose. *Photo Courtesy Walker Art Studios.*

Decorated buffalo robe worn by Chief Colorow. *Photo by H. S. Poley. Courtesy of Denver Public Library Western Collection.*

Woven Indian water bottle, drum, pottery canteen—1895. *Photo by H. S. Poley. Courtesy of Denver Public Library Western Collection.*

Embroidered vest—1895. *Photo by H. S. Poley. Courtesy of Denver Public Library Western Collection.*

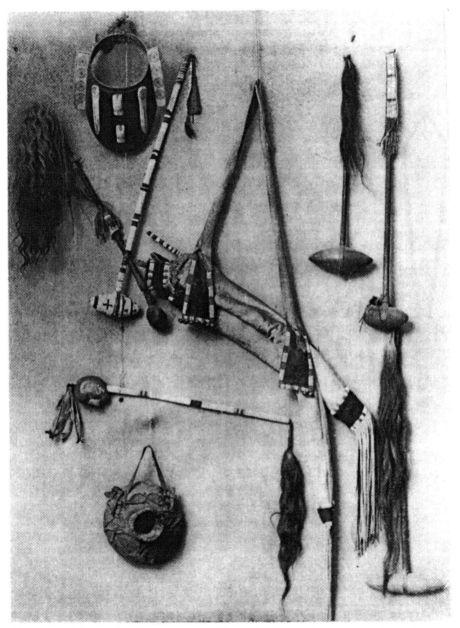

Ute war clubs, arrow holder, etc. *Photo by H. S. Poley. Courtesy of Denver Public Library Western Collection.*

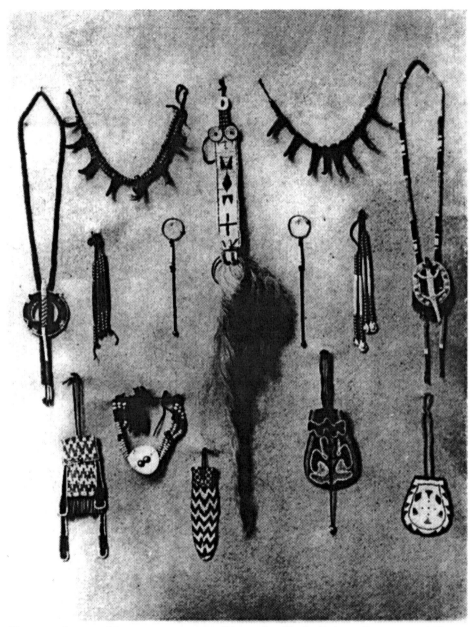

Ute pouches, necklaces, ornaments. *Photo by H. S. Poley. Courtesy of Denver Public Library Western Collection.*

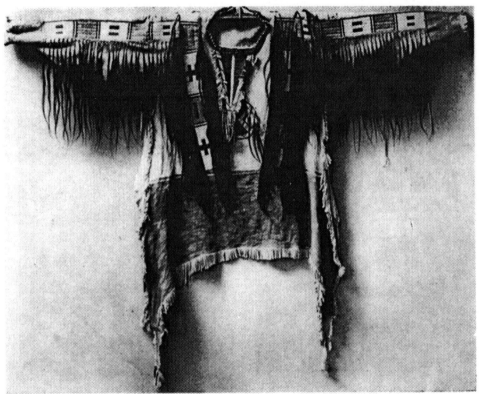

Ute embroidered buckskin coat and long hair decoration. *Photo by H. S. Poley.*
Courtesy of Denver Public Library Western Collection.

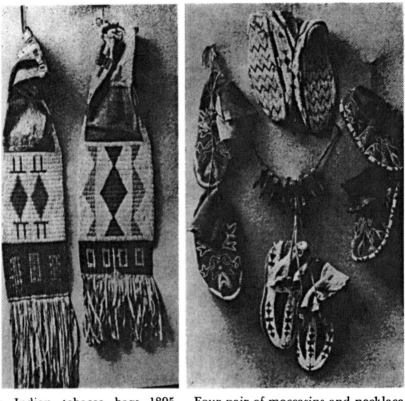

Two Indian tobacco bags—1895. *Photo by H. S. Poley. Courtesy of Denver Public Library Western Collection.*

Four pair of moccasins and necklace— 1895. Photo by H. S. Poley. *Courtesy of Denver Public Library Western Collection.*

buckskin bag, which contained the umbilical cord, saved from birth.

To throw away the navel cord or to forget to place it either in an ant hill or this buckskin bag tied to the cradle resulted, according to the Ute belief, in the child becoming foolish when he grew up. After the child has outgrown the board, this bag was worn around his neck on a leather string.

On the right side of the papoose board was often attached a toy, such as a ribbon or a little bell. The cradle board was carried by means of a broad strap across the mother's shoulders.

When the child was able to walk and had outgrown the cradle, the mother carried the infant upon her back within the folds of her shawl.[7]

Ute women made the clothing, provided the lodge and household utensils, cooked the meals, looked after the children, and did most of the work in moving camp. The men spent their time hunting, making raids in enemy territory, and fighting. They also made the weapons and ceremonial implements and conducted most of the ceremonies.

The bow and arrow was originally the Indian's most important weapon. It had a deadly range up to seventy yards, and a Ute hunter could shoot it about as rapidly as the average white man can shoot a revolver.[8]

The lance consisted of a shaft six or seven feet long, tipped with a sharp point of flint, iron, or steel. It was used both in war and when hunting buffalo. When in battle warriors sometimes carried shields made of dried bull-hide.

In riding horseback the Utes used a piece of rope, made of twisted hair from the horse or buffalo. This rope was tied about the horse's jaw. In battle or while hunting the Indians rode bareback, but they did have saddles which they used occasionally at other times.

One type of saddle was a flat buffalo-skin bag filled with grass or buffalo hair. This riding pad served as both blanket and saddle. Another common type of saddle was one that had a high cantel and pommel, the front and back being made of elk-horn prongs or forked sticks covered with rawhide.[9] The stirrups were short and made of wood, covered with fresh hide.

Indian saddles were often decorated with bead work and leather fringe.

In traveling the Utes used the "travois," which, like their riding equipment, was adopted from the plains Indians. The travois was made up of two long poles, the small ends of which crossed above the horse's shoulders and the large ends dragged behind on the ground. Two braces, placed several feet apart in back of the horse, held the poles apart. To these braces was attached a rawhide net capable of carrying several hundred pounds. On this wheelless wagon the Utes transported their camp equipment, tepee covers, buffalo robes, small children, and old and sick people.[10]

FOOTNOTES

[1]Frances Densmore, *Northern Ute Music,* p. 25.

[2]Ernest Ingersoll,, *Knocking Around the Rockies,* p. 97.

[3]J. Monaghan, *Moffat County Interviews,* Book I, 1933-34, CWA Workers, Pamphlet 356, Doc. 1-73 incl., pp. 74-83.

[4]Leroy R. and Ann W. Hafen, *Colorado,* p. 62.

[5]Helen Sloan Daniels, "Ute Costume," *The Ute Indians of Southwestern Colorado,* p. 118.

[6]Monaghan, *op cit.*

[7]Daniels, *op. cit.,* p. 90.

[8]Hafen, *op. cit.,* p. 63.

[9]*Ibid.,* p. 65.

[10]*Ibid.*

INDUSTRIES, FOOD, ORGANIZATION

The Utes made in limited quantities undecorated pottery of inferior quality. However, most of their pottery was obtained from the Jicarilla Apaches and the Pueblo Indians in New Mexico.

The Utes were more skilled in making baskets which they constructed from willows. The most characteristic of these was the water jug, which was an urn-shaped basket covered with a waterproof coating of pinon pitch.

Medicine and wedding baskets were large and shallow with the background in natural cream, and decorations in red and black. A little more of the yellow was used in coloring the wedding baskets, which were also slightly larger than the medicine baskets.[1]

Among other types of baskets made by the Utes were bowls, burden baskets, harvesting fans and basket caps, used by the squaws for everyday wear.

The Utes were also excellent craftsmen in the manufacture of bags, such as tobacco pouches, vanity bags, awl cases, and paint bags.

The tobacco pouch was a long, fringed buckskin bag, ornately beaded and containing a draw string at the top.[2] The vanity bag, carried by both men and women, was made of heavy leather with two stripes of blue beads on each side and a green stripe on the bottom. Small cone-like metal objects were at-

tached to the bottom of the bag as well as on the buckskin flap
which covered the opening. These caused the bag to jingle
musically when being moved or carried.[3] A small bag of beaded
buckskin, fashioned in the shape of a rawhide cone, was used
to carry awls—the sewing tools for buckskin—and was known
as an awl case. The paint bag consisted of a slender triangle of
beaded buckskin to which a string of blue beads, a brass button,
and a stone arrowhead were attached. A small envelope inside
the bag about the size of a cigarette paper held the paint and a
smooth stick for application. The paint was a brilliant vermil-
lion powder.

The Utes did a large amount of bead work, obtaining the
beads from white traders. They specialized in the use of yellow, light blue, and light green. The most common articles
which were beaded in recent times were arm bands, purses,
rabbit feet, dolls, moccasins, gauntlets, watch fobs, cradle
boards, vests, neck ties, collars, leggings and chaps.

In pre-reservation days before the government began allot-
ting the Utes food and clothing, their diet consisted primarily
of meat killed in the hunt. This was cooked on coals or broiled
on a rack of sticks built over the fire. Some of the meat was
jerked for future use. They were also very fond of the cleansed,
dressed, and broiled entrails of animals.

A limited amount of food to supplement the meat diet was
obtained from fishing and gathering wild native plants, such as
yucca fruit, camas, tobacco roots, grass seeds, pinon nuts, wild
potatoes, serviceberries, and chokecherries.[4] Chokecherries,
serviceberries, and seeds were dried and then ground on metates
or pounded in mortars. Pinon nuts were parched in hot ashes
after which the shells were removed and the nuts pounded on a
stone.

Corn, which was about the only agricultural product occasionally known to be raised among the early Utes, was ground
by placing it on a broad flat stone and grinding it under a long
round stone. This corn meal was then mixed with water and
baked on heated earth from which the ashes of a fire had been
removed.[5]

The Ute tribe was divided into a loose confederation of seven bands, each with its chief and council. The council was made up of certain distinguished elderly men of the band, and all important questions were considered by them as advisors to the chief.[6]

This chief and council type of organization broke down, however, when no one man could acquire control of a band. For example, after the death of Nevava in the 1870's, no one Ute was strong enough to get control of any of the three bands among the Northern Utes. Consequently, any man who could secure a following of more than his own family assumed the title of chief. The most prominent of these were Antelope, Douglass, Jack, Colorow, Johnson, Sahurtz, and Bennet. Douglass, Jack, and Colorow were the most popular and had the greatest following. Nevertheless, with the authority so divided, the oldtime council ceased to function.

The Tabeguache or Uncompahgre band and the three bands of the Southern Utes continued to function under the chief and council system long after it had broken down among their tribesmen to the north.

When anything of general interest was to be considered such as a raid, a general meeting was called of all the men in the band. There the matter was discussed freely, and then it was referred to the council. The chief met with the council, listened carefully to its advice, and ultimately made the final decision.[7]

FOOTNOTES

[1]Helen Sloan Daniels, "Ute Costume," *The Ute Indians of Southwestern Colorado,* p. 106.

[2]*Ibid.,* p. 123.

[3]*Ibid.,* p. 119

[4]Albert McCall, "An Outline of Indian Culture," *The Ute Indians of Southwestern Colo.,* p. 98.

[5]Frances Densmore, *Northern Ute Music,* p. 26.

[6]Wm. N. Byers, "History of the Ute Nation," *Rocky Mountain News,* April 16, 1880. Article in U. S. Randall Scrap Book, pp. 13-14. In possession of State Historical Society of Colorado.

[7]Ernest Ingersoll, *Knocking Around the Rockies,* p. 93.

RELIGION, MEDICINE MEN, AND BURIALS

The religious ideas of the Utes were not highly developed. Around the lodge fire they learned from their parents and grandparents that there was one supreme being, who was a good, personal God. Subordinate to him were other gods, including a God of War, a God of Peace, a God of Floods, a God of Thunder and Lightning, and a God of Blood who heals the sick.[1]

The Utes were sincere believers in immortality. They had a child-like faith that when an Indian died—whether he was good or bad—he went to the Happy Hunting Ground.[2] They did believe that immediately after death there was an evil spirit who competed with the good spirit (Sin-o'-Wap) for possession of the soul. However, they felt that Sin-o'-Wap nearly always won out, so there was really nothing to worry about. After the good spirit had chased away the evil spirit, he conducted the Indian's soul to the Happy Hunting Ground.[3]

These beliefs, while very real to the Utes, were never expressed in ceremonies or prayers.

The Ute traditional story of the creation of the world and of the flood was apparently the result of Jesuit teaching which was passed on to them by their Indian neighbors in New Mexico, who came in frequent contact with the Spanish priests.[4]

The untrained minds of the Ute Indians were clouded by superstitions, and their primitive religious life centered pri-

marily around the medicine men. The principal objectve of
the medicine man was to heal the sick, and the Indians supposed that he acquired his power from communication with the
spirits of dead Indians, eagles, bears, birds, or imaginary supernatural little green men similar to elves.

The medicine men used two methods in treating the sick. In
both there was a dependence on supernatural help, but in one
herbs or other material remedies were also made use of.[5]

The most respected medicine men used supernatural powers
only, which consisted of singing curative songs and attempting
occasionally to suck out through the patient's skin imaginary
objects which were causing the sickness or pain. Each medicine man composed his own songs, usually under the inspira-
tion of dreams or communion with the supernatural.

In treating a patient the medicine man usually knelt beside
the sick person with his back to the spectators. He then sang in
a series of high-keyed grunts gradually reducing the pitch to a
lower and more solemn tone. It was a weird sound when the
family joined in, and the yipping could be heard sometimes for
a mile. The songs were invariably ended with a gargling sound
as if the singers' mouths were full of water.

In critical cases a medicine man often sang all day and night
—not only to heal the patient but also to frighten away the
evil spirit in case of death so that the good spirit Sin-o'-Wap
would have an easier time getting possession of the soul.[6]

The sweat house was a common thing in all Ute camps. It
was built close to a stream and consisted of a low hut of willow
bushes or brush built over a shallow pit. When a patient was to
be treated, a small fire was built in the pit and several stones
were placed in the coals to heat. When the stones were red hot,
the patient, wearing only a blanket over his shoulders, would
pour water over the rocks until a lot of steam was emitted.
Then, holding the blanket around him, he would squat over
the pit. When he was sweating most profusely, the patient
would throw the blanket down, and running out of the sweat
house, he would plunge into the cold water of the stream. In
serious cases such heroic treatment often resulted in instant
death. But the theory of the ordeal was to make the body so

uninhabitable that the evil spirit causing the sickness would take flight.[7]

The Utes buried their dead secretly in caves, crevices, arroyos, or shallow graves, usually wrapping the deceased in blankets and carrying him on horseback at night to his grave. The remains were then well covered with pieces of rock or dirt. Certain personal goods of the dead man, such as his implements of war and his clothing, were buried with him. His dogs and two of his horses were usually killed by the grave as a burial sacrifice.[8] The Indians were afraid of the dead; so burials were usually made as quickly as possible.[9]

Ceremonies conducted on the death of a squaw were the same except that there was no destruction of property and no weapons were buried with the corpse.

FOOTNOTES

[1]Sidney Jocknick, *Early Days on the Western Slope of Colorado,* p. 297.

[2]*Ibid.,* p. 298.

[3]Ernest Ingersoll, *Knocking Around the Rockies,* p. 103.

[4]*Ibid.,* pp. 102-103. Also see D. B. Huntington, *Vocabulary of the Utah and Sho-Sho-Ne or Snake Dialects with Indian Legends and Traditions,* pp. 24-26.

[5]Frances Densmore, *Northern Ute Music,* pp. 127-130.

[6]Ingersoll, *op. ct.,* p. 104.

[7]*Ibid.,* p. 102.

[8]*Ibid.,* p. 104.

[9]For a somewhat different version of the Ute burials, see Helen Sloan Daniels, "Ute Burial," *The Ute Indians of Southwestern Colo.,* pp. 133-135.

COURTING, MARRIAGE, AND GAMES

Marriage and divorce were rather casual affairs among the Utes. There were no ceremonies. Marriage was limited in meaning strictly to cohabitation, and whenever one or the other desired it, separation occurred. Youths engaged in intercourse at a very early age. Separation was frequent among young "married" couples, but when middle age approached, there was more of a tendency toward stability in this relationship. It was common for the Utes to intermarry with the Jicarilla Apaches to the south of them and with the Bannocks and Snakes to the west of them.[1]

An ancient Ute method of courting was for a young buck to conceal himself near his girl's wigwam and then serenade her with a love flute or flageolet. The flageolet was about two inches in diameter and 1½ to 3½ feet long with several holes near one end and the blowing end tapered for the mouth. It was highly colored and covered with designs. It was made to fit the voice of the serenader, who would alternately play and sing, making up the words as he went along and frequently using the girl's name so that she would know that the music was for her benefit.

The girl thus honored usually sat idly around the camp trying to figure out the word content of the musical messages. A curious girl might locate her hidden admirer, and if her efforts were successful, it made for an informal introduction between the two.

The flageolet was used only for philandering, and more serious advances were withheld until after a series of such romantic affairs.[2]

During the Bear Dance the women took the lead in choosing partners, as already explained. A more serious advance was made if she tossed a stick or a stone into a man's lap. This gesture was an invitation to visit her camp at night. These clandestine visits were held secretly, and sexual intimacy often occurred. Illegitimate births were fairly common, but there was no stigma attached to illegitimacy.

When a man really became serious about a girl, he would dress himself in his best attire and visit the girl's parents. He would completely ignore his prospective bride and direct his entire conversation toward the members of her family. The significance of these tactics, however, was understood by all, and after his departure, the suitor's availability and desirability were discussed. The girl's relatives gave their opinion, but the final decision was up to her.

After several such visits if the suitor believed that his chances were favorable, a customary way of bringing the matter to a head was for him to go on a hunt and return with the body of a deer packed on his horse. He would then tie his horse near the tepee of the desired girl and enter, often not noticing her.

If the girl had decided to accept his proposal, she would water and feed the horse and then skin and dress the deer. After cooking some of the venison, she would invite the visitor to eat some with her. The two would then start living together with no more ado.[3] While there were, of course, other methods of getting married, this is a good illustration of the informality of the ceremony.

The husband and wife usually began their married venture in the tepee of the bride's mother, the groom becoming a part of the girl's family. However, after several children were born the pair eventually constructed a tepee of their own.

The Utes were polygamous at one time but never to any great extent because of the even number of sexes in the tribe.

The men married at about eighteen years of age and the women at from fourteen to sixteen.

Divorce was just as informal as marriage. Whenever one of the couple returned alone to the camp of his parents, the divorce was considered final.[4]

Common games among the Utes were dice and gambling sticks, hoop and pole, ball juggling, double ball, and shinny.

Dice and gambling sticks were played extensively, and large stakes were often involved. Singers, pounding on hand drums or on a horizontal pole, sang appropriate songs as the games progressed.

The contestants, consisting of five or six or sometimes a dozen men, faced each other on either side of a blanket. A bundle of pointed sticks was placed before each man, and each couple was provided with two cylindrical bone dice, one being white and the other black or occasionally just ornamented with a black band. The gambler holding the dice played one hand above the other and juggled the dice back and forth, reversing his hands again and again while so doing in order to confuse his opponent as to which hand the dice were in.

During this performance the other player would cross his arms and place each hand under the opposite arm. Then, he would sway back and forth in time to the music of the drummers as he watched the passing of the dice. After a few minutes he would suddenly point with one hand toward the opposite hand of his opponent at the same time hitting himself under the pointing arm with the other hand. His opponent would then open the hand selected and if the dice were in it the guesser took the dice and started juggling them in the same way. If the dice did not happen to be in the hand chosen the guesser would forfeit a stick from his bundle. The game continued until one of the players had lost all of his sticks.[5]

The Utes took a lot of pride in their horses and each man had a racer on which he would gamble about anything. Indian race tracks were always straight and the distance only a few hundred yards.

At a signal the competitors would all start out together. With one arm holding on to the bridle and the other vigorously hitting his horses' hips each horseman would come galloping down the stretch yelling and frantically kicking his horse's ribs with his heels.

Sometimes a horse failed to stop after passing the finish line but would stampede across the hills while the spectators laughed at the rider's predicament.[6]

FOOTNOTES

[1]Albert M. McCall, "An Outline of Ute Indian Culture," *The Ute Indians of Southwestern Colorado*, pp. 104-105.

[2]Ralph Linton, *Acculturation in Seven American Indian Tribes*, pp. 147-148.

[3]Sidney Jocknick, *Early Days on the Western Slope of Colorado*, pp. 291-292.

[4]Linton, *op. cit.*, p. 151.

[5]Frances Densmore, *Northern Ute Music*, pp. 174-175.

[6]Ernest Ingersoll, *Knocking Around the Rockies*, p. 101.

EARLIEST WHITE PENETRATIONS
INTO UTE TERRITORY

It was not until after the United States defeated Mexico in 1848 and took over her large empire, which included the Western Slope of Colorado, that the Utes started meeting the full impact of white civilization. This period ushered in long years of defeat, territorial loss, and disillusionment. Prior to 1848 the Utes came in only occasional contact with missionaries, explorers, traders, and hunters who ventured into their wild and unknown domain.

Don Juan Rivera's expedition in 1765, ten years before the outbreak of the Revolutionary War, was the earliest recorded exploration into the wilderness of Western Colorado. During that year Governor Cachupin of New Mexico, which was then a part of Spanish territory, sent Rivera to explore the unknown lands to the north. Rivera and his group of explorers traveled northward through southwestern Colorado to the Uncompahgre River, which the Spaniards followed to its junction with the Gunnison at the present site of Delta.

While camped there Rivera made some carvings on a cottonwood tree as a landmark for future travelers. Escalante referred to these marks in his journal when he journeyed through that area eleven years later:

Farther down the river [Uncompahgre] and about four leagues
north of this plain of San Augustine, the river forms a junction
with a larger one, called by the people of our party the River
of San Javier [today it is known as the Gunnison] and by the
Yutas [Utes] the River Tomchi. There came to these two rivers
in the year 1765 Don Juan Maria de Rivera. . . . The place
where he said he cut the figure of a cross on a young poplar
tree, with the initials of his name and the year of his expedition,
are still found at the junction of these rivers on the southern
bank, as we were informed by our interpreter.[1]

While no reference is made to the Ute Indians, Rivera and
his party undoubtedly had some contact with them during their
long trek through the southern Colorado mountains.

The next outstanding expedition into the land of the Utes
was made in 1776 by two Spanish priests, Fathers Escalante and
Dominguez, with twelve companions. The purpose of this trip
was to chart an overland route from Santa Fe, New Mexico, to
the Spanish missions which Junipero Serra had established in
Monterey, California.

Escalante and Dominguez made their way into southern Colorado near the present location of Pagosa Springs. In order to
avoid the high mountains to the north, the Spaniards pursued a
westerly course through the present site of Durango to the
Dolores River. They were forced to ford many rivers between
Pagosa Springs and the Dolores River, including the Piedra,[2]
Los Pinos,[3] Florida,[4] Animas,[5] and the Mancos.[6] The two
priests named many of these rivers.

The two friars then followed the Dolores River[7] through the
Disappointment country as far north as the present village of
Bedrock.[8] The roughness of the country north of them forced
the travelers southeastward to what is now Naturita.

In this vicinity on one of the creeks which flows into the San
Miguel, the Spaniards were overtaken by a Ute, the first Indian
that they had seen since leaving New Mexico.[9] Escalante wrote
in his journal:

We gave the Indian something to eat and to smoke, and afterward through an interpreter we asked him various questions
concerning the land ahead, the rivers, and their courses.[10]

Escalante likewise questioned him concerning the whereabouts of Indian tribes in the neighborhood:

> At first he appeared ignorant of everything, even of the country in which he lived, but after he had recovered somewhat from his fear and suspicion . . . [he told the newcomers a great deal].

> We asked him if he would guide us to the camp of a chief said by our interpreter and others to be very friendly toward the Spaniards and to know a great deal about the country.[11] He consented on condition that we should wait for him until the afternoon of the next day.[12]

> Before twelve o'clock the Yuta reached the place where we were awaiting him, accompanied by his family, two other women, and five children, two at the breast and three from eight to ten years old, all good looking and very agreeable. They thought we had come to trade and therefore they had brought tanned deerskins and other articles for barter. Among other things, they brought dried berries of the black manzanita, which are very savory and similar to those of the little grape. . . . We informed them that we did not come to trade and had no goods to trade with. . . . We gave food to all of them, and the wife of our [prospective] guide presented us with a little dried venison and two plates of manzanita berries, which we paid for with flour.

> After midday we gave the Yuta what he requested for guiding us—two hunting knives and sixteen strings of white glass beads. He gave them to his wife who with the others went to their rancheros [while] we departed with our guide. . . .[13]

The Ute guide led the missionaries northeastward over the Uncompahgre Plateau to the Uncompahgre River, a short distance south of the present town of Montrose.[14] After traveling northward down the Uncompahgre a short distance they met another Ute and his family.[51] After a lengthy visit with the Indian by means of their interpreter in which the whites learned nothing useful, they continued northeast to where the town of Austin now stands along the Gunnison River. Here camp was made, and the interpreter and the Ute guide went in search of other Indians to assist the Spaniards on their journey.

About ten o'clock the next morning five Utes appeared on
the opposite side of the river. The explorers at first thought
that they were the Indians whom the guide and interpreter had
gone in search of, but after visiting with them through another
interpreter, they proved to be merely passing by. In his journal
Escalante recounts the event . . .

> We gave them something to eat and to smoke but after a long
> conversation about the difficulties they had during the summer
> with the Comanches we could not get from them anything use-
> ful to our interests because their design was to make us afraid,
> exaggerating the danger to which we were exposing ourselves,
> as the Comanches would kill us if we continued on this course.
> We destroyed the force of the pretexts with which they tried to
> stop our progress by saying to them that our God, which is
> above all, would defend us in case of an encounter with our
> enemies.[16]

The following morning the chief interpreter and the Ute
guide arrived with five Utes and one Laguna Indian. After the
explorers had given them plenty of food and tobacco, the Spaniards explained that they needed a guide to take them to the
camp of the Laguna tribe, which Indians were said to be friendly to the whites.

The Indians replied that to reach the Lagunas the Spaniards
would have to pass through country occupied by the hostile
Comanches. They also pretended that they did not know the
way. However, when Escalante displayed to the Laguna Indian
a woolen cloak, a hunting knife, and some white glass beads, he
said that in exchange for the articles he would guide the newcomers to his country. After the Indian had been presented
with the gifts, some of the Utes confessed that they also knew
the way. Before parting, the Utes insisted that the white men
visit their camp on what today is known as Muddy Creek some
miles north of the present coal mining town of Oliver.[17] The
five Utes, who were with the Laguna, said that they would accompany the Spaniards as far as this village.

The new guide escorted the party on up the Gunnison River
to its junction with the North Fork. The group then followed

up the North Fork to where Leroux Creek flows into it a short way below the present town of Hotchkiss, where they pitched camp.

The next morning they continued their journey on up the North Fork River past the present sites of Hotchkiss and Paonia to where the town of Bowie now stands. From this point the Laguna led them northward and that evening camp was made east of the present Overland Reservoir.[18]

One of the Utes who was accompanying the Spaniards gorged himself so ravenously at supper that he became violently ill, and for a time it looked as if he might die. However, after throwing up some of the surplus, he felt much better.

On the following morning the travelers reached Muddy Creek, where the Ute camp, consisting of about thirty tepees, was located. On the way the Spaniards met about eighty Ute warriors on horseback, most of whom were from this camp. They told Escalante that they were out on a hunt, but the explorer concluded that they were riding together in such a large number to make a show of force and to ascertain whether any more palefaces were following.

While camp was being set up on Muddy Creek below the Indian village, Father Fray Francisco Atanasio went with an interpreter to see the chief. He entered the chief's tepee and greeted him and his sons after which he asked the chief to assemble the other Indians so that he could talk to them.

After the Indians had gathered, the missionary, through his interpreter, told them about the gospel. Afterwards, he informed the chief that if he and his people would accept Christianity that he and his fellow priests would come back to instruct them and arrange for their baptism.

Father Atanasio went on to tell the Ute that Indians should not name themselves after wild animals and explained the purpose for which man was created. He also said that it was wrong for them to have more than one wife.[19]

After completing his spiritual messages, the missionary turned to more earthy subjects. He traded some glass beads for dried buffalo meat. He also made arrangements with the chief to exchange some lame horses for sound ones so that they could more easily continue their long journey.

Shortly before sunset the chief, some old men, and many others visited the white men's camp. The visitors urged them to turn back, warning them of the dangers ahead from unfriendly Indians.

Early the next morning even more Utes appeared and again tried to dissuade the explorers from continuing on.[20] During the preceding night they had persuaded the Laguna Indian not to guide the Spaniards further, and he returned the gifts which had been presented to him.

After arguing with the Utes and the guide for more than an hour and a half without success, Escalante told them that he was going to continue on his journey, guide or no guide. He went on to say that the Laguna had consented voluntarily to accompany the Spaniards as far as his country and that if he refused to keep his word they would no longer consider him or the Utes as friends.[21]

This threat caused the Utes to change their position, and after much arguing, they finally persuaded the confused Laguna to continue on as guide. The Utes then broke camp and departed. The uncertain guide remained at the site of the Ute camp, pretending to be looking for a saddle to put on the horse the explorers had given him.

While the Laguna dallied, Escalante and his party started to follow the route taken by the Utes. When the guide did not appear, Escalante sent the interpreter back to look for him. The Indian told the interpreter that the whites were headed in the wrong direction and to bring them back. The missionaries returned to find their guide saying goodbye to several of his countrymen who were remaining with the Utes. One of the Lagunas, who was still a boy, at the last moment decided to accompany the travelers back to his home territory. Since the boy had no horse, one of the Spaniards let him ride behind on his mount.

The explorers gladly left the trail of the Utes, and with the two Lagunas crossed over Grand Mesa, stopping for the night some distance east of the present town of Collbran on what is now known as Buzzard Creek. The next day they crossed the Colorado River near the site of present DeBeque.

In this vicinity they encountered three Ute women and a child drying berries which they had gathered along arroyos and creeks. Escalante and Dominguez visited with them, and the women gave them some berries which Escalante describes in his journal as:

.... chokecherry, garambullo, and some of this year's pinon. The garambullo which grows in these parts is very bitter while on the bushes, but when dried in the sun as these Yutas had done, it is bitter-sweet and very savory.[22]

After crossing the Colorado River, the friars traveled northwestward through the present site of Rangely, and then journeyed into northeastern Utah to the land of the Lagunas, where they arrived on September 23, 1776.

Here they changed guides and plodded onward, but when they reached Utah Lake two weeks later, on October 8th, winter had begun to set in and they were getting low on provisions.[23] So, the Spaniards decided to give up the trip and turn homeward to Santa Fe, where they arrived on January 2, 1777.

This expedition ranks as the most outstanding exploration of Western Colorado until the coming of Captain Gunnison in 1853.

For fifty years after Escalante's penetration of this little-known region, there is no record of any white explorers invading the land of the Utes. However, occasional unrecorded expeditions were made by the Spaniards to spread the gospel, pursue runaway slaves, punish marauders, hunt, and trade with the Indians.

In the 1830's beaver pelts became quite valuable, and many trappers came into western Colorado looking for beaver. Brown's Park, an almost level valley thirty miles long and five miles wide lying in the extreme northwestern corner of Colorado, became a rendezvous for the Mountain Men about 1830 when Baptiste Brown, a French-Canadian fur trader, settled here.

A one-story trading post was built here out of mud and cottonwood logs in 1837 by Philip Thompson and William Craig on the north bank of the Green River. This post was called Fort Davy Crockett.[24]

At about the same time Fort Uncompahgre was constructed just below the junction of the Uncompahgre and Gunnison rivers near the present town of Delta by Antoine Robidoux, a French trader from St. Louis.

These two trading posts were the only white settlements on the Western Slope of Colorado at this time. They were used primarily as general outfitting and trading headquarters for beaver trappers, and unlike trading posts east of the mountains, little, if any, trading was done with the Indians.

Neither post prospered. Within a short time after Fort Uncompahgre was built, the Utes set fire to the log buildings. Captain Gunnison noted its ruins when he passed by on his fatal exploration in 1853. Lieutenant Beckwith, a member of the group, recorded:

> We crossed the point of land lying between the Uncompahgre and Grand [Gunnison] rivers reaching the latter at Roubideau's [Robidoux] old trading fort, now entirely fallen to ruins.[25]

Fort Davy Crockett fared little better. It had such a difficult time that trappers referred to it as Fort Misery. Dr. F. A. Wislizenus of Germany, author of "A Journey to the Rocky Mountains in 1839," visited the post. He found its hungry inhabitants contentedly eating a lean dog that they had purchased the day before. Wislizenus reported that the dog meat was not so bad.

This trading post was abandoned about 1840, and the Mountain Men and their Indian squaws departed.

In the fall and winter of 1839-40 Jim Baker and Kit Carson headquartered at Fort Davy Crockett while hunting in northeastern Utah. Three years later in 1842 thirty-six trappers under the leadership of Henry Fraeb were working the Little Snake River valley northeast of Brown's Park.

Jim Bridger, a partner of Fraeb, was trapping on the Green River in Utah at the time, and heard that the Sioux and Cheyennes in Wyoming had recently gone on the warpath. So, he sent Jim Baker, then a young man of twenty, with two companions to warn Fraeb.[26]

Just as Baker reached Fraeb's camp near the present site of Slater, Colorado, one of Fraeb's trappers came staggering into camp badly wounded. He said that he and his party had been attacked by Indians who had killed several men and stolen ninety horses.

The trappers hastily threw up a fortification on what is now known as Battle Creek. The next morning about five hundred Arapahoe and Cheyenne Indians appeared and attacked this improvised fort. The fight lasted for several hours, and four trappers, including Fraeb, were killed and many others wounded. The deadly rifles of the besieged little group of frontiersmen took a heavy toll of Indians.

Early on the following morning the Cheyennes and Arapahoes made another short attack and then galloped away, carrying their dead and wounded with them. The squaws, who had been quartered on what has since been called Squaw Mountain also left. The trappers hurriedly buried their four comrades in one grave and made their escape down the river to Bridger's camp on the Green.[27]

Two years later in 1844 John C. Fremont and his party passed by the grave of the four trappers. On this, his second expedition through Colorado, Fremont crossed over the border into Wyoming and continued eastward to the North Platte, which he followed southward through North Park (Jackson County). He then traveled over the mountains into Middle Park (Grand County), camping one night at the head of a branch of Big Muddy Creek.

Upon reaching the Colorado River a short way east where the town of Kremmling now stands, Fremont and his men ferried down the Colorado to its junction with the Blue River at present Kremmling. They then proceeded up the Blue through what are now Grand and Summit Counties and crossed the Continental Divide at Hoosier Pass south of the present town of Breckenridge. The famous explorer continued on to Pueblo and thence eastward to Missouri.[28]

Another early explorer was the Oregon missionary, Marcus

Whitman, who rode through western Colorado in the fall of 1842. He and a companion named Lovejoy crossed the Colorado River near the present site of Grand Junction and journeyed up the Gunnison. In the mountains east of the present town of Gunnison they lost their way. Lovejoy reported that Whitman knelt in the snow and prayed for help. He then mounted his mule, dropped the reins, and the animal carried him to safety.[29]

With the exception of such occasional contacts with white trappers, missionaries, and explorers, the Utes were left to themselves to lead their free and nomadical life until the start of the Mexican War in 1846. From this time on they started feeling the gradually increasing impact of white civilization.

FOOTNOTES

[1]W. R. Harris, *The Catholic Church in Utah (1776-1909)*, p. 146. (Escalante's journal.)

[2]*Ibid.*, p. 130. ". . . and a league farther on we arrived at another river called the Piedra at a point near its junction with the Navajo."

[3]*Ibid.*, p. 131. "Crossing the river [the Piedra] we traveled two leagues to the west and a little more than two to the west-northwest and arrived at the eastern bank of the river . . . the Rio de los Pinos because of the pine trees growing on its banks."

[4]*Ibid.*, "We left the River Pinos . . . and . . . arrived at the River Florida which is much smaller. . . ."

[5]*Ibid.* "Passing the River Florida we . . . came to the River de los Animas [River of Souls]. . . ."

[6]*Ibid.*, p. 133. "We left the River Animas . . . and were obliged to stop by the first of two small streams which made up the San Lozaro, otherwise called Las Mancos."

[7]*Ibid.* "We passed through a piece of burnt-over woodland with scant pasturage and turned to the north, crossing the Rio de Neustra Sonora de los Dolores [River of our Lady of Sorrows]."

[8]*Ibid.*, pp. 137-140. "Wishing to cross the ridge of high and rocky table lands, for the river bed now became impassable, one of the men went on ahead to see if the road was passable. He found that we could not travel the northwest road but discovered another path to the southeast . . . we came to the Rio San Pedro [the San Miguel]

. . . which runs toward the north, turns to the northwest, and then to the west until it unites with the Dolores."

[9]Herbert E. Bolton, *Pageant in the Wilderness,* p. 148.

[10]*Ibid.*

[11]Escalante explains later on in this journal that the friendly chief was the head of what he refers to as the Laguna tribe living near Utah Lake in Utah.

[12]Bolton, *op. cit.,* pp. 148-149.

[13]*Ibid.*

[14]Harris, *op. cit.,* p. 143. "We now began to cross the mountains in a northeasterly direction. . . . We finished the descent of the mountains and entered the pleasant valley of the River of San Francisco . . . called by the Yutas the Ancapogari [Uncompahgre], which the interpreter tells us means Colorado [red] lake from the fact that near its source there is a spring of reddish water, hot and disagreeable to the taste."

[15]*Ibid.* "We . . . journeyed down the river in a northwesterly direction, and having traveled a short distance we met a Yuta by the name of Surdo [the Deaf One] and his family."

[16]*Ibid.,* p. 147.

[17]Bolton, *op. cit.,* p. 154.

[18]*Ibid.,* p. 155.

[19]*Ibid.,* p. 157.

[20]*Ibid.,* p. 159.

[21]*Ibid.,* p. 160.

[22]*Ibid.,* p. 162.

[23]Harris, *op. cit.,* pp. 192-193.

[24]*Colorado,* Colo. Writers Project of W.P.A., pp. 289-290.

[25]Beckwith, *Reports of Explorations and Surveys,* Vol. II, p. 56.

[26]Charles H. Leckenby, *The Tread of Pioneers,* pp. 37-40.

[27]In 1873 Jim Baker took up a permanent home on the Little Snake River near the scene of the battle and resided there until his death in 1898. When he moved there, he built a two-story bullet-proof house with a turreted second story. The building stood near Slater for several years after Baker's death but later was moved and is now preserved as a historic relic by the State of Wyoming.

[28]Leckenby, *op. cit.,* p. 104.

[29]Leroy R. and Ann W. Hafen, *Colorado,* p. 101.

FIRST NEGOTIATIONS WITH THE UTES

Within a month after the conquest of New Mexico by General Kearney on August 18, 1846, the United States Army sent William Gilpin, who fifteen years later became Colorado's first territorial governor, north from Santa Fe to confer with the Utes. Gilpin brought back sixty Ute leaders from the San Luis Valley, and this delegation met Colonel Doniphan on October 13th and agreed to remain peaceful.[1]

On December 30, 1849, a year after the defeat of Mexico, the first official treaty between the Utes and the United States was negotiated at Abiquiu, New Mexico.[2] Indian Agent James S. Calhoun represented the United States. By this treaty the Utes recognized the sovereignty of the United States and agreed not to depart from their accustomed habitat without permission. However, no boundaries were defined.

An agency was opened at Taos, New Mexico, a year following this treaty. John Greiner served as agent from 1851 to 1853, but the agency proved unsuccessful due to lack of money.[3] The agency was reopened early in December, 1853, to serve the Capote band, and Kit Carson, the celebrated trapper and former Indian fighter, was named agent. He had charge of the agency until 1859.[4] The Mouache band camped much of the time in this area and was also served by the Taos agency. However, members of the Weeminuche band, then as now, were highly individualistic and came in as little contact as possible with the white race.

The Tabeguache Utes heard of the infrequent gifts which Carson gave to the Capote and Mouache bands; so in 1856 the Tabeguaches made a trip to the agency in search of presents. Carson recommended that an agency be set up for this band, but his request was ignored for some time.[5]

According to the Treaty of Guadalupe Hidalgo, which ended this nation's war with Mexico on February 2, 1848, land and property rights of Mexicans in Colorado, as well as elsewhere, were to be fully respected. The Mexican government had made several large land grants in the San Luis Valley before the United States took over possession.

In 1851 the Mexicans started a settlement on one of these grants. This new town of San Luis was located on the Culebra River in present Costilla County. In 1852 and 1853 San Pedro and San Acacio were also started. These three towns were the first permanent settlements in Colorado.

To safeguard these settlements Fort Massachusetts was established north of them in 1852. This fort was built on Ute Creek near the base of Mount Blanca and was the first United States military post in Colorado. In 1858 it was replaced by Fort Garland, six miles to the south.

Early in the year 1855 the Utes went on the warpath and began attacking settlements in the San Luis Valley. Mexicans were killed, cattle and sheep were driven away, and even Fort Massachusetts was threatened. Trees and branches were removed from around the fort, additional breastworks were thrown up, and sentinels kept a day and night vigil.[6] General Garland at Santa Fe organized six companies of mounted volunteers and sent these and regular troops into the San Luis Valley to put down the Ute uprising. Colonel Thomas T. Fauntleroy led the campaign, and Kit Carson went along as head scout.

Fauntleroy's forces joined those at Fort Massachusetts, and they went in search of the hostile Utes. The first Ute war party was encountered in the Saguache Valley on March 19, 1855. The Indians under the leadership of Chief Tierra Blanco, who

stood out because of the red woolen shirt he wore, retreated in
the face of greater numbers. In the running fight toward
Cochetopa Pass most of them escaped.

The troops moved northward and crossed Poncha Pass, and
near the present town of Salida Fauntleroy surprised a band of
Utes. The soldiers killed forty, captured others, and recovered
some horses, sheep and supplies.[7] This battle took place on
April 29, and it was followed by other minor skirmishes during
May and June. By this time the Utes had taken such a beating
that they asked for peace. A treaty was concluded in the fall of
1855. and from that time on the Ute tribe was generally on
friendly terms with the whites.

During this troublesome period with the Utes, Captain
John W. Gunnison made the most outstanding exploration of
western Colorado since the Escalante expedition seventy-seven
years before. In 1853 Jefferson Davis, who was then Secretary
of War, sent Captain Gunnison, assisted by Lieutenant E. G.
Beckwith, into this region to determine the most practical
route for a railroad to connect the Mississippi Valley with the
Pacific Ocean.

Captain Morris with a detachment of thirty soldiers from
Fort Leavenworth, Kansas, went in advance of the group as an
escort, building roads where necessary. Then followed sixteen
wagons, each drawn by a six-mule team. An ambulance wagon
and a small vehicle loaded with surveying instruments brought
up the rear.[8]

Captain Gunnison was a rather short, handsome, well-built
man with a ruddy complexion, brown hair and a prepossessing
manner. He and his party of engineers crossed the Continental
Divide at what is now known as Cochetopa Pass. He then proceeded north to Tomichi Creek, which stream he followed to its
junction with the Taylor River near the present town of Gunnison, where the Gunnison River, which was later named in his
honor, has its beginning.

The explorers followed the Gunnison to where it starts flowing through the Black Canyon, which measures from 1725 feet
to 2240 feet in depth and 1000 to 3000 feet in width.[9]

Unable to go through this high, narrow gorge, the white men

went around its southern border over what is now known as Blue Mesa. During this part of the journey they were kept under constant surveillance by the Utes, who followed the expedition. The Indians were continually yelling and making a lot of noise. Roads had to be built over the rough terrain and temporary bridges were constructed. Gunnison had considerable difficulty moving his wagons over the mountainous country. The Uncompahgre River was finally reached on September 15th.

Lt. Beckwith's report mentions the excursion around the Black Canyon:

> The canyon which we have been so many days passing around terminates several miles above the junction of the Uncompahgre with the Grand River (Gunnison).[10]

The engineers followed the Uncompahgre to its junction with the Gunnison, passing near the present sites of Montrose, Olathe, and Delta. Just below the site of Delta they passed Robidoux' old trading post which they found in ruins.[11] They traveled on down the Gunnison to its junction with the Colorado River where Grand Junction now stands. They continued westward along the Colorado into Utah, and Beckwith was so unfavorably impressed by the barrenness of the country that he wrote:

> No part of the route thus far from San Luis Valley . . . offers a spot of any considerable extent suitable for settlement.[12]

On October 24th while camped in central Utah Captain Gunnison was told by a passing traveler that some of the Piute Indians in that area were on the warpath because of the unwarranted killing of several of their number by emigrants who were passing through the country.[13]

Ignoring this warning, Gunnison with four companions and an escort of seven soldiers left the main camp on the following day and started out to explore Sevier Lake, which the white men believed to be about sixteen miles away. Indian signal fires were seen frequently throughout the day, but the explorers had traveled so far in the midst of hostile savages without trouble that no alarm was felt.

That evening camp was made along the Sevier River. No precaution was taken that night except for the usual camp sentinels, each man, including Captain Gunnison, taking his turn.

While the men were eating breakfast early the next morning, the Piutes made a surprise attack. The savages used both rifles and bows, shooting from the surrounding willows.

The white men were confused and startled by this unexpected assault. While the others sprang for their guns, Captain Gunnison rushed out of his tent and extended a hand in a token of peace. He was instantly pierced by fifteen arrows and sank to the ground mortally wounded.

One of the captain's companions had fallen at the first volley, but the remaining nine men fled for Lieutenant Beckwith's camp fourteen miles distant with the Indians in close pursuit.

Only four made their escape. One of these staggered into Beckwith's camp, bearing the tragic news. In less than thirty minutes the rescue party was on its way to the scene of the massacre. They arrived too late to find all of the missing men before dark; so a big bonfire was kept burning all the night to guide any more survivors.

At daybreak the search was resumed. The mutilated bodies of the dead were finally discovered. None had been scalped, but several, including Captain Gunnison, were found with their arms severed at the elbow. It was difficult to identify the remains because of the mutilations made by the Indians and the wolves.[14]

In 1858, five years after the fateful Gunnison expedition, gold was discovered near the present site of Denver. The white population increased so rapidly that by 1861 the Territory of Colorado was organized, and the territorial governor was made ex-officio Superintendent of Indian Affairs.

The governor gave the Tabeguache band an agency in 1861 at Conejos. Lafayette Head was appointed the first agent, but because of inadequate funds, he was unable to do his work efficiently.[15]

On the following year in 1862 Congress authorized an agency

for the Northern Ute bands, but it was not until April, 1863, that Simeon Whiteley, the agent, arrived to open the agency at Hot Sulphur Springs. Whiteley appointed Uriah Curtis as interpreter and sent him out to locate the Indians.

The Taos Agency in New Mexico continued to serve the Southern Utes.

As friction increased between the advancing settlers and the Utes, a conference was held on October 1, 1863, at Conejos for the purpose of moving the Utes to a new locality. Members of the commission representing the United States included Simeon Whiteley, agent of the newly created agency at Hot Sulphur Springs for the Northern Utes; Lafayette Head, agent at Conejos for the Tabeguache band; Superintendent Michael Steck, head of the New Mexico agency for the Southern Utes; and Governor John Evans of the Colorado Territory. John Nicolay, President Abraham Lincoln's secretary from Washington, D. C., served as secretary for the commission.[16]

Due to lack of sufficient representation from the Northern and Southern Utes, the commission dealt only with the Tabeguache band. The Tabeguaches refused to be moved to a new location, but they did finally agree to a treaty which specified the boundaries of their reservation.

The described boundary followed the Uncompahgre River from its beginning through present Montrose to its junction with the Gunnison. From this point the line continued down the Gunnison to where it joins the Colorado, and then on up the Colorado to where the Roaring Fork flows into it at the present site of Glenwood Springs. The boundary line turned up the Roaring Fork to its source near what is now known as Independence Pass above Aspen. Thence it was drawn along the summit of the Sawatch Range to its intersection with the Sangre de Cristo Range and south along the summit to the source of Sand Arena Creek of the San Luis Valley. Thence westward in a straight line to a point where the Rio Grande crosses the 106th degree of longitude. Then up the Rio Grande to the 107th degree of longitude and south along this longitudinal line to the summit of the Continental Divide. Thence westerly along the summit to a point due south of the Uncom-

pahgre River, and then due north to the source of the Uncompahgre.[17]

This was the first time that any definite boundary line was
agreed on to restrict the nomadic Utes in their wanderings.
This treaty also provided that the Mouache band be placed
upon this reservation with the Tabeguaches.

The land which the Tabeguache band gave up included
much of the area settled by the white race and mining sites. In
return for surrendering title to this territory the Tabeguaches
were to receive cattle not to exceed 150 head annually for five
years starting with the ratification of the treaty (the treaty was
ratified in 1864), and sheep not to exceed 1000 head annually
for the first two years after ratification and 500 head a year
during the next three years if the Indians showed some interest
in agriculture and ranching.[18]

The government also promised to furnish a blacksmith and
to give the band ten thousand dollars a year in goods and ten
thousand dollars in provisions for ten years.

Ten Tabeguache leaders, including Ouray, signed the treaty.
It was witnessed by five army officers and John Nicolay. After
the meeting was concluded, Governor Evans presented seven of
the more friendly Indians with silver medals.[19]

In the fall of 1864 a big snowstorm prevented the Tabeguache band from going to the plains country and obtaining
their winter's supply of meat and hides. The hungry Utes assembled around Colorado City near present Colorado Springs
and begged for food. The residents finally gave them ten sacks
of flour, and ninety-five additional sacks were distributed to
them by their agent at Conejos to keep them away from the
white settlements.

The government failed to fulfill any of its obligations as
provided in the Treaty of 1863 and did not even provide the
band with an agency building. Fortunately, the game supply
was still sufficient at this time to keep the Indians independent
of government rations.

The Tabeguaches and the Latin-American settlers of the
San Luis Valley continued to have trouble. A Ute killed a Mexican, and two Indians were murdered in retaliation. Governor

Evans immediately sent gifts to the families of those killed in an effort to maintain peace.

FOOTNOTES

[1]Leroy R. and Ann W. Hafen, *Colorado*, p. 130.

[2]*U. S. Statutes at Large*, Vol. 9, p. 984.

[3]Ralph Linton, *Acculturation in Seven American Indian Tribes*, p. 177.

[4]*Ibid.*

[5]James Warren Covington, "Federal Relations with the Colorado Utes," *The Colorado Magazine*, Oct., 1951.

[6]Hafen, *op. cit.,* p. 132.

[7]*Ibid.,* p. 133.

[8]*Reports of Explorations and Surveys . . . from the Mississippi River to the Pacific Ocean . . .* 1853-54, II, 12, Senate Ex. Doc. No. 78, 33rd Congress. Also see Lois Borland, *Historical Sketches of Early Gunnison,* June 1, 1916.

[9]This canyon was established as a National Monument on March 2, 1933, by proclamation of President Herbert Hoover.

[10]Beckwith, *Reports of Explorations and Surveys,* Vol. II, p. 56.

[11]*Ibid.*

[12]*Ibid.,* p. 59.

[13]Nolie Mumey, "John Williams Gunnison," *Colorado Magazine,* Jan., 1954, p. 32

[14]Captain Gunnison's body was taken to Fillmore, Utah, for burial.

[15]James Warren Covington, "Federal Relations with the Colorado Utes," *The Colorado Magazine,* Oct., 1951, p. 258.

[16]*Ibid.,* p. 261.

[17]Frank Hall, *History of the State of Colorado,* Vol. 4, p. 60. Also see *U. S. Statutes at Large,* Vol. 13, p. 673.

[18]Covington, *op. cit.,* p. 262.

[19]*Ibid.,* p. 263.

THE TREATY OF 1868

It was primarily to get the Utes out of the San Luis Valley that a treaty was negotiated on March 2, 1868, at Washington, D. C., between representatives of the seven bands and commissioners N. G. Taylor, A. Hunt, and Kit Carson.

By this treaty the entire Ute tribe was placed on a reservation which extended north from the southern border of the Colorado Territory along the 107th meridian of longitude to a point fifteen miles due north of where this line intersects the fortieth parallel of latitude. The boundary line then ran due west to the western border of the Territory, thence south to its southern border and thence directly eastward to the place of beginning.[1]

Roughly speaking, the outer limits of the reservation ran northward from Colorado's southern boundary past the present towns of Pagosa Springs, Gunnison, Crested Butte, and Basalt to a point ten or twelve miles south of where Steamboat Springs now stands and then west to the Utah line. The sites of Gunnison and Crested Butte lay a little to the east of the reservation line.

An agency for the three bands of Northern Utes was established on White River near the present town of Meeker. Another agency was to be built on the Los Pinos River in La Plata County for the Tabeguache band and the three Southern Ute bands. However, when the Tabeguaches arrived at a branch

U-in-ta Utes, living in the U-in-ta Valley, on the Western Slope of the Wasatch Mountains, in Utah. Home of Ta-vah-puts. (Survey of J. W. Powell and A. H. Thompson.) *Photo by Hillers. Courtesy of Denver Public Library Western Collection.*

Ute blanket, saddle, bridle, and stirrups. (Woman's saddle.) *Photo by H. S. Poley. Courtesy of Denver Public Library Western Collection.*

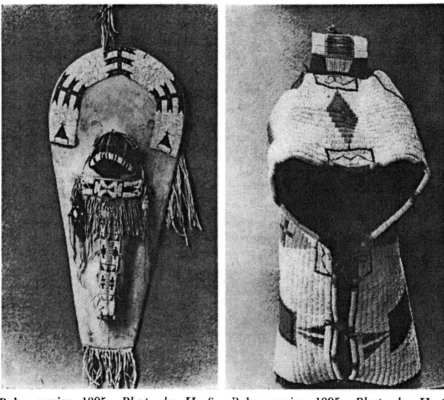

Baby carrier—1895. *Photo by H. S. Poley. Courtesy of Denver Public Library Western Collection.*

Baby carrier—1895. *Photo by H. S. Poley. Courtesy of Denver Public Library Western Collection.*

Cotoan, presumed to be son of Ouray. *Photo Courtesy Bureau of American Ethnology.*

Ute Bear Dance on reservation, music on Morache—1890. *Photo by H. S. Poley. Courtesy of Denver Public Library Western Collection*

Ute Bear Dance on Reservation—1890. *Photo by H. S. Poley. Courtesy of Denver Public Library Western Collection.*

The Bear Dance. Held in the spring of each year, it is the most ancient and typical of the Ute dances. *Photo courtesy of Thorne Studios.*

Signers of the Treaty of 1880 which forced the Northern and Uncompahgre Utes out of Western Colorado. This picture was taken in Washington, D. C., on March 6, 1880. *Left to right:* Galota, Otto Mears (interpreter), Savero. Shavanoux, Col. H. Page (agent of the Southern Utes), Jocknick, Ignacio, Hon. C. Schurs (Secretary of the Interior), Woretsiz, Ouray, Gen. Chas. Adams (special agent), Chipeta, Olio Blanco, Wm. H. Berry (last agent of the Uncompahgre Agency near Montrose), Tapuch. Capt. Jack, Tim Johnson, Sowerwick. Henry Jim, Buckskin Charlie, Wass, Wm. Burns, Alhandra. *Photo Courtesy George A. Gallagher.*

An old Indian lookout on the west side of Shavano Valley about seven miles west of Montrose. This point affords a view of the surrounding country for a long distance. Just beyond it is an old camp ground used by the Indians for many years. *Photo courtesy Walker Art Studios.*

Ouray as a young man. *Photo Courtesy Walker Art Studios.*

of Cochetopa Creek about 55 miles west of Saguache in western
Saguache County, which was sixty miles north of the Los Pinos
River, they refused to go further; so at this spot, which later
proved to be a number of miles east of the reservation boundary, the Los Pinos agency was set up. The tributary to Cochetopa Creek on which it was established was named Los Pinos
Creek in order to make the place of location conform to the
name of the stream specified in the treaty.[2]

The treaty gave full assurance that the reservation, compris-
ing about one-third of Colorado, would forever remain in possession of the Utes. It also provided for education, allotment of
lands in severalty, and annuities in clothing, blankets, utilities
and food up to $60,000 a year until the Indians were capable of
supporting themselves. Herds of sheep and cattle were to be
brought in by the government, and the Indians were to be
taught agriculture.

Since the new agency was so far north from the habitat of the
Southern Utes, they continued getting their rations and supplies from their old agency in New Mexico despite the terms of
the 1868 treaty.[3] The Southern Ute Agency at Ignacio was not
started until 1877.[4] Henry Page was appointed the first agent.
He, with the help of Edgar G. Bates who was one of the early
settlers on Pine River, built the first log cabin at the Ignacio
agency.[5]

In addition to the two agencies in western Colorado, a
third agency was started in Denver on January 17, 1871, with
Major James B. Thompson as agent for whatever Utes might
happen to be in Denver. Buffalo was still plentiful at that time
on the Eastern Slope of Colorado, and the Utes still made fall
hunting excursions into this area to shoot buffalo.

The favorite camping grounds of the Utes while on these
expeditions was in the Platte bottoms just across the river
from the mouth of Cherry Cheek. Here they would set up
their tepees and sometimes remain for several weeks, coming
into Denver almost every day to sell their hides and to patron-
ize the stores with the money thus received.[6]

While the Utes had no real right to the lands outside of their
reservation, the government deemed it best to allow them to

make these fall hunting trips in order to augment their winter supply of meat and hides.

By 1876 the buffalo had been largely exterminated, and, as a result, the Denver agency for the Utes was discontinued since the Indians no longer had any spending money from the sale of hides and, therefore, became a source of trouble about town.[7]

FOOTNOTES

[1]*Senate Documents*, Vol. II, p. 990.

[2]Frank Hall, *History of Colorado*, Vol. 4, pp. 144-146.

[3]Alonzo Hartman, *Memories and Experiences with the Utes in Colorado*, original manuscript copied in master's thesis of John B. Lloyd, *The Uncompahgre Utes*, Western State College, Mar. 24, 1939, pp. 5-15. In possession of Western History Dept., Denver Public Library.

[4]Edward Gulhume, *A History of La Plata County*, Master's Thesis, University of Colorado, 1934. In possession of Western History Dept., Denver Public Library.

[5]Martin Bates, *C.W.A. Interviews*, 1933-34, La Plata County, p. 17. In possession of State Historical Society of Colorado.

[6]Thomas F. Dawson, "Major Thompson, Chief Ouray, and the Utes," *Colorado Magazine*, May, 1930, p. 115.

[7]*Ibid.*, p. 122.

THE LOS PINOS AGENCY

The first agent at the Los Pinos Agency in Saguache County was Second Lieutenant Calvin T. Speer of the 11th United States Infantry. He arrived on July 31, 1869, and arranged for the construction of the agency buildings. Around a 200 foot quadrangle or parade ground, he supervised the construction of houses for the agent, resident farmer, miller, carpenter, and blacksmith. He also built a corral, mill, stable, cellar, Fairbanks platform scales, warehouse, schoolhouse, and combined carpenter and blacksmith shop.[1]

While it was easy to transport incoming goods as far as Saguache, the road from there to the agency was bad. It took annuity goods around eleven days to travel the fifty-five miles from Saguache to the agency.

Chief Ouray's house, also built during Speer's term of office, was a short distance south and east of the quadrangle. This original cabin, containing four rooms, burned down with all the chief's belongings. He was reimbursed $400 by the government, and a new cabin was constructed.

In 1871 the agency cow camp was started near the present site of Gunnison with James P. Kelley in charge until Alonzo Hartman was appointed. Charles F. Holt and John Kerr drove in the first government livestock, consisting of 640 cows and 1160 sheep.

It was customary for various church boards to recommend

agents for the various Indian reservations. The Los Pinos
Agency was under the auspices of the Unitarian Church of
Boston. In 1871 this church recommended the appointment of
Jabez Nelson Trask, a graduate of Harvard, to relieve Speer at
the usual $1500 a year salary. The new agent reached Denver
on April 23, 1871. After reporting to the territorial governor
to learn about his duties, he walked the 250 trackless miles to
the agency without waiting for the transportation which the
governor was trying to arrange.

While Trask was a man of Puritanic habits and character,
his peculiar dress and eccentric mannerisms made him a butt of
ridicule among the Indians.[2] He was usually dressed in a
swallow-tailed, navy blue coat with brass buttons and out-of-
date trousers which fitted skin-tight above and below the knees
while flaring out in a funnel-shape at the angles. This attire
was topped off by an old-fashioned beaver hat, enormous green
goggles, and a buck thorn walking stick.[3]

Trask was a highly educated man. After getting his degree at
Harvard he spent two years at Cambridge, graduating from the
Divinity School in 1866. He was very proficient in his knowledge of botany, geology, and astronomy, understanding these
subjects much better than he did the Indians. In keeping with
his unusual character, he bequeathed his estate to the Society
for the Protection of Dumb Animals and willed his body to the
Harvard Medical School.[4]

The Utes, through their spokesmen, sent in complaints about
the new agent, claiming that he didn't associate with them, refused to issue rations as needed, and treated them as inferiors.
They said that they wanted him replaced by an agent whom
they could respect and rely on for counsel and advice such as
Colonel Albert Pfeiffer, a sub-agent in New Mexico with whom
they had once dealt.[5]

On July 29, 1871, J. F. Jocknick, possibly Sidney Jocknick's
father, was sent out from Washington, D. C., to investigate
Trask's accounts. Jocknick found the agent's bookkeeping in
considerable confusion. Inexperience and ignorance rather
than dishonesty were the reasons for this incompetency. As a
matter of fact, he was overly economical in his expenditures

since his successor found $25,000 in a Denver bank upon which Trask could have drawn.

After Jocknick's report, the Unitarian Church realized that the job was too much for the Harvard scholar, so the church recommended General Charles Adams as his successor. As a result, in the summer of 1872 General Adams became the third Los Pinos agent at a salary of $1500 a year. This was supplemented, however, by a thousand dollars a year which his wife received as the agency teacher, although the schoolhouse was not used. Adams' actual name was Karl Adam Schwanbeck. He was a German by birth, and his real name being so difficult to pronounce, he took the simple English name of Adams. He did not attain the rank of general in the Army. The Colorado Territory was divided into four military districts soon after the Civil War with provisions for a brigadier general chosen from the civilians to be in charge of each district. Governor McCook appointed Adams to one of these posts. Consequently, he was only a militia general.[6]

Adams discharged all of the former employees at the agency with the exception of James P. Kelley who had charge of the agency's cow camp near the present town of Gunnison.[7] Adams later on assigned this job to Alonzo Hartman, but Kelley was retained as his assistant. Herman Luders handled the book work at the camp and was theoretically the manager, but Hartman was actually the head man.

Luders built one of the cabins at the cow camp and all of the stock corrals. The first cabin was built by Alonzo Hartman who arrived at the camp in 1872. These cabins were located a mile below the present town of Gunnison. The agency cowboys who resided here ran about 1000 head of cattle for the Tabeguache band.[8]

In addition to Hartman, Luders, and Kelley, Sidney Jocknick, who had formerly served as a cook at the agency, also helped out with the cowpunching.

Adams brought to his office a background of many years of experience with Indians, which he had acquired while engaged in military service at Fort Union, New Mexico. The Utes, Navajos, and Apaches all knew him.

During the summer of 1872 Otto Mears contracted to supply the Los Pinos Agency with one hundred head of cattle per month for beef to feed members of the Tabeguache band. He also contracted to supply them not later than November 16th with flour, 75,000 pounds of potatoes, 10,000 pounds of beans, and oats and hay.[9] In order to deliver these supplies Mears had to repair the 55-mile stretch of road from Saguache to the agency so that these loads could be hauled over the mountains. In a report by Territorial Governor Edward Mc-Cook on October 16, 1869, he wrote that it took eleven days to transport provisions and goods from Saguache to the Los Pinos Agency—five miles a day.[10]

There was an ox train of ten wagons due at the agency about October 1, 1872, from Fort Garland with blankets, tents, clothes, scissors, needles, thread, and many other goods from Washington, D. C., for the Utes. Adams was depending on Mears to have his road in shape by October so that this ox train could get through to the agency.

During the summer months the agent gave the Tabeguache band flour, blankets, tents, beans, potatoes, rice, sugar, coffee, and beef on the hoof. The Utes came to the agency in great numbers on ration day. Beginning at sunrise, groups of Indians with their wives and children would come riding in to the agency until by nine o'clock nearly 2,000 men, women, and children had assembled. When it was time to distribute the rations, the Indians would sit down and several of the older men would help pass out the provisions and goods.[11] The squaws then packed these supplies on horses.

As soon as these rations had been given out, the male Indians threw off their blankets, took rifles and revolvers, mounted their horses and gathered in groups about the corral.[12] One beef cow was given to the members of each tepee, and the cattle in the corral varied from ten to fifty.[13]

The beef cows were then "booed" out of the gate, and the Utes whooped and yelled to make them stampede. When they were going at a good rate of speed, the Indians in hot pursuit, started shooting at them as if they were wild buffalo on the plains. Sometimes a running horse would step in a hole and turn a somersault. If the rider wasn't killed, the post doctor usually had him fixed up for the next ration day.

It was impossible for the Indians to use all the meat at one time, but they used what they needed and dried and cured the rest for winter. This meat was cut in long strips and hung over a smoke fire in the sun to dry. This kept the flies away and also cured the meat.

When the Utes left the Los Pinos Agency around the last of October or the first of November to spend the winter along the Uncompahgre and Gunnison rivers, their horses were loaded with provisions and dried beef. This lasted them until the next spring when they returned to spend the summer months in the mountains near the agency.

FOOTNOTES

[1]Lois Borland, "Sale of the San Juan," *Colorado Magazine*, April, 1951, pp. 110-111.

[2]Sidney Jocknick, *Early Days on the Western Slope of Colorado*, p. 25.

[3]*Ibid.*, p. 37.

[4]Borland, *op. cit.*, p. 113.

[5]Other reasons for the Utes' dislike of Trask might have resulted partly from the agent's refusal to give gifts to the Indians to secure their cooperation, which was an old government practice, and because he insisted that Sunday be respected as a day of rest.

[6]Thomas F. Dawson, "Major Thompson, Chief Ouray and the Utes," *Colorado Magazine*, May, 1930, p. 122.

[7]Jocknick, *op. cit.*, p. 39.

[8]Frank Hall, *History of Colorado*, Vol. 4, pp. 144-146.

[9]Alonzo Hartman, "Memories and Experiences with the Utes in Colorado," original manuscript copied in master's thesis of John B. Lloyd entitled *The Uncompahgre Utes*, Western State College, Mar. 24, 1939, pp. 5-15. In possession of Western History Dept. of Denver Public Library.

[10]Borland, *op. cit.*, p. 111.

[11]Ernest Ingersoll, *Knocking Around the Rockies*, pp. 92-95.

[12]*Ibid.*, p. 94.

[13]Hartman, *op. cit.*

OUTSTANDING TABEGUACHE CHIEFS

The most famous chief of the Tabeguache band and the spokesman for all of the seven Ute bands was Chief Ouray. According to most historians Ouray was born at Taos, New Mexico in 1833.[1] His father was a Jicarilla Apache by the name of Guera Murah, who was adopted into the Ute tribe, and his mother was a member of the Tabeguache band.[2]

Ouray once told Major James B. Thompson, agent for the Denver Utes, that there was no meaning to his name. He said that "Ooay" was the first word he spoke as a child; so his parents called him that. The whites corrupted the word into "Ouray," but his own people who had difficulty pronouncing the letter "r" called him "Oolay" or "Ulay."[3]

Ouray's boyhood was spent among the better class of Mexican ranchers as a sheepherder in the present state of New Mexico.[4] During these formative years he became familiar with the Spanish language. Ouray could talk understandable English but he had a much better knowledge of Spanish.

At the age of eighteen he gave up his work as a sheep herder and came into western Colorado to become a full-fledged member of the Tabeguache band of Utes in which his father was a leader. From then until 1860 he lived like a typical wild Indian,, hunting, fighting the plains Indians, and visiting the other Ute bands.

In stature Ouray was about five feet seven inches tall, and he became quite portly in his later years. His head was large and well shaped with regular features. His face, while stern and dignified in repose, lighted up pleasantly when he talked. He had a refined, polished manner and enjoyed meeting and visiting with white men. He ordinarily wore a civilized attire of black broadcloth and usually wore boots instead of moccasins. However, he never cut off his long hair which he bound up in two braids that hung on his chest in Ute Indian fashion.

While still a young man Ouray married a Tabeguache maiden, and they had a son. One fall when the baby was about five years old, Ouray went on a buffalo hunt twenty-five miles north of Denver. While the men were out hunting, a group of Sioux raided the Ute camp on the Platte River near the present site of Fort Lupton and kidnapped Ouray's boy.[5]

After his first wife's death, Ouray married a Tabeguache girl by the name of Chipeta in 1859. She was sixteen and Ouray twenty-six at the time of their marriage.

Ouray first came into prominence in 1863 when a treaty was negotiated with the Tabeguache band at Conejos defining the boundaries of the band's reservation. During the negotiations Ouray translated the speeches of his people into Spanish from which came the English version through the government interpreter. To this treaty Ouray signed his name "U-ray." Five years later at Washington, D. C., when the Treaty of 1868 was being discussed, the federal government recognized Ouray as spokesman for all seven of the Ute bands. To the original Treaty of 1868 his name was signed "U-re" but to the amendment it was signed "Ouray."

Ouray's hold upon his people was always precarious except for the members of his own band, who were usually loyal to him. He accomplished his objectives primarily through patience, diplomacy, and the strength of his personality rather than by any power that he might have had as head chief of the tribe.

Many of the Ute chiefs were jealous of Ouray's position, and he had many enemies among his own people. The Northern Ute chiefs were particularly hostile, believing that the federal government should have chosen one of them as spokesman for the Ute nation, and it took them a long time to accept Ouray.

Even in his own band there was some resentment. Once in 1872 at the Los Pinos Agency five sub-chiefs of the Tabeguache band tried to kill Ouray. The one chosen as leader of the group was Sapowanero, a brother of Chipeta and the man who usually took charge of the Tabeguache band whenever Ouray was away. The would-be assassins hid in the agency's blacksmith shop as Ouray led his horse across the plaza to get it shod. As he tied his horse to the hitching post, George Hardman, the blacksmith, gave Ouray a warning wink.

Ouray was put on his guard just in time, for seconds later Sapowanero ran out of the shop, brandishing an ax. Ouray jumped behind the post as Sapowanero swung the ax at him, the blow missing the great chief's head only by inches. Ouray kept the post between him and his assailant, and when Sapowanero struck again, the ax handle hit the post and broke.

Without his weapon Sapowanero was no match for his powerful brother-in-law. Ouray threw him down into an irrigation ditch that ran past the blacksmith shop. Grasping Sapowanero's throat, Ouray reached for his knife to dispose of the fallen Indian, but Chipeta, who happened to be nearby, pulled the knife from its scabbard just as her husband grabbed for it, thereby saving her brother's life. Seeing how Sapowanero fared, his accomplices in the blacksmith shop took to their heels.[6]

In spite of this altercation in front of the blacksmith shop, Sapowanero was usually very loyal to Ouray. Whenever Ouray was away from the agency for any length of time, he left Sapowanero in charge.[7] Besides visiting the other Ute bands, Ouray and Chipeta once a year would pack their camping outfits and ride up in the mountains to hunt for a few days, never more than a week. Sapowanero always knew where he could find them, but he never disturbed them on these trips except in emergencies.

After the Meeker Massacre Sapowanero was chosen by Ouray as his representative to go with General Adams to rescue the women and children who had been kidnapped at the Meeker Agency. The little village near the mouth of the Black Canyon in Gunnison County was named in honor of this Ute chief.[8] He died shortly after the Tabeguache band was moved to the new agency in Utah in the fall of 1881.

Curicata, another promrinent Tabeguache chief, was well along in years when the Los Pinos Agency was started in 1869. Consequently he did not take an active part in the general activities, but he always attended the council meetings held once a year.[9]

Curicata had a twin brother named Kanneatche, and they usually led the annual Bear Dance each spring in Denver during the agency days there (1871-1876). They were inseperable and roamed and hunted all over the Colorado Territory together. Curicata was a man of Puritanic habits. He never drank, and although an excellent dancer he was indifferent to the squaws. He didn't marry until late in life and had only one wife. Kanneatche, on the other hand, was quite a carouser. He had many wives and was a heavy drinker.[10]

One time when he was in Denver, Kanneatche walked into the office of the *Rocky Mountain Herald*. A printer gave him an old plug hat which had once ben worn by O. J. Goldrich, the proprietor of the paper. A large label entitled "Superior Cocktail Bitters" was pasted around the side of the hat. For many days Kanneatche, wearing his plug hat, paraded proudly up and down the streets of Denver to the admiration of the Indians and the amusement of the whites.[11]

When Kanneatche died a few years later, Curicata inherited the plug hat. Ten years after his brother's death, Curicata also died. Curecanti Creek, a well-known fishing stream which flows into the Black Canyon of the Gunnison River, was named after this chief and has perpetuated his memory.

Other outstanding chiefs of the Tabeguache band were McCook, Shavano, and Piah. John McCook, one of Chipeta's brothers, took an active part in the band's activities. One fall day in 1872 Ouray wished to send an urgent message to a camp of Utes about one hundred miles away. He asked Chief McCook to carry the important message to its destination and gave him a fine looking, but only half-broken, horse to ride. The bronco threw McCook and galloped away to join the other horses about a mile distant. McCook lay unconscious on the ground, and the Indians thought that he was seriously hurt. However, he came to in a short time, and, catching another horse, he rode off with the message.

Alonzo Hartman, a newcomer who had arrived the day before with Otto Mears, roped the runaway horse and led him back to where Ouray was standing. After removing the saddle, Hartman asked Ouray what he should do with the outlaw.[12]

Ouray told Hartman to turn the bronco loose, saying that if McCook could not ride him no one could.

"Do you want him ridden?" Hartman questioned.

"Yes," said Ouray, "but who can do?"

"I think maybe I can," Hartman said as he carefully replaced the saddle.

A crowd, composed of all the agency employees and about 200 Indians, quickly gathered to see the fun. The white man swung himself on, and the horse ducked his head and began squealing and pitching. He was strong and lively on his feet, but Hartman, who had spent most of his life on a cattle ranch, soon brought the outlaw under control. Hartman was later made manager of the agency's cow camp which had just recently been started one mile below the present site of Gunnison.

McCook was with Ouray when the great chief died while on a visit to the Southern Ute Agency in the fall of 1880. McCook helped bury him secretly in a cavern two miles below the agency. On March, 1925, McCook helped escort Chipeta's remains from its burial place in Utah to her mausoleum at the Ouray Memorial Park two miles south of Montrose. In 1937 when McCook died, his body was buried beside the tomb of his sister.

Chief Shavano, a mild looking, grandfatherly sort of Indian, took a prominent part in the discussion when the Treaty of 1873 was being negotiated. Oftentimes on ration day at the Los Pinos Agency Shavano would appear on the ridge-pole of the government's storehouse, and with his blanket wrapped majestically around him, he would give directions as to how the Indians should assemble for the distribution of the goods. He spoke in the usual low voice of a Ute, which while nearly inaudible to a white man was clearly understood by the sharp ears of an Indian. When everyone was seated and quiet prevailed, Shavano would ask several of the older Utes to help him pass out the flour, beans, coffee, tobacco, and other rations.[13]

Piah was originally a member of one of the Northern Ute bands, but after he killed a prominent chief by the name of Johnson, he fled and joined the Tabeguache band. The name Johnson was then taken by another Northern Ute chief, who later attacked Nathan C. Meeker when the agent started plowing a field which Johnson had been using for a horse pasture.[14]

One fall in the early 1870's a fight occurred on the Republican River in eastern Colorado between Piah's band of buffalo hunters and a group of Arapahoes under the leadership of Chief Moonface. The Utes won the battle and took the scalps of the defeated plains Indians, including that of Chief Moonface. The sheriff of Denver, the Ute interpreter, and others persuaded Piah to celebrate the Utes' victory with a war dance in the city. A famous animal trainer, Mr. Bartholomew, offered his tent for the exhibition.[15]

The promoters asked the Ute agent at Denver, Major James B. Thompson, for permission to give the performance, and Thompson wrote the Commissioner of Indian Affairs concerning the matter.

The Commissioner wired, "Prevent the exhibition at all hazards. It will arouse the jealousy of the Arapahoes. Call on U. S. Marshal if necessary."[16]

The promoters, however, ignored Thompson's orders and decided to put on the victory dance, anyway. Thompson appealed to the U. S. marshal, who refused to act. Next the agent looked up the Denver marshal and showed him the Indian Commissioner's wire. The Denver marshal told Thompson that he wasn't taking orders from the Indian Commissioner. Thompson was, thereupon, put in the difficult position of having to stop the exhibition completely by himself, if he were to follow the orders of his superior in Washington.

Meanwhile, Piah at the head of his band and followed by the promoters, wearing plug hats, started marching down Fifteenth Street. Their route to the animal trainer's tent, where the dance was scheduled to take place, took them past Thompson's office. As Piah passed by, the Indian agent suddenly jumped out from the crowd in front of the Ute chief with a loaded revolver in each hand.

With a terrifying cry, he yelled at Piah, "Vamoose, presto!"

Startled, Piah promptly complied, followed by the others. In their haste to get away, the Utes stampeded into the rear guard of white promoters, who lost their dignity as well as their plug hats.[17]

The U. S. marshal and the Ute interpreter at the Denver agency lost their jobs because of their refusal to help Thompson carry out the Commissioner's orders. If the performance had been staged, it would undoubtedly have antagonized not only the Arapahoes but the Cheyennes, the Kiowas, the Comanches, and the Sioux as well.

In the summer of 1874 Hayden's geological and geographical survey expedition camped at the Los Pinos Agency. While the white men were visiting with the Utes, it suddenly began to rain and most of the surveyors sought refuge in Piah's tepee, where they sat on the hides of wild animals until the shower had stopped. The squaws were quiet, but Piah more than kept up his end of the conversation with the white men. While he talked, he pulled out from an otter-skin pouch, where he carried a great assortment of articles, a small round looking-glass and a shallow box containing vermilion. Piah was a short man with an unusually small head and face, and as he crouched upon his haunches and beamed at the white men over the top of his mirror with little piggish eyes, he looked more like an elf than an influential chief.[18]

Rubbing some tallow on the palms of his hands, he patted down his shining, jet-black hair until it was pasted to his small boyish-like skull. Behind, his hair was done up in two long braids, which hung on his chest. To these braids were entwined strips of otter-skin, lengthening the plaits until they reached nearly to his hips. He did not touch the braids but proceeded to tint the straight parting in the middle of his head with yellow-ochre.

Then he folded some buckskin over the end of his finger, dipped it into the shallow box containing the vermilion, and rubbed the paint upon his face until two large red spots appeared on his extraordinarily dark cheeks. Then he added some lines upon his forehead and chin.

When the shower finally passed over, Piah took a last scrutinizing look at himself in the mirror. Apparently everything meeting with aproval, he replaced his toilet articles in the carry-all pouch, and pulling his Navajo blanket around his shoulders, he stalked out of the tepee with all the drama of a Shakespearean actor.

FOOTNOTES

[1]Frank Hall, *History of Colorado*, Vol. 2, p. 135.

[2]Thomas F. Dawson, "Major Thompson, Chief Ouray, and the Utes," *Colorado Magazine*, May, 1930, p. 118.

[3]*Ibid.*, p. 121.

[4]Hall, *op. cit.*, pp. 506-513.

[5]Ann Woodbury Hafen, "Efforts to Recover the Stolen Son of Chief Ouray," *Colorado Magazine*, Mar., 1939, p. 54.

[6]Sidney Jocknick, *Early Days on the Western Slope of Colorado*, pp. 116-117.

[7]Alonzo Hartman, "Memories and Experiences with the Utes in Colorado," original manuscript copied in master's thesis of John B. Lloyd entitled *The Uncompahgre Utes*, Western State College, Mar. 24, 1939, p. 9. In possession of Western History Dept. of Denver Public Library.

[8]Sapinero.

[9]Hartman, *op. cit.*, p. 10.

[10]Jocknick, *op. cit.*, p. 294.

[11]*Ibid.*, p. 295.

[12]Hartman, *op. cit.*, pp. 6-8.

[13]Ernest Ingersoll, *Knocking Around the Rockies*, pp. 93-94.

[14]Wm. N., Byers, "History of the Ute Nation," *Rocky Mountain News*, April 16, 1880, J. S. Randall Scrap Book, p. 13. In possession of Colorado State Historical Society.

[15]Jocknick, *op. cit.*, pp. 30-32.

[16]*Ibid.*, p. 30.

[17]*Ibid.*, p. 31.

[18]Ingersoll, *op. cit.*, p. 98.

TREATY OF 1873

In 1870 and 1871 small gold discoveries were made in the San Juan region of southwestern Colorado near the present town of Silverton. By 1872 prospectors and miners were over-running this portion of the Ute reservation. Twice government troops were sent in to force out the trespassers, but they kept coming back. A lot of pressure was exerted against the government to draw up a new treaty on the basis that this mountain area which was so valuable to the whites was practically worth-less to the Indians.

Congress acted favorably upon a recommendation of the Secretary of Interior to authorize him the power to appoint a committee to negotiate with the Utes for relinquishing some of this valuable mining land. Three commissioners were ac-cordingly appointed, and a council was ordered to be held at the Los Pinos Agency in August, 1872.[1]

At this meeting Chief Ouray and his followers opposed giv-ing up any of the reservation as established by the Treaty of 1868. Ouray won the day for his people by exposing the viola-tion of the government's pledges, and he pointed out the moral injustice of its attempting to nullify a treaty which had been deliberately framed, signed, and ratified by the United States Senate. The commission returned to Washington defeated.

Charles Adams, the agent at Los Pinos, was requested by the Commisioner of Indian Affairs to bring a delegation of Utes,

selected by Chief Ouray, to Washington, D. C., for a conference
with the Indian Department and to meet President U. S. Grant.
Ouray's first selection was Sapowanero, and together they chose
seven others, who with Ouray's wife Chipeta made ten Indians
in all. Ouray asked Otto Mears to accompany them as an interpreter, and Adams named three other white men to go along
and help Mears in the difficult job of looking after the delegation.[2]

On November 10, 1872, the group left the agency, traveling
in a covered wagon, drawn by a team of mules, to Colorado
City, near present Colorado Springs, where they boarded a train
for Washington, D. C. The delegation spent ten days in the
national capitol, where they met President and Mrs. U. S.
Grant in the White House.

The Utes also visited New York City, Baltimore, Boston,
Philadelphia, and other big cities of the east. While in New
York they were taken to a circus, where they were fascinated by
the trick riding and astonished at the other performances in the
arena. They much preferred the circus to the theater where
they saw "The Black Crook." At Central Park they took great
interest in the animals, being especially impressed by the camels
which, they were told, were ridden like horses by people in far-
away lands. The Utes made fun of the small, scrawny buffaloes
in the park. They called the elephant by a title which translated by Mears meant "the big high animal with a tail at each
end." The monkeys and baboons startled them at first, but
within a short time they were laughing at their antics. The
Indians referred to them as "the long-armed creatures who try
to look like men." The Utes thought that the stuffed bird and
animal exhibits in the museum were shams and prided themselves in detecting the deception.[3]

The Utes finally arrived home at the Los Pinos Agency on
January 10, 1873, after a sixty-day trip.[4]

The Utes were instructed to assemble about the middle of
August, 1873, to hold another council with a new commission
from Washington to discuss the San Juan problem. Felix
Brunot, head of the new commission, had been told by Ouray
at the first gathering on the previous year that some ten years

ago his only son had been kidnapped by the Sioux. Ouray said that a Mexican who traded with the Sioux had told him that one of the chiefs of that tribe now had this boy who was called Friday. This story was confirmed, Ouray added, by a Mexican woman who was married to a Sioux.[5]

Brunot had responded to this information by sending letters immediately to the various Indian agencies in an attempt to find the lost boy. His investigations showed that the boy had passed from the Sioux into the hands of the Northern Arapahoes on the North Platte, and after several years he had been taken over by the Southern Arapahoes. He was a young man of about sixteen or seventeen and to all appearance a full-fledged Arapahoe, the members of which tribe were deadly enemies of the Utes.

Brunot worked hard to get hold of the youth, believing that if he could deliver him to Ouray the chief would reciprocate by using his great influence to obtain his people's consent to relinquish the disputed San Juan lands. Brunot hoped to bring the boy along with the newly appointed commissioners, who were once more going to try negotiating a treaty with the Utes.

The agent of the Northern Arapahoes learned from the head chief information concerning the capture of the lost boy, and this corresponded to most of the facts furnished by Ouray. The Northern Arapahoe chief told the agent that Friday was now with the Southern Arapahoes.[6]

Around 1800 Ute Indians gathered at the Los Pinos Agency about the middle of August, but the commissioners did not arrive until Septeber 5th. Brunot explained that the delay was caused by their stopping at Colorado Springs and other places while enroute in order to wait for the expected arrival of Ouray's son, who had somehow managed to elude the agents who had gone to get him.

Ouray was greatly disappointed, but Brunot promised to continue the search. The council met on the morning of September 8, 1873. Primarily through the efforts of Ouray a treaty was agreed upon by the seven Ute bands on September 13th.

By this Treaty of 1873, the Utes ceded to the United States

their rights to most of the San Juan country.[7] The Utes surrendered most or all of the present counties of San Miguel, Dolores, Montezuma, La Plata, Archuleta, Ouray, Hinsdale and San Juan. They continued to keep most or all of the present counties of Rio Blanco, Garfield, Mesa, Delta and Montrose, as well as parts of Gunnison, Pitkin and Eagle.[8]

The new reservation boundary left a strip of territory roughly fifteen miles wide and one hundred miles long to the Utes along the Colorado-New Mexico border, where the Southern Utes now reside. Another long strip about twenty miles wide and eighty miles long was left to the Utes along the Colorado-Utah border.

The Utes were allowed to hunt upon the lands taken away from them so long as they remained at peace with the whites. In consideration for the cession, the government agreed to set apart and hold in perpetual trust for the Utes a sum sufficient to produce $25,000 interest per year. This was to be distributed or invested by the President for the use and benefit of the Indians.

For his services as head of the confederated bands of Utes the treaty provided that Ouray was to receive $1,000 a year for as long as he remained head chief and his people remained at peace with the United States.

The Treaty of 1873 was ratified by the United States Senate on April 29, 1874.

It was while the Treaty of 1873 was pending that Captain John Moss drew up a private treaty with Ignacio, a chief of the Southern Utes, for the right to farm and mine thirty-six square miles of the San Juan area with the central point at what a short time later became Parrott City near the present village of Hesperus. In return one hundred ponies and many blankets were given to the Indians. Parrott City was designated in 1876 as the county seat of La Plata County. This designation brought the town an ephemeral boom, which faded gradually into a ghost town with the establishment of Durango and the coming of its railroad.

John Moss looked like an Indian and dressed like one. He understood Indian character and spoke many Indian languages.

The Utes called him "Captain." His friendship with Ignacio kept the Southern Utes peaceful to the residents of his little settlement.

After the Utes signed the Treaty of 1873, Felix Brunot kept his promise to bring Ouray and the boy Friday together. He made arrangements to have a delegation of Arapahoes and a delegation of Utes arrive in Washington, D. C. about the same time. There, representatives of these two enemy tribes, including Ouray and Friday, met in the office of the Board of Indian Commissioners. At this dramatic meeting Brunot tried to get Friday to recognize Ouray as his father and to make peace between the age-old enemy tribes.[9]

He explained to the youth that the head chief of the Utes had his son captured a long time ago and that evidence pointed to the probability that Friday was the lost boy.

Speaking through an interpreter, Ouray asked Friday if he could remember his Ute name. Friday said that the only name he could recall was the one that the Arapahoes had given him.

One of the younger representatives of the Ute delegation told Friday that they were cousins and had played together as children. He informed Friday that his Ute name was Cotan.

However, in spite of all these pleas Friday refused to admit that he was a member of the tribe which he had been taught to hate. He returned to his reservation, apparently still believing that he was an Arapahoe.

FOOTNOTES

[1]Frank Hall, *History of Colorado*, Vol. 2, p. 508.

[2]Alonzo Hartman, "Memories and Experiences with the Utes in Colorado," original manuscript copied in master's thesis of John B. Lloyd entitled *The Uncompahgre Utes*, Western State College, Mar. 24, 1939, p. 13. In possession of Western History Dept., Denver Public Library.

[3]Helen M. Searcy, "Otto Mears and the Utes," *Pioneers of the San Juan*, Vol. I, p. 24.

[4]Hartman, *op. cit.*, p. 13.

[5]Report of the Board of Indian Commissioners, 1872, p. 109, official document found among unpublshed papers of the Indian

Bureau now housed in the National Archives Building. Also, see
Ann Woodbury Hafen, "Efforts to Recover the Stolen Son of Chief
Ouray," *Colorado Magazine*, Mar. 1939, p. 54.

[6]Hafen, *op. cit.*, p. 56.

[7]The land ceded was described in the treaty as follows: "Beginning at a point on the eastern boundary of said reservation, 15 miles
due north of the southern boundary of the Territory of Colorado,
and running thence west on a line parallel to the said southern
boundary to a point on said line twenty miles due east of the western boundary of Colorado Territory; thence north by a line parallel
with the western boundary to a point ten miles north of the point
where said line intersects the 38th parallel of north latitude; thence
east to the eastern boundary of the Ute reservation; and thence
south along said boundary to the place of beginning. . . ."

[8]*Senate Documents*, Vol. I, p. 151.

[9]Hafen, *op. cit.*, p. 57.

AFTERMATHS OF THE TREATY

The Utes still roamed at large through the San Juan country after the signing of the Brunot Treaty, and they became increasingly hostile as the settlers increased and more and more land in the valleys was taken up.

In the mountainous areas where no farms were practical, the newcomers brought in cattle to graze on the rich, abundant grass. The cattle competed against the wild game which helped support the Indians, causing further conflict of interest between the two races.

The miners and ranchers lived in constant fear of the Utes, never knowing when their resentment against the flood of settlers might cause the Indians to go on the warpath.

One evening in 1874 several members of the Hayden Survey sat by their campfire on a wooded bluff overlooking the new mining town of Howardsville. At that time rumors abounded that the Utes were in open rebellion and had burned ranches, murdered stockmen, hunters, and prospectors, and were preparing to raid Howardsville![1]

Around the campfire sat Ernest Ingersoll, a recorder of the famous expedition; F. M. Endlich, a French cook; a young horse packer called Bob; and a general servant. The other members of the surveying party were away on a side trip.

"If them red bastards show up tonight," Bob commented,

patting the .44 caliber Sharps rifle that he held in his lap, "I'll really put the fear of God into 'em with this shootin' iron."

"I wouldn't take too seriously all this talk about the Utes bein' on the warpath," Ingersoll said. "They have always been a peaceful tribe."

"Yuh can never trust a redskin," Bob said knowingly. "It don't take much to get 'em roused up."

"You talk like an old Indian fighter," Endlich remarked with a smile. "Have you had a lot of dealings with the critters?"

"Well, I've read a little about 'em, and I've always had a hankerin' to be an Indian fighter."

"If the rumors prove true, you'll probably get your chance tonight, Bob," Ingersoll said, amused at the young horse packer's attitude.

The group retired as usual about nine o'clock that night. An hour or so later they were rudely awakened by earsplitting, diabolical shrieks and yells, accompanied by the echoing roar of guns. Pandemonium had broken loose in Howardsville.

Ingersoll leaped to his feet. There in the moonlight he saw Bob standing half dressed, his face the personification of terror. His rifle hung limply in his hand.

"There they come!" he gasped. "Oh, my God!" He disappeared into the night and was not seen again until the following day when everything had quieted down.

The next morning the rest of the party walked down to Howardsville to see what had happened. They discovered that the whole affair was a frame-up. In a successful effort to get rid of an unpopular easterner, a number of miners had disguised themselves as Indians and staged a mock raid.

The whites violated the Treaty of 1873 by trespassing continually on the reservation strip along the Colorado-New Mexico border. The Southern Utes became increasingly hostile as herds of cattle were driven from both directions across their reservation, eating up most of the sparse quantities of pasture. In order to prevent open hostilities a fort was established near Pagosa Hot Springs in 1878. The post was called Fort Lewis in honor of Lieutenant Colonel Lewis who had been killed in action against the Cheyenne Indians in 1877. The military reservation comprised an area six miles square on both sides of the San Juan River with Pagosa Hot Springs in the southwest corner.

The San Juan Treaty of 1873 reopened all of the old bitterness against Ouray. The Northern Utes believed that the head chief of the Ute confederation should have been selected from one of their bands. As early as 1875 some of them planned the overthrow of Ouray. If it could not be accomplished peaceably, they proposed to kill him and talked openly of it.[2]

Certain leaders of the three Northern Ute bands charged that Ouray had sold the Ute tribe down the river in the Treaty of 1873 for the $1,000 a year salary provided for him in the treaty. When the federal government failed to live up to its obligation of paying the Utes $25,000 per year, Ouray took a lot of the blame from his people. They claimed that Ouray and certain white officials were conspiring to misappropriate the money and annuities which the government had promised the Utes. Their plots and smear campaigns against Ouray, however, failed to overthrow the great chief, and they finally became reconciled, if not cordial, to him.

Many of the Southern Utes felt for a time the same reseptment and envy toward Ouray. One of these had been a student at the Carlisle Indian School. He acquired the name of Hot Stuff at school because of an explosive accident which he had in his chemistry class. When Hot Stuff got out of the hospital, he went back to the reservation to live the life of a wild Indian.

He was bitter toward the whites and hated Ouray for being so cooperative and friendly with them. One day Ouray was informed by his secret police that Hot Stuff was on his way to the Uncompahgre Agency to kill him.

Late on the afternoon of the following day Chipeta happened to see Hot Stuff riding toward Ouray's home on a calico horse. The rider was approaching through a heavy growth of brush so as not to be seen. Chipeta pointed him out to her husband, who got his rifle. When Hot Stuff got within shooting range of the chief's adobe house, Ouray drew a bead on his enemy and shot him through the neck.[3]

Ouray was forced to kill four other rebellious Utes who

strenuously opposed his policies.[4] His severe method of disposing of his opponents was probably without parallel in the history of the American Indian, and this was one of the primary reasons that he kept his redmen so well in line. He understood Indian nature and was capable of dealing with it. If it hadn't been for Ouray's discipline and influence on the Utes, there would undoubtedly have been many serious and bloody outbreaks among his dissatisfied and primitive people.

FOOTNOTES

[1]Mary Ayers, "Howardsville in the San Juan," *Colorado Magazine,* Oct. 1951, pp. 250-251.

[2]Wm. N. Byers, "History of the Ute Nation," *Rocky Mountain News,* April 16, 1880. Article in U. S. Randall Scrap Book, p. 13. In possession of State Historical Society of Colorado.

[3]Sidney Jocknick, *Early Days on the Western Slope of Colorado,* p. 119.

[4]*Ibid.,* p. 118.

THE UNCOMPAHGRE AGENCY

For some time removal of the Los Pinos Agency to a new location had been contemplated. The agency was not on the Ute reservation although it was believed to have been when first established. Due to the extreme cold during the winter, the Indians remained at the agency for only a few months out of the year, which wasn't long enough to make progress in either agriculture or education.

Ouray thought that his band could not be persuaded to move farther away than the agency cow-camp at the junction of the Gunnison and Tomichi. The Cebolla Valley between the present towns of Gunnison and Sapinero was also given serious consideration for the new location. However, the site finally decided upon was the Uncompahgre Valley where the village of Colona now stands, twelve miles south of Montrose.

The 1200-head of government cattle were moved first. They were herded from Taylor Park north of the present site of Gunnison to where Cow Creek[1] flows into the Uncompahgre River about seven miles south of the new agency site. It took the agency cowboys[2] ten days to make the 110-mile drive. Upon arriving they proceeded to build a corral and cabin.[3]

Transfer of equipment from Los Pinos to the Uncompahgre Agency over seventy-five miles of mountainous terrain was no small task. It took twelve men, four wagons, nine yoke of oxen, and one mule team three weeks to remove the sawmill.

Hundreds of Indian ponies, part of them heavily packed with Ute belongings, took part in the evacuation. The removal was finally completed about November 20, 1875.[4]

Ouray was given a four-hundred acre ranch at the new agency and the government built him and Chipeta an adobe house on the southern outskirts of present Montrose. This house was furnished with beds, tables, chairs, rugs and stoves.[5]

During the summer of 1875, shortly before orders were received from Washington to move the agency, Charles Adams was replaced as agent by the Reverend Henry F. Bond, a graduate of Harvard.[6]

Accoring to a current policy, various churches recommended agents for the Indian reservations. The Indian Department, as already mentioned, had allocated the Los Pinos Agency to the Unitarian Church of Boston. Adams had been appointed because of his military record and experience with the Indians. At the time of his appointment it was generally believed that he was a Unitarian. When it was discovered that he was a Catholic, the Unitarian Church secured his removal in order to appoint a member of its own sect.

Within a short time after Bond took over management of the agency, it was removed to the Uncompahgre River. The Los Pinos Agency served as a sub-agency from 1875 to 1879 when it was abandoned. An auction was held, and everything movable was disposed of. The last building to stand was Ouray's old adobe house. In 1882 John McDonough bought the agency location. Today all that remains of the Indian days is the Ute race track, which can still be plainly seen east and south of the ranch house.

When a count was made of the government cattle driven over from the Gunnison country, there was found a shortage of two hundred head of steers. These had apparently strayed back from the Uncompahgre to their old range in Taylor Park, where they had been appropriated by settlers, prospectors, and miners.[7]

Because of this shortage, Bond was requested to resign. He was succeeded by Major W. D. Wheeler, who arrived from Washington in the fall of 1876. Wheeler was an ex-army paymaster and well-fitted for the job. He was tall and portly with a military bearing which made him highly respected by his employees and the Indians. He was stern and exacting, and while a member of the Unitarian Church, he was not deeply religious.

One of the interesting diversions from the daily routine of agency life on the Uncompahgre was carrying of the mail. This duty fell by turns to each of the employees except the cook.

The mail carrier was equipped with a saddle horse and a pack mule, and he rode through seventy-five miles of mountain country to reach the Lake City road, which was the nearest connecting link with civilization.[8]

Once when Sidney Jocknick, an agency cowboy, was returning with the mail bags, he was stopped by a group of Indians who insisted that he get out a letter addressed to the agency and read it to them.

When Jocknick refused, they tried to take the pouches away from him. The cowboy then threatened to inform Chief Ouray of their actions, and the Utes rode away. The presence of Ouray at the agency was always a stabilizing influence on the Indians.

In the fall of 1876—the year that Colorado became a state— the Uncompahgre Agency became a central headquarters for the outgoing and incoming mail to the nearby San Juan mines. Otto Mears handled bids of the various contractors. He divided the seventy-five mile route to the Lake City road into three sections with a cabin located every twenty-five miles.

With the coming of winter tall, bushy sticks were stuck in the snow at equal distances, which helped the mail carriers follow the same trail after each snowfall. Before long this path became packed from continuous use and resembled a raised highway. If a carrier tried stepping off of this road to take a shortcut, he would go down neck-deep in the soft, deep snow.

The snow often covered the carriers' cabins so completely that only the chimneys were visible. Many times the chimneys had to be used for entrances and exits into the cabins.

An old prospector by the name of Stewart Daniells, who had once been employed as a mail carrier of the Hudson Bay Fur

Company, suggested to Otto Mears that dogs be used to transport the mail during the winter months. Daniells was thereupon given a contract to carry the mail by dog-team from the Cimarron River to the Lake City road.

George Beckwith, a nephew of the famous scout Jim Beckwith, was given a contract by Mears to carry the mail by pack-mule from the Uncompahgre Agency to the Cimarron, where the dog route began.[9]

A week before Christmas, 1876, Beckwith's pack mule went lame; so he saddled his horse and rode out in search of the agency horses, which he found out on the open range. He roped one of the horses, which he planned to use as a substitute for his pack mule. After catching the mustang he tied the end of his lariat rope to his saddle horn. Something frightened the horse he was riding, who began bucking around in a circle. Beckwith was thrown, and the rope entwined both horses. In struggling to get loose from each other, the horses kicked and trampled the unfortunate rider. He died a few days later and was buried Christmas day on the top of a hill about a mile northwest of the agency.

Major Wheeler[10] conducted the last rites in a raging snowstorm, reading the burial service from an Episcopal prayer book. Seven Indians, who had followed the group of white men to the grave, stood a short distance away watching the ceremony. After the service was over and the agency employees started homeward, these Indians rode past the grave with both hands raised in the air as a last farewell to the dead mail carrier.[11]

After the Meeker Massacre, Colonel R. S. MacKenzie at Fort Garland was ordered to move with part of his command to the Uncompahgre Valley to prevent any outbreak in that area. The first troops arrived in the valley on May 25, 1880, and consisted of four companies of the 4th Cavalry, five companies of the 19th Infantry, and two companies of the 23rd Infantry. A cantonment, or quarters for the troops, was established four miles north of the agency, which would be eight miles south of present Montrose. It was known as the "Military Cantonment" until March 12, 1884, when the name was changed by presidential order to Fort Crawford in memory of Captain Emmett

Crawford of the 3rd Infantry, who was killed by the Apaches in Arizona.[12] The post was finally abandoned in 1890, nine years after the Tabeguache band was taken out of Colorado.[13]

FOOTNOTES

[1]Cow Creek was named by the cowboys who drove the cattle over.

[2]The cowboys who made the drive were Alonzo Hartman, who was wagon boss, John B. McIntire, Jim Bishop, George Beckwith, Jim Kelley, Antonio Madrill, and Sidney Jocknick.

[3]Sidney Jocknick, *Early Days on the Western Slope of Colorado*, p. 85.

[4]Lois Borland, "Sale of the San Juan," *Colorado Magazine*, April, 1951, p. 126.

[5]The house still stands at Ouray Memorial Park just south of Montrose. Its original location was about one hundred yards north of where it is now situated.

[6]Jocknick, *op. cit.*, p. 81.

[7]*Ibid.*, p. 107.

[8]*Ibid.*, p. 122.

[9]*Ibid.*, p. 126.

[10]Agents at the Uncompahgre Agency who followed Wheeler were Major W. M. Kelley, the seventh agent for the Tabeguache band; Captain Stanley, the eighth; and Major William H. Berry, the last. Berry was agent when the Uncompahgre Utes were moved to their new agency in Utah in the fall of 1881.

[11]Jocknick, *op. cit.*, p. 131.

[12]Frank Hall, *History of Colorado*, p. 237.

[13]*Colorado Magazine*, Vol. 18-19, 1941, p. 29 (Place Names).

THE WHITE RIVER AGENCY

In 1868 an agency was started for the Northern Utes on White River not far from where the town of Meeker now stands. During the fall of 1869 Major D. C. Oakes, the first agent, arrived with an outfit of wagons, supplies, and tools from Rawlins, Wyoming. Runners were sent out to notify the Indians and bring them to the site of their new agency. Log cabins were erected with one dwelling for each of the six white men of the party.[1]

Lieutenant Parry succeeded Major Oakes as agent. Then followed Captain Beck and a Mr. Brown. In 1875 the Reverend E. H. Danforth was appointed agent, and it was he who introduced farming among the Northern Utes. This program proved to be very unpopular with them.[2] Nathan C. Meeker succeeded Danforth in the spring of 1878.

Meeker was a tall, thin man with a pleasing personality to casual acquaintances.[3] He was well-known as a poet before the Civil War. During the war he served as a correspondent for the New York *Tribune,* and after the war Horace Greeley, editor of the *Tribune,* sent him west. The letters Meeker wrote about his travels were featured in the newspaper.[4]

While in Colorado Meeker was much impressed with the Pikes Peak region, and when he returned to New York, he suggested to Greeley that they colonize that area. Greeley agreed to help and solicited subscriptions in the *Tribune* for the enterprise. Before long $100,000 was raised, and in 1870 Meeker set out for Colorado to found a colony.[5] Instead of locating near Pike's Peak as originally planned, he established his colony one hundred miles north of Pike's Peak on the Cache la Poudre River where more land could be irrigated. The newly found town was named Greeley and became Colorado's most famous colony.

Although the colony proved to be a success, it was not a money-maker, and Meeker lost money in the venture. So, when he was offered the job of Indian agent at the White River Agency, he gladly accepted. Because of his outstanding background as a journalist and colonizer, much was expected of him.

Meeker arrived at his post on May 15, 1878, and entered enthusiastically into his duties. At this time northwestern Colorado was a new frontier. North of the reservation Charlie Perkins had a trading post on Snake River along the Colorado-Wyoming border near the present site of Baggs, Wyoming. He was a short, heavy-set man with a pocked face and crochety disposition.[6] He shipped to Denver hundreds of deer hides that he obtained from the Utes for whiskey. The road from Rawlins, Wyoming, to the White River Agency went by his place, and he also carried on quite an extensive trade with the freighters. Once a freighter traded a hundred quarters of elk meat for whiskey, and Perkins shipped the meat to Denver. Perkins was also in charge of the mail deliveries from Rawlins to Dixon (later known as Baggs) and from Dixon to the agency. Although the little trader was a clever business man, he died broke. At one time in a moment of weakness he deeded all of his property to his wife, and she refused to give it back to him.

Big Joe Morgan and his brothers, Dave and Charlie, had a log trading post a short distance east of the present town of Craig. The post was located east of Elkhead Creek where it flows into the Yampa River. The store was built of logs with a dirt roof. There was no counter, and the floor was covered with bags of coffee, sugar, flour, tobacco, powder, and bullets. The Morgans traded muzzle loader guns, powder, lead, and caps to the Indians for buckskin. Joseph, who could speak the Ute language, did most of the trading. The buckskin was sent to

Denver to a man who paid for it in money and guns. Unlike Perkins, the Morgan brothers never sold whiskey to the Indians.[7]

The Morgans were popular with the Utes, and Joe, a big, powerful man, often had friendly wrestling matches, usually for wagers, with the redskins who traded there. After Joe had thrown all of the Northern Utes who wanted to wrestle with him, a gigantic Southern Ute was brought up to test his strength and skill against the white wrestler. It was a close contest, and for a time it looked as if neither contestant could win. Suddenly, Joe lifted his heavy adversary into the air, and staggering as he whirled, the white man threw his opponent from him with terrific force. The Ute landed in a heap and died from internal injuries within a few hours.[8]

Also, on the Yampa River was a postoffice and store, where the ranches of Bert Smart and Major James B. Thompson[9] joined. Thompson named the place Hayden in honor of Professor F. V. Hayden, the famous surveyor, who had camped in that vicinity during the summer of 1874. A man by the name of Peck also had a ranch and a little trading post on the Yampa a few miles beyond Hayden.

Northeast of the reservation was the small mining town of Hahns Peak close to the Wyoming-Colorado border; and Steamboat Springs east of Hayden was just getting started.

These sparsely populated settlements and trading posts, along with the approximate dozen employees at the White River Agency and the ten or twelve freighters who drove ox teams from Rawlins to the agency, accounted for about all of the white population in northwestern Colorado when Meeker took over. The few stockmen who grazed their herds on the Yampa and Snake Rivers could be counted on the fingers of one hand.[10]

In spite of Meeker's high moral character, outstanding background, and pleasant manner, events proved that he had only a slight understanding of Indians and little ability to manage them.

His first major move to reform and civilize the Utes was moving the agency some fifteen miles to a new location in Powell's Valley about four-and-a-half miles down the White River from the present site of Meeker. This valley was in a more favorable location for agricultural pursuits, which the agent had made an important part of his program. The Indians had been pasturing their horses on the lush grass of Powell's Valley and were very much opposed to fencing and plowing up the area.[11]

One faction of the Northern Utes under the leadership of Captain Jack, a Ute chief with the tall, lithe figure of an Arapahoe, refused to move to the newly established site of the agency. The other faction, led by Chief Douglass, a short, chunky man with a sparse mustache, accompanied Meeker to Powell's Valley. Removal of the agency was begun in July, 1878, and continued into the spring of 1879 when several of the buildings were transported to the new location.

Since an irrigation ditch was needed for his farming project, Meeker persuaded the reluctant Utes to spend $3,000 of their money for its construction. The Indians showed no enthusiasm for digging the canal, and only about fifteen of them stayed consistently with the work. The same unwillingness was noticed in building fences, grubbing, plowing, and planting.

Meeker reported, "A great deal of talking and entreaty were required all the time; once in about a week all would stop work without apparent cause, though evidently in bad humor, but after a few days they would be at work again."[12]

Crops of grain were planted that spring, and immediately afterward a group of some one hundred Utes started north to their summer hunting grounds. It was customary for the Utes to ride up to the Yampa River from their reservation every spring and camp there until the snow disappeared from the mountains to the north. When white men visited their camps, they and the Indians would sit in a circle and pass around a pipe. Visitors had to take a puff to show that they were friendly. On these hunting excursions off their reservation the men all carried guns while the boys brought bows and arrows.[13]

From five to six hundred Utes usually camped during the summer near Steamboat Springs. They were friendly with James Crawford, founder of the town, and made a habit of coming to his home for nearly everything they needed, including medical and surgical aid. They often begged for bread, sugar, and other provisions. In return for these favors the Indians occasionally gave the Crawfords bows and arrows, moccasins, and hides.

A sub-chief by the name of Yahmonite was especially friendly, and a creek, a mountain, and an addition to the town were named in his honor.[14]

On July 5th Meeker sent Chief Douglass and Frank Dresser, an employee of the agency, after the Indians who had left their farm work to go hunting. The messengers caught up with the Utes in four and a half days and talked them into returning to the reservation. On his return Dresser said that the Utes had killed several hundred antelope and eighteen buffalo. He also reported that the Indians were setting fire to timber.

On July 15, 1879, Meeker wrote to the Commissioner of Indian Affairs:

> In many parts of the Bear (Yampa) River Valley and all the way up to its head in Egeria Park, the country is well burned over. At Hayden, where reside the families of Smart and Thompson the fires were so near the houses that the women, whose husbands were away, were on the watch two days and carried their household goods to a place of safety. The grass range on which their cows and cattle fed is destroyed. I have previously reported to you that the Indians are destroying timber everywhere; last winter something like one hundred acres of beautiful cottonwood groves were burned close to the agency. Their object here is to get dry wood (for) next winter. At the present time the timber on the mountains north and south is burning, and one valley is filled with smoke. These fires are built to drive the deer to one place that they may be easily killed and thereby the destruction of pine, cedar, and aspen is immense while the fire ruins the grass . . .[15]

The Utes contended that they had not started any fires off their reservation and pointed out that most of the fires were caused by the negligence of white men who were cutting ties for a railroad.

The Indians were great beggars when on their summer and fall hunting trips on the Yampa and Snake Rivers. Late one summer in 1876 Colorow, a tremendously fat, blustering leader

of a group of young Ute renegades, rode up to the cabin of
John Mack near Hayden. Colorow and his party were on their
way back to the reservation from the Snake River country. As
they passed, Colorow got off his horse, and, leaving his gun outside, walked into the cabin.

"Build fire," he said to Mack, "cook dinner. Me got squaw.
Bring meat. You cook him."

Mack refused. Colorow scowled and went outside. He
mounted his horse and rode away. Mack told Bert Smart, the
Hayden postmaster, about the incident, and Smart said, "You
got off lucky. Colorow killed a man on the Gore range because
he would not cook for him."[16]

In order to prevent the Utes from taking long excursions off
their reservation, Meeker made a ruling that rations would
be issued once a week and that the head of each family had to
be present before his family could receive anything. This
weekly attendance kept the Utes from taking their customary
trips and was very distasteful to them.[17]

Meeker also objected to the Utes obtaining guns, ammunition, and whiskey at the trading posts off the reservation.
There was no store at the agency, and the Indians carried on a
prolific trade with Charlie Perkins on the Snake River and
with the Morgan brothers on the Yampa.

The growing resentment against Meeker and the white race
was aggravated by the government's shameful neglect in the
delivery of annuities to the Utes.

All supplies for the Northern Utes were sent to Rawlins,
Wyoming, where they were stored in warehouses until transported to the agency. Often it took months to get needed food
and clothing from the warehouses to the White River Agency.
Sometimes the destitute Indians would go to Rawlins where
they would discover a trainload of clothing, provisions, and
annuity goods which should have been distributed months before.[18]

One winter's provisions were sent to Rawlins by rail with a
contract that they be hauled by wagon from there to the White
River Agency. After the goods arrived in Rawlins, the contractor decided that he had bid too low. In an effort to make up

for his prospective loss, he stole and sold some bags of beans in the shipment. Government agents caught him in the act and requested him to redeem the stolen property. The contractor then refused to deliver any of the goods. The government brought action to force him to carry out his contract, and in the long court struggle that followed the Indians were forgotten. During this period some of the provisions rotted at the railway station, some were stolen, and a large quantity was taken for storage charges. Nearly a year after the rations had arrived in Rawlins, a small portion of the goods finally were delivered to the agency.[19]

The Los Pinos Agency had similar difficulties. About this same time a shipment of annuity goods was sent to the Tabeguache band at Los Pinos. At Pueblo the shipment was misrouted and was carried to Denver, where it remained lost for a number of months.

During these trying times at the White River Agency, an unfortunate event occurred which added further fuel to the grievances of the Northern Utes and was undoubtedly an important motive for the Meeker uprising.

Although Meeker tried to keep the Utes on the reservation, a number of them wandered into Middle Park or Grand County in July, 1879. They camped on a meadow which was a part of what was then known as the Junction Ranch near the present town of Fraser.[20] Junction Ranch, a stage station, was so named because it was located at the junction of two roads leading across the Continental Divide—namely, the Rollin and Berthoud highways which had just recently been constructed.

John Turner, the proprietor of Junction Ranch, asked the Indians to get out of the meadow which was used for pasturing the stage-coach horses kept at the ranch.

The Utes refused to leave; so Turner rode to Hot Sulphur Springs and notified the sheriff. When Sheriff Marker and his posse of eighteen men arrived at Junction Ranch, the Indians were racing their horses on an improvised track across the river.[21] The white men took all the guns and ammunition from the tepees, which were still on the meadow, and awaited the return of the Indians.

As the Utes approached, one of them raised his rifle. Thinking that he was going to shoot, Frank Addison, a trigger-happy member of the posse, shot the young Indian, who fell from his horse mortally wounded.[22] The dead man's name was Tabernash, and he was the son of a Ute chief.

The Utes started toward Hot Sulphur Springs, carrying the body of Tabernash. A short distance from Junction Ranch they stopped long enough to bury him. Two horses were shot and laid on both sides of the shallow grave.

The sheriff sent out couriers to notify all settlers about the occurrence so that they would be prepared for trouble from the enraged Indians. Among those notified was Abraham Elliott and his wife and son, Tom, who were living on a cattle ranch a few miles south of the present site of Kremmling.

Mrs. Elliott was worried about the danger, and her husband promised to round up his cattle and leave the country until conditions became more settled.

One evening as he was cutting wood a day or so after the killing of Tabernash, the Utes passed unobserved by his ranch. One of them dismounted on a nearby hill about two hundred yards away from the woodcutter and shot him in the back. Elliott died instantly. A fiendish laugh was the only evidence that the Indians were passing. A young hired hand, who was living with the family, saddled his horse and galloped away in search of help.

That night a posse of twenty-six men gathered at a ranch near the present town of Kremmling. At daylight the group started after the Utes and chased them all the way to the White River Agency. It was impossible to punish them after they reached their reservation, but the posse returned to Middle Park with seven horses that the Utes had stolen.

The seriousness of conditions was evidenced by an experience of Charlie Beck, who carried the mail during 1878 and 1879 from Junction Ranch to Hayden. One evening when he arrived at Hayden with his mail bags, Bert Smart, the postmaster, asked him to go to Peck's trading post and get some medicine for his sick wife. As the mail-carrier rode toward Peck's ranch a few miles away, a Ute suddenly stepped out into the trail from behind a large, jutting rock. His face was colored yellow and black—the war paint of the Utes. Two long braids of coarse black hair, interwoven with strings of colored beads, hung over his chest.

"Where you bound for?" the Ute asked.

"Down to Peck's place to get some things for Mrs. Smart. She's sick."

"All right, Charlie, go ahead."

Beck had occasionally met this Indian on his mail route, but his war regalia surprised and worried him. The Indian was apparently stationed behind the rock as a scout or guard.

Beck discovered more than five hundred Indian horses around Peck's store, which the Utes had traded for Winchester repeating rifles—a pony for a rifle. Peck had been shipping in rifles and ammunition by the wagon-load to carry on this trade.[23]

As the tension at the White River Agency neared the breaking point, Major James Thompson of Hayden was advised by some of the older Utes, whom he had known in Denver when he was Ute agent, to move farther away from the reservation. They complained of Meeker's treatment of them and said that if he persisted in his present course that there would be serious trouble. In case of an uprising they explained that it would be hard to control all the younger and more hot-headed bucks who might even attack Thompson and his family.[24]

Chief Yahmonite also advised his friend James Crawford, founder of Steamboat Springs, that trouble was pending and suggested that he and his family move to North Park (Jackson County) until conditions settled down.[25]

FOOTNOTES

[1]Frank Farley, "Meeker Massacre," *Rocky Mountain News*, July 7, 1929.

[2]Rio Blanco County, C.W.A. Interviews, 1933-34, pp. 1-2. In possession of the State Historical Society of Colorado.

[3]Moffat County, C.W.A. Interviews, 1933-34, A. G. Wallihan account, pp. 136-139. In possession of the State Historical Society of Colorado.

[4]Sidney Jocknick, *Early Days on the Western Slope of Colorado,* pp. 182-183.

[5]Leroy R. and Ann W., Hafen, *Colorado,* p. 227.

[6]Moffat County, C.W.A. Interviews, 1933-34, accounts of Madeline Adams and Jennie Reische (daughters of Jim Baker). In possession of the State Historical Society of Colorado.

[7]*Ibid.,* p. 17.

[8]Arthur H. Carhart, *Colorado,* p. 267.

[9]After Thompson resigned his position as agent for the Denver Utes in 1876, he and his family took up this ranch.

[10]Moffat County, C.W.A. Interviews, 1933-34, p. 259. In possession of the State Historical Society of Colorado.

[11]Marshall D. Moody, "The Meeker Massacre," *Colorado Magazine,* April, 1953, p. 93.

[12]Commission of Indian Affairs, Annual Report, Washington, 1879.

[13]John Mack, "Early Days on Bear River," Moffat County C.W.A. Interviews, 1933-34. In possession of the State Historical Society of Colorado.

[14]Charles H. Leckenby, *Tread of Pioneers.*

[15]Meeker to Commissioner of Indian Affairs, July 15, 1879. Records of the Bureau of Indian Affairs, Letters Received 1879, Colorado M 1509. National Archives Record Group 75.

[16]Mack, *op cit.*

[17]Wm. N. Byers, "History of the Ute Nation," *Rocky Mountain News,* April 16, 1880. Article in Randall Scrap Book, pp. 13-14. In possession of the State Historical Society of Colorado.

[18]Mary Lyons Cairns, *The Pioneers,* pp. 45-55.

[19]*Ibid.*

[20]*Middle Park Times,* June 20, 1940.

[21]Leckenby, *op. cit.*

[22]Lafayette Hanchett, *The Old Sheriff and Other True Tales.*

[23]Cairns, *op. cit.*

[24]Thomas F. Dawson, "Major Thompson, Chief Ouray, and the Utes," *Colorado Magazine,* May, 1930, p. 121.

[25]Leckenby, *op. cit.*

THE AMBUSH

In spite of all these warning signals, Meeker kept right on with his unpopular farming program. During the summer of 1879 he had another eighty acres of land fenced, plowed, and irrigated.[1] Again in early September Meeker ordered some more plowing to be done.

A Ute by the name of Johnson, who had been somewhat of a favorite at the agency, unexpectedly became the ringleader of a group of Indians who started taking a firm stand against any more plowing. Johnson had 150 horses which grazed on the land Meeker was fencing and plowing, and the Indian didn't want any more of his pasture destroyed. He told the agent that he could continue plowing on less desirable land, which was spotted with alkali. Meeker refused and told the plowman to proceed.

Before the plowman had progressed far, two Indians carrying guns ordered him to stop. This was reported to the agent who directed that the plowing continue.[2] Shortly thereafter the plowman was fired upon from a small bunch of sagebrush, and this halted the plowing for a time.

Meeker sent a message to Captain Jack asking him and his followers to come to the agency. When they arrived, the agent had a general council with them and with Chief Douglass and his men. After a long discussion the Indians agreed to let Meeker continue with his project.

So, the plowing was resumed the following day, but some of the Utes began protesting again. Jack was again sent for, and another meeting was held that afternoon. Once more it was agreed that the land could be plowed providing that Meeker would remove the corral, dig a well, help build a log house, and give a stove to the Utes.

Johnson apparently was not in accord with the majority decision since a few days later the Indian strode into Meeker's house and grabbed hold of the agent in the presence of Mrs. Meeker. Pushing Meeker outside, the Ute gave him a terrific beating.[3] Agency employees came to the victim's rescue before he was killed. Meeker reported this incident to the Commissioner of Indian Affairs:

> White River Agency, Colo
> September 10, 1879.

Hon. E. A. Hoyt
Commissioner, Washington, D. C.

I have been assaulted by a leading chief, Johnson, forced out of my own house, and injured badly, but was rescued by employees. It is now revealed that Johnson originated all the trouble stated in letter September 8th. His son shot at the plowman, and the opposition to plowing is wide. Plowing stops. Life of self, family, and employees not safe; want protection immediately; have asked Governor Pitkin to confer with General Pope.

> N. C. Meeker
> Indian Agent[4]

Meeker was notified on September 15th that the War Department had been requested to send troops for his protection and that the leaders of the disturbance would be arrested when the soldiers arrived.

Major T. T. Thornburg was ordered from Fort Steele, Wyoming Territory, to the White River Agency. He marched southward from Rawlins with two companies of cavalry, two companies of infantry, and a wagon train. This amounted to a total of 140 men and thirty-three wagons.

Upon reaching Fortification Creek north of the present site of Craig, the soldiers followed the stream to where it turns west-

ward. Here they crossed over the Flats and reached the Yampa
River (then called the Bear River) at its junction with Elkhead Creek, sixty-five miles north of the agency.[5]

While Thornburg was camped here, Captain Jack, accompanied by nine Utes, unexpectedly appeared and inquired
about the purpose of the expedition. The Indians then learned
for the first time that troops were on their way to the White
River Agency at the request of Meeker.[6] Jack and his braves,
while appearing friendly and unconcerned, were greatly
alarmed and distressed at this development. They left about
nightfall and spread the news of the approaching soldiers.

The next morning Thornburg continued up the Yampa to
the present site of Cary Ranch, where the troops forded the
river. They then proceeded over the hogback to Williams
Fork, arriving there on September 27th. At this point Captain
Jack and his followers again rode into camp.

Jack proposed that Major Thornburg take an escort of five
soldiers and accompany the Indians to the agency to talk matters over. It was evident that the Utes did not want so many
troops to come on to their reservation.

Joseph Rankin, head scout of the expedition, feared some
sort of Indian trickery and advised Thornburg to refuse the
request.

Acting upon this advice, Thornburg told Jack that he was
going to march his men to within hailing distance of the agency,
where he would accept their proposition.[7]

Jack suggested that the troops be halted fifty miles from the
agency. Again Thornburg refused, and the ten Utes departed.[8]

The command marched southward from Williams Fork to
Milk Creek. As the troops neared the border of the Ute reservation twenty miles north of the present town of Meeker, the road
led through a mountain pass surrounded on each side by high
bluffs. The soldiers entered this pass about ten o'clock on the
morning of September 29, 1879. The wagon train followed
three-fourths of a mile behind.[9]

As the troops approached a much narrower defile inside the
pass, Joe Rankin galloped up to Thornburg.

"That gulch just ahead would be an ideal place for an ambush, sir. I suggest that we go around it."

Thornburg laughed at Rankin's fears, but being a good sport, he ordered his men off the road in order to bypass the gully. If he had not done so, every man in his command would have been killed, for there were around 300 Ute warriors lying in wait here for the soldiers.[10]

Colorow, a ponderous, over-rated, blustering Ute; Antelope, a son of the great Chief Navava, who had died a few years before, were leaders along with Captain Jack in this ambuscade.

When the Indians saw the troops unexpectedly leave the road to circle the arroyo, Captain Jack and Antelope quickly reorganized their forces. Colorow, a great coward when real danger threatened, remained too far in the background to be of any assistance.

Thornburg could see the Indians moving about, and while incredulous of their intent to attack, he ordered his troops back toward the wagon train three-quarters of a mile to their rear.

The Utes started moving rapidly between the soldiers and the train, and Rankin, an experienced Indian fighter, advised Thornburg to open fire. The commanding officer, however, had explicit orders from Washington not to molest the Utes in any way unless they fired on him first.

After the Utes had flanked the troops, they began shooting from both the front and rear of the retreating men. Thornburg hastily assembled twenty cavalrymen, and riding at their head, he charged the flanking Indians in a desperate attempt to open up a hole to the wagons.

Thornburg and thirteen of his cavalry were killed in this courageous charge, but they succeeded in driving a wedge into the Utes' line so that the rest of soldiers could reach the wagon train, which was hurriedly being formed into an irregular circle.[11] Every officer except one had been wounded and more than 150 mules killed at the first onslaught.

The scene of the attack was well fitted for Indian warfare. Some five hundred yards on one side of the pass a mountain offered the attackers ample protection and enabled them to keep up a continual fire without exposing themselves. On the other side the mountains were more distant but still within easy rifle range.

The command was corralled on a small plateau on the right bank of Milk Creek about one hundred yards from the stream.[12] After Thornburg's death Captain Payne of the Fifth Cavalry, though wounded, took charge. He set about using the dead animals and the wagons and their contents for breastworks. Within this ghastly enclosure a deep circular rifle pit was dug with implements found in the wagons. The wounded were placed inside this pit and made as comfortable as possible.

During all this time a galling fire poured down on the beleaguered men from the surrounding bluffs. The cries of the wounded and the dying could be heard above the continual roar of the rifles, The medical officer, though wounded himself, dressed the wounds of those most needing attention.

A new danger threatened when a strong wind arose soon after the attack was begun. Taking advantage of the occasion, the Indians started setting fire to the dry grass and brush to the windward of the improvised fort, hoping to burn the defenders out. No water being at hand, the soldiers had to smother the flames with whatever was available. After many of the wagons were badly burned, the troops finally got the fire under control.

About four o'clock in the afternoon the savages made a furious attack on the breastworks, but they were repulsed and retired to the surrounding hills, where they resumed the old tactics of picking the white men off one by one whenever the opportunity offered.[13] The Utes believed that starvation and thirst would in a short time so weaken the defenders that they would be unable to resist another charge.

During the night defenses were strengthened, and a little water was obtained from Milk Creek by the hard-pressed soldiers. Joseph Rankin and several other couriers galloped off into the darkness, gambling against death that some of them might get through the barricade of Indians and obtain help before it was too late.

For some strange reason the Ute sentinels did not see the horsemen depart. One of the couriers had been informed that Captain F. S. Dodge with one company of colored cavalry were on their way to the agency from Middle Park to act under the direction of Meeker in breaking up illegitimate trading and forcing a return of the Utes to their reservation. This messenger left a note on a piece of sagebrush by the side of a wagon road leading from Middle Park to Steamboat Springs which read, "Hurry up! The troops have been defeated at the agency E. E. C."[14]

Captain Dodge found the paper on September 30th and hurried on to Hayden, which he found deserted. While he was looking through the few buildings, a group of fearful residents appeared from where they had been hiding out north of town. They told Dodge that the courier had informed them about the siege.

Dodge continued down the Yampa River as rapidly as possible until 4:30 P. M. when he made camp. At eight-thirty that night he repacked the wagons and sent them to a supply station on Fortification Creek with a guard of eight men.[15] He then started with the rest of his company for Milk Creek, taking with him thirty-five negro cavalrymen, four white guides, and another officer.

The night was bright and cold, and the company kept up a steady, mile-consuming jog. About four o'clock the next morning the men had ridden within five miles of their destination. A half-hour later, on the third day of the siege, Dodge's cavalry reached the besieged soldiers. The Utes, apparently believing that it was a much stronger force and not wishing to expose themselves, did not fire at the newcomers until the riders were inside the wagon corral. Then, the Indians began shooting and kept it up intermittently for the next three days. Of the forty-two horses taken into the entrenchments at this time, all were killed by this gunfire except four and these were wounded.[16] While arrival of Dodge's reinforcement strengthened and encouraged Payne's beleaguered command, it was too small to change the tide of the battle.

During this siege the soldiers lived primarily on corn. Milk Creek was about one hundred yards away, and armed groups frequently ran the gauntlet of fire to secure badly needed water.

Each night the defensive works were strengthened and each

day defended against renewed assaults. The greatest difficulty was in hauling out the dead animals at night and watering and feeding those that still lived.

At night some of the Indians would occasionally crawl up the creek bottom and open fire at closer range in an effort to hinder these nightly activities.

FOOTNOTES

[1]Marshall D. Moody, "The Meeker Massacre," *Colorado Magazine*, April, 1953, p. 94.

[2]Meeker to Commissioner of Indian Affairs, September 8, 1879, Records of the Bureau of Indian Affairs, Letters received 1879, Colorado M 1862.

[3]A few days before he was attacked, a wagon had fallen on Meeker, crippling him so that he was unable to give a good account of himself in the fight.

[4]Bureau of Indian Affairs, Letters Received 1879, Colorado M 1862.

[5]Account of A. G. Wallihan, Rio Blanco County, C.W.A. Interviews, 1933-34, Pamphlet 356, Doc. 1-73 incl., J. Monaghan interviewer, pp. 136-139. In possession of the State Historical Society of Colorado.

[6]Moody, *op. cit.,* p. 98.

[7]Thomas F. Dawson, and F. J. V. Skiff, "The Ute War—a History of the White River Massacre and the Privations of the Captive White Women among the Hostiles on Grand River," *Denver Tribune*, 1879. Article recorded in Sidney Jocknick, *Early Days on the Western Slope of Colorado*, pp. 184-185.

[8]Moody, *op. cit.,* p. 98.

[9]Dawson and Skiff, *op. cit.* (Jocknick, p. 185).

[10]*Ibid.*

[11]*Ibid* (Jocknick, p. 186).

[12]A letter by F. S. Dodge, Capt. Ninth Infantry, Commanding Co. D, at Fort Union, New Mexico, to Asst. Adj. General, Fort Leavenworth, Missouri. Letter reproduced in Rio Blanco Co., C.W.A. Interviews, 1933-34, pp. 60-67.

[13]General Wesley Merritt, "Three Indian Campaigns," *Harper's New Monthly Magazine*, 1889, reproduced in Rio Blanco County, C.W.A. Interviews, pp. 67-70. In possession of the State Historical Society of Colorado. See Appendix for Merritt's account in full.

[14]A letter by F. S. Dodge, Captain Ninth Cavalry, Commanding Co. D, at Fort Union, New Mexico, to Asst. Adj. General, Fort Leavenworth, Missouri. Letter reproduced in Rio Blanco Co., C.W.A. Interviews, 1933-34, pp. 60-67.

[15]*Ibid.*

[16]Merritt, *op. cit.*

THE RESCUE

Joe Rankin, one of the couriers who escaped into the night, rode the 160 miles from Milk Creek to Rawlins, Wyoming, in twenty-eight hours.

Within a short time after Rankin reported the disastrous news, a telegram reached the garrison at Fort Russell, Wyoming Territory, which read:

> Major Thornburg is killed; Captain Payne and two other officers, including the surgeon of the command, are wounded. The command is surrounded and constantly pressed by the hostiles; fifty men are killed and wounded, and all the horses are killed.[1]

Within four hours after the telegram arrived at Fort Russell, General Wesley Merritt, one of Sheridan's most successful commanders, had all the available cavalry troops with their horses and equipment on a train headed for Rawlins.

By the next morning on October 2nd a force of about 200 cavalry troops and 150 infantry troops had assembled at Rawlins. Teams and light wagons were collected in the neighborhood to carry the infantry, since the soldiers couldn't walk the 160 miles to Milk Creek in time to rescue Payne's sorely pressed command, whose provisions were sufficient to last for only three more days.

Merritt and his troops left Rawlins at 10:30 on the morning

of October 2nd. They traveled forty miles that day. The second day, Friday, they made fifty miles. On Saturday they rode seventy miles, traveling day and night.

Early Sunday morning about 5:30 they unexpectedly came upon a blackened heap of ashes intermixed with fragments of iron and chains and pieces of harness. The charred wreckage proved to be George Gordon's freight outfit, loaded with a mowing machine and provisions for the agency. The freight train had been just a few miles behind Thornburg's troops at the time of the ambush. The bodies of Gordon and a fellow teamster were found farther on with distorted features and staring eyes.[2]

Upon seeing the burned ruins of Gordon's freight wagons, the guide turned to General Merritt and said, "We must be getting close. Payne can't be far from here."

Merritt brought his troops to a halt, and everyone strained his eyes and ears for a glimpse or sound of the besieged garrison or the attacking Indians. Nothing revealed the presence of either, and Merritt feared that perhaps he had arrived too late.

"It looks bad," he said to the bugler, "but go ahead and sound the Officers' Call." The Officers' Call was the night signal for the Fifth Infantry and would be recognized by any soldier of Payne's group who might still be living.

The clear notes of the trumpet broke the ominous stillness of the early dawn and eased the tension of the morning. The last notes echoed and re-echoed through the mountains and was followed by a blanketing silence. Every man in Merritt's command waited expectantly for an answering sound.

Within a few, hour-long seconds came the joyous reply of Payne's bugler, followed by the ringing cheers and glad cries of the rescued men as they rushed from their rifle pits.[3]

Merritt and his men hurried forward to greet the entrenched soldiers who had been under fire for six days.[4] Wounded men were hobbling in every direction. Nearly two hundred dead horses and mules lay within thirty feet of the breastworks filling the air with the almost intolerable stench.[5] Captain Payne hobbled forward and threw his arms around General Merritt as a child would embrace his father. Each knew that it was almost a miracle that every man in Thornburg's command was not killed.

Almost simultaneously with the arrival of Merritt's troops, Sapowanero, Ouray's trusted messenger, arrived with orders from the Chief to cease fighting. These two events caused the rebellious Utes to give up the struggle, and they disappeared in the mountains.

The body of Major Thornburg was found stripped and mutilated where he had fallen. His remains were carried to Rawlins and shipped to Omaha, Nebraska, for burial.

After the rest of the dead were buried on the battlefield and the wounded were cared for, Captains Dodge and Payne took the remnants of their troops back to Rawlins under a strong guard. General Merritt continued on to the agency.

Twenty and one-half miles northeast of Meeker a monument was erected in memory of the officers, soldiers, and civilians who were killed and wounded in this battle.

FOOTNOTES

[1]General Wesley Merritt, "Three Indian Campaigns," *Harper's New Monthly Magazine,* 1889. Article reproduced in Rio Blanco Co., C.W.A. interviews, 1933-34, pp. 67-70. In possession of the State Historical Society of Colorado. See Appendix for Merritt's account in full.

[2]Five years later in the summer of 1884 Abram Fiske and his son Charles, who had homesteaded land at Hayden, went to the battleground and got the cylinder, bull wheel, and tumbling rod of the burned mowing machine. That fall they used these parts to assemble an improvised mowing machine to do what little threshing that needed to be done around Hayden. That winter the Fiskes made further improvements on the mower, and this machine did the threshing for the valley for more than a dozen years. It was then sold to William L. Youst of Willam Park who made use of the relic on his ranch. Finally, in the early 1940's citizens of Hayden purchased the historic mower and removed it to the Routt County Fair Grounds, where it stands beside the first county court house as a monument to pioneer days.

[3]Merritt, *op. cit.*

[4]From September 29, 1879 to October 5, 1879.

[5]Thomas F. Dawson and F. J. V. Skiff, "The Ute War—a History of the White River Massacre and the Privations of the Captive White Women among the Hostiles on Grand River," *Denver Tribune*, 1879. Article recorded in Sidney Jocknick, *Early Days on the Western Slope of Colorado*, pp. 190-191.

THE MEEKER MASSACRE

On the morning of September 29th the whites and possibly even the Indians at the White River Agency were unaware of Captain Jack's attack on Thornburg's troops at Milk Creek. Everything was calm and peaceful, and at one o'clock that afternoon Meeker sent a message to Thornburg by Wilmer E. Eskridge, a saw-mill operator at the agency. The note said:

> I expect to leave in the morning with Douglass and Sherrick to meet you; things are peaceable, and Douglass flies the United States flag. If you have trouble in getting through the canyon today, let me know in what force. We have been on guard three nights and shall be tonight, not because we know there is danger but because there might be.[1]

Douglass seemed to be in a more friendly mood when he talked with the agent that morning. He discussed the possibility of sending his son Frederick to school with Meeker's daughter, Josephine, and he accepted some food around noon that the family gave him. Several other Utes also came to the agent's house around dinner time in hope of getting their usual handouts.[2]

After dinner the agency employees went about their respective duties. Arthur L. Thompson, Frank G. Dresser, and Shadrick Price resumed their work of putting a roof on a building. Thompson climbed up on top, and Dresser and Price began pitching up dirt to him.[3] W. H. Post was carrying sacks of flour into one of the warehouses, and the other men were performing various tasks.

As Meeker's wife and his daughter Josephine were putting away the last of the dishes, they saw twenty or twenty-five Utes appear and begin shooting at the white men while they were at work. It was a little after one o'clock, and the Utes at the agency had apparently just learned about Captain Jack's attack on Thornburg and his troops.

Most of the agency employees were killed before they could find shelter, but Frank Dresser, Mrs. Meeker, Josephine Meeker, and Mrs. Shadrick Price, wife of the agency's blacksmith, and her two children ran over to the milk house, which stood a short distance away from Meeker's home. They remained there all afternoon listening to the intermittent shooting and activities of the Indians, but they were unable to see any of the horrors. The Utes set fire to several of the nearby buildings, and the smoke drifted into the milk house, making it difficult to breathe. When the smoke became unbearable, the little group ran over to the agent's house while the Indians were busy plundering and carrying off supplies.[4]

Realizing that the savages would eventually come into the agent's headquarters, the frightened survivors watched for an opportunity to make a get-away and hide in the surrounding territory. When they thought no one was watching, they made a dash for it, sprinting across the street and entering the plowed field to the north of the building where they had been hiding.

One of the Utes saw them, and in a few moments all of the Indians were in close pursuit, yelling and shouting. They easily caught the women and children, but Dresser outran the pursuers. The Indians shot at him before giving up the chase. Mortally wounded, he crawled into a small cave to hide.

Mrs. Price, a buxom, good-looking young woman, was overtaken by three Indians whom she did not know. Her captors took her down to White River and placed her on a pile of blankets.

Mrs. Meeker was taken prisoner by a Ute whom she was not acquainted with who turned her over to Douglass, the recognized leader of the massacre. As Douglass led her past her house, she asked the Indian if she might enter to get some medicine, a book, blankets, and a few other things. Douglass consented on the condition that she bring out all of the money that she could find.

She went into the house followed by an Indian and returned with her equipment and thirty dollars which she handed to Douglass. Douglass kept twenty-six dollars and distributed four dollars in silver to the other Utes in the group.

When Mrs. Meeker saw the mutilated body of her husband lying on his back about two-hundred yards from the house, she started to kneel down and kiss him a last goodbye. However, noting the hadred on the faces of her captors, she was afraid to do so.

Josephine Meeker was taken prisoner by an Indian named Persune, who escorted her down to the bank of the river, where the other two women and Mrs. Price's two children were sitting on a pile of blankets.

After a time the women and children were put on horses and taken to a small canyon four or five miles distant where everyone dismounted. The Indians had been drinking continuously during the afternoon and many were intoxicated. They amused themselves by threatening the women with their guns and saying they were soldiers. Douglass drunkenly made fun of the way the guard had been kept at the agency.

A little later the party rode ten or twelve miles farther on to Douglass' camp from where they started southward to Plateau Creek in the Plateau Valley about thirty-five miles northeast of Grand Junction.

On October 11th General Merritt arrived at the White River Agency. His most fearful expectations were realized. All of the buildings except the house that had been built for Johnson were burned down, and the site was one of utter desolation. The soldiers located all the dead bodies of the victims.

The body of Wilmer E. Eskridge, who had left with the message to Thornburg just a few minutes before Douglass made his attack, was found two miles north of the agency. In a pocket was found the note written by Meeker which said that all was well at the agency and that he would meet Thornburg in the morning.[5]

Frank Dresser, who, although shot, had outrun the Utes in his dash for freedom, was found lying dead in a cave near the agency, his coat folded under his head for a pillow.[6]

The body of Carl Goldstein, an itinerant Jew who was not in the employ of the agency, was found in a ditch some distance from the agency buildings. The body of another transient, Julius Moore, was also reported to have been found.[7]

At the agency the naked, mutilated body of Nathan Meeker was found lying on his back about two hundred yards from his house. One side of his head was bashed in, and a long barrel stave splinter had been driven through his mouth.[8]

Other bodies found were those of William Post, Harry Dresser, Albert Woodbury, Shadrick Price, husband of the kidnapped woman, Arthur Thompson, Fred Shepard, and George Eaton.[9]

Mounds of earth were shoveled over the bodies where they lay. That fall they were removed by relatives.[10]

Edwin L. Mansfield was the only employee of the agency who escaped death. The reason for his good fortune was that three days before the massacre he had been sent with a dispatch to Captain Dodge.[11]

General Merritt established a military camp about four and one-half miles up the river from the ruined agency. The troops built their quarters in the customary army fashion with the buildings facing the quadrangle or parade grounds. On the north side of the parade ground the officers constructed their quarters out of logs in the form of one-story buildings, each divided in the middle by a center hallway with rooms on either side. On the south side of the parade ground the enlisted men built long adobe buildings for their barracks.[12]

This cantonment became known as the "Camp on the White River." The establishment was maintained until August, 1883, when the buildings and other government property were auctioned off to the residents of the valley. These buildings sold for thirty-three dollars to ninety dollars each, and the new inhabitants had a ready-made town which they named Meeker after the murdered agent. The parade ground was fenced off and made into a public park. The large enlisted men's barracks south of the parade ground were used for stores and other business houses, while the officers' private quarters north of the parade ground were reconstructed into private homes.

In 1927 the Meeker Monument was erected three miles west of the town in a memorial to the sincere but misguided agent.

FOOTNOTES

[1] Commissioner of Indian Affairs, *Annual Report,* 1879, XXXII.

[2] Marshall D. Moody, "The Meeker Massacre," *Colorado Magazine,* April, 1953, pp. 98-99.

[3] Elizabeth Agnes Spiva, "The Utes in Colorado (1863-1880)," 1929, p. 106, Master's Thesis, Western State College. Manuscript in possession of Western History Department of the Denver Public Library.

[4] Moody, *op. cit.,* p. 99.

[5] Dawson and Skiff, *op. cit.,* p. 192.

[6] *Ibid.*

[7] Moody, *op cit.,* p. 101.

[8] Dawson and Skiff, *op. cit.*

[9] Records of the Bureau of Indian Affairs, Roster of Agency Employees, 1879-80, p. 65.

[10] Rio Blanco County, C.W.A. Interviews, 1933-34, a letter from H. A. Wildhack, April 8, 1921, p. 192. In possession of the State Historical Society of Colorado.

[11] Mansfield to Commissioner of Indian Affairs, Oct. 18, 1879. Bureau of Indian Affairs, Letters Received 1879, Colorado M. 209L.

[12] Rio Blanco County, C.W.A. Interviews, 1933-34, pp. 162-165. In possession of the State Historical Society of Colorado.

INDIAN SCARES

News of the Meeker massacre caused grave fears among the pioneers of western Colorado that there would be a general Indian uprising. This tense state of mind among the settlers was illustrated by numerous Indian scares which occurred immediately after the outbreak.

On the night of October 7, 1879, election returns were being counted at Howardsville, the county seat of San Juan County at that time. Suddenly a horseman galloped up the quiet streets and rode into the door of Jimmie Soward's saloon.

"Git up and out o' here," the rider cried. "The Indians have massacred everybody in Animas City and are moving on Silverton. I've got dispatches to the governor for arms and troops and am going to Antelope Springs before daylight. Jimmie, give me a drink."[1]

After showing his dispatches, he was given his drink. Then, he dramatically galloped off into the night.

Messengers were immediately sent to Animas Forks, another little mining town, to warn the residents. Others started out for Silverton to help repel the forthcoming attack. On the way they came across the camp of a group of men who were constructing a telegraph line.

When they were told that the Indians were on the warpath, the boss of the gang said, "From now on every man is on his own."

The telegraph builders broke camp without delay. Some of them started for the mountains to hide. Others headed for Del Norte, and the remainder accompanied the Howardsville party to Silverton. No more construction was done there that fall.

Upon reaching Silverton, the true nature of the horseman's mission was learned. He was the bearer of an appeal to the governor to send arms to Animas City so that the residents could defend themselves in case of an attack. He was bound for Del Norte via the wagon road across Stony Pass. There had been no uprising, but he had apparently told his wild tale about an Indian insurrection in order to get a free drink of whiskey, knowing that no one would hesitate to donate a drink to a man on such a mission of mercy with a forty mile ride before him.[2]

Within a short time after this incident, about six hundred troops under the command of General Edward Hatch marched from Fort Lewis at Pagosa Springs to Animas City.[3] The citizens had already formed a company of men and built a stockade on the west side of the Animas River just south of the bridge. They also built a fort on top of the hill facing the river and a sod fort on the Gaines ranch in Animas Valley.

It took the Fort Lewis soldiers three days to make the sixty-mile journey from Pagosa Springs. The soldiers arrived early in October and remained until the following January, 1880.[4]

Soldiers marching and soldiers practicing on the rifle range became a daily sight to the Southern Utes around Animas City, and this display of military power quieted any desires that they may have had to follow in the rebellious footsteps of their northern kinsmen.

On the following July, 1880, Fort Lewis was moved from Pagosa Springs to a more central location on the La Plata River about twelve miles southwest of the present town of Durango. Five companies of the 13th Infantry came with supplies and equipment in one hundred wagons, each drawn by six mules. The enlisted men's barracks were constructed first, followed by the officers' quarters. The fort was largely completed by the late fall of 1880.[5] In that same year Otto Mears established a toll road from Animas City to Fort Lewis. He collected fifty cents a trip for each wagon drawn by a single team and more for the heavier army wagons pulled by five or six mules. Soldiers and civilians riding horseback usually took another trail to avoid paying toll.

The new Fort Lewis on the La Plata became the scene of many gay social activities, and when it was abandoned in 1891, a Durango newspaper bemoaned the loss of the social life afforded by the officers and soldiers at the fort.

In 1892 the deserted buildings of the old military post were transformed into an Indian school for children of the Southern Utes. However, the young Utes did not take kindly to forcible education and burned the buildings to the ground. In 1910 the Fort Lewis School of Agriculture was established as a junior college of Colorado Aggies at Fort Collins.[6]

A day or so after the massacre on White River a group of cowboys were racing horses with some Southern Utes on a track near the present site of McPhee. Jim Nash rode in a race against an Indian on which many wagers were made, the Indians betting blankets and the cowboys, money. Judges consisted of both white men and redskins since the stakes were high.

As the two contestants neared the finish line, Nash's horse began to pull ahead. Seeing that he was beaten, the Ute wheeled off to one side. The Indians then began grabbing their blankets and some of the money as if their horse had won. Nash lost his temper, and jumping off his horse, he began quirting every Indian he could reach.

Before the Indians had time to retaliate, several horsemen came galloping up to the group.

"The Utes have killed everyone at the White River Agency," one of them shouted as they raced by. "Warn the settlers!"

The Utes snatched up their blankets, and the argument ended with the cowboys fleeing in one direction and the Indians in another.[7]

News of the massacre also had repercussions on the inhabitants of Rico. Believing that the outbreak might spread, all of the women and children were placed in a new log cabin to which no doors or windows had as yet been constructed. The only means of entrance was through the partially completed roof.

Guards were staioned below town near the site of the old Grand View smelter. Men also gathered in Frank Raymond's store and set up hay bales and empty beer cases around the doors and windows for breastworks.

One night while everyone was waiting fearfully for the Utes to attack, hoof beats suddenly sounded along the road to town. A frightened guard pulled up his rifle and fired in the direction of the approaching hoofs. The bullet struck one of the burros in a heavily loaded pack train. The burro puncher took after the retreating guard and caught him as he was crossing Silver Creek. Results of the night's adventure were one dead burro and a whipped tenderfoot.[8]

Settlers in the northern part of the state along the Yampa and Snake Rivers also had the jitters. Joe Rankin, Thornburg's scout, had warned the settlers around Hayden of the uprising as he was hastening to Rawlins for help, and George Fuhr had carried the news up the Snake River, advising the pioneers to run for their lives.

The Snake River people congregated at Charles Perkins' store near the present site of Baggs, ready to start up the Muddy if necessary. Meanwhile, a caravan of ranchers from the Yampa River country came riding past Perkins' store and camped twelve miles up the Muddy, waiting for General Merritt's command, which they intended to follow back.

The settlers around Steamboat Springs assembled at the home of James H. Crawford, founder of the town, where a state of siege was maintained for many days.[9] No Indians appeared, but the settlers decided to move away until conditions became more stable. Crawford and his family moved to Boulder, returning the next spring.[10]

When the Meeker trouble occurred, a resident of Hahn's Peak, a rival town for the county seat of Routt County, collected all of the county records at Hayden and took them to Hahn's Peak for safe keeping. The people of Hayden later tried to get the records back but were unable to do so.[11]

When news of the Meeker massacre reached Grand Lake, the

people who were spending the summer and fall there prepared immediately to depart. Judge Wescott, an old trapper who lived near the lake, tried to quiet their fears, explaining that the Utes had a superstitious fear of the lake and would not venture near it even in case of a general uprising. Nevertheless, within a week everyone except Wescott started for Denver. All of the men were armed and rode in the front, rear, and on each side of the wagons which carried the women and children.[12]

During this anxious period, A. J. Chitwood, a cowboy, was looking for stray catle down on the Mesa Mountains below Ignacio. As he rode along with his head down looking for tracks, there was an unexpected loud clatter of hoofs, and twenty Ute horsemen galloped out of the scrub pine and surrounded him.

The suddenness of the onslaught so startled Chitwood that he thought his time had come. One of the Indians rode directly up to him, and the cowboy's trembling hand felt for the butt of his six-shooter.

"Whiskey?" the Ute asked.

"No whiskey," Chitwood replied, feeling a little relieved.

"Tobacco?"

"No tobacco."

The Ute grinned, and he and his companions rode away.[13]

When the people in and around Parrott City learned of the Meeker killings, they were suddenly glad that they had the good will not only of Chief Ignacio, from whom Captain John Moss had purchased their land, but also of Chief Red Jacket.

Chief Red Jacket and a group of Southern Utes usually camped for several months each summer a mile and a half below Parrott City. He was a frequent visitor at the homes of the early settlers in this area who for expediency gave him handouts. In return, he sometimes brought his white friends venison or hides. His friendship for the Parrott City residents began when Henry Smith divided with Red Jacket his last few pounds of flour to save the life of the Indian's sick squaw. The nearest place to obtain flour was at Tierra Amarilla, 125 miles away. Smith's generosity won for the pioneers a friend whose services were often needed.[14]

FOOTNOTES

[1]Mary C. Ayers, "Howardsville in the San Juan," *Colorado Magazine*, October, 1951, p. 252.

[2]*Ibid.*

[3]Animas City was located about three miles north of the present site of Durango. When Durango was started in the fall of 1880, Animas City was gradually absorbed into the new town.

[4]Helen M. Searcy, "The Military," *Pioneers of the San Juan*, Vol. I, pp. 65-68.

[5]The garrison at Pagosa Springs was continued until 1882 although most of the troops were removed some time before the fort was abandoned. After all the troops were gone, the little settlement of Pagosa Springs moved gradually across the river to the higher and better site which had been occupied by the fort.

[6]*The Colorado Magazine*, Jan., 1941, pp. 29-30.

[7]Erastus Thomas Account, Otero and Montezume Counties, C.W.A. Interviews, 1933-34, pp. 532-533. In possession of the State Historical Society of Colorado.

[8]Louise Hecks, "Milestones in Rico's History," *Pioneers of the San Juan*, Vol. 3, pp. 138-139.

[9]Byron T. Skelton, "History of Hayden Valley," reproduced in *The Tread of Pioneers* by Charles H. Leckenby, pp. 63-64.

[10]E. A. Brooks Account, Routt and Arapahoe Counties, C.W.A. Interviews, 1933-34.

[11]John Mack, "Early Days on Bear River," Moffat County, C.W.A. Interviews, 1933-34. In possession of the State Historical Society of Colorado.

[12]Mary Lyons Cairns, *The Pioneers*, Chapter III.

[13]"Account of A. J. Chitwood," *Pioneers of the San Juan* Vol. I, pp. 34-35.

[14]Mary C. Ayres, *Pioneers of the San Juan*, Vol. 3, p. 164.

RELEASE OF THE CAPTIVES

Ralph Meeker of New York, son of the dead agent, was appointed to take charge of the government property at the White River Agency and to secure the money, papers, and effects of the murdered men. He received no compensation but was allowed five dollars a day for hotel expenses, meals, and lodgings.[1]

Charles Adams, an employee of the Post Office Department and a former agent at the Los Pinos Agency, was made a special agent on October 14, 1879, to recover the three women and two children who had been kidnapped by Douglass and his followers. Adams left Denver on October 15th and proceeded to the Uncompahgre Agency to get Chief Ouray's advice and help.[2]

On October 19th Adams started out to find Douglass' camp, which Ouray said was somewhere on Plateau Creek between the present towns of Palisade and De Beque. He was accompanied by three chiefs—Sapowanero, Shavano, and a son of Colorow, and by Captain M. W. Cline and a Mr. Sherman, who were connected with the Uncompahgre Agency. In addition to this official delegation, Count Von Doenhoff, a member of the German legation at Washington, became interested in the mission and went along as a spectator.[3] Adams carried orders from Ouray for immediate cessation of hostilities and for the surrender of the captives.[4]

Two days later about ten o'clock in the morning the little

Left to right: Back row—Washington (a leading Northern Ute Chief), Susan (sister of Chief Ouray), Johnson No. 2 (Susan's husband), Capt. Jack (leader of Thornburg ambush five years later), John. Middle Row—Uriah Curtis (first interpreter for Northern Utes), J. B. Thompson (agent at the Denver Ute Agency), Chas. Adams (agent of the Los Pinos Agency 1872-75), Otto Mears.

Front Row—Guero (possibly Ouray's father), Chipeta, Ouray, Piah (Tabeguache Ute Chief). Presented to State Historical Society of Colorado by Major J. B. Thompson, who said picture was taken about 1874. *Photo courtesy State Historical Society of Colorado.*

Douglass and Johnson. Johnson assaulted Nathan Meeker for plowing up his horse pasture. This attack caused Meeker to ask for the aid of troops, which in turn, precipitated the Thornburg ambush and Meeker massacre. Douglass was the leader in the Meeker massacre at the White River Agency.

Photo Courtesy of State Historical Society of Colorado.

SUSAN
—SARAH, SISTER OF OURAY.

Susan—Chief Ouray's young sister—who befriended the captive
survivors of the Meeker massacre. This drawing appeared in
Frank Leslie's Illustrated Newspaper on Nov. 15, 1879. *Photo
Courtesy Denver Public Library Western Collection.*

Josephine Meeker. *Photo Courtesy State Historical Society of Colorado.*

Nathan C. Meeker, *Photo Courtesy State Historical Society of Colorado.*

Mrs. N. C. Meeker. *Courtesy of R. S. Ball, founder of the old Meeker Hotel.*

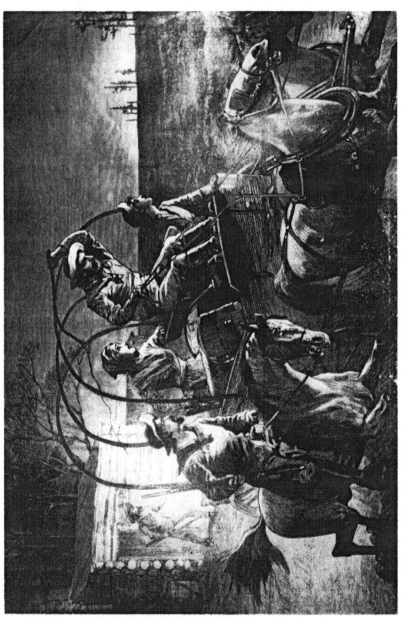

Ute War of 1887. Settlers abandoning their ranches and flying to Meeker for safety. *Source: Frank Leslie's Illustrated Newspaper, Sept. 3, 1887. Photo Courtesy Denver Public Library Western Collection.*

This drawing of the burned White River Agency appeared in *Frank Leslie's Illustrated Newspaper* on Dec. 6, 1879. *Photo Courtesy of Denver Public Library Western Collection.*

DEATH OF MAJOR THORNBURGH WHILE LEADING A CHARGE TO SECURE THE WAGON TRAIN.

COMPANY D, OF THE NINTH CAVALRY (COLORED), UNDER CAPTAIN DODGE, FORCING THEIR WAY TO THE RELIEF OF THE BELEAGUERED SURVIVORS.

COLORADO.—THE UTE OUTBREAK AND MASSACRE NEAR THE WHITE RIVER AGENCY.—FROM SKETCHES BY OUR SPECIAL AGENT.—SEE PAGE 156.

Source: *Frank Leslie's Illustrated Newspaper*, Nov. 8, 1879.
Photo Courtesy Denver Library Western Collection.

A portrait of Major T. T. Thornburg, who was ambushed while on his way to the aid of Meeker. Thornburg and thirteen of his troops were killed in the initial attack. *Photo courtesy of State Historical Society of Colorado.*

Joseph P. Rankin. *Photo Courtesy State Historical Society of Colorado.*

Captain Jack—leader of the Thornburg ambush. *Photo Courtesy of State Historical Society of Colorado.*

Chief Coloro—a participant in the Thornburg ambush. *Photo Courtesy of Denver Public Library Western Collection.*

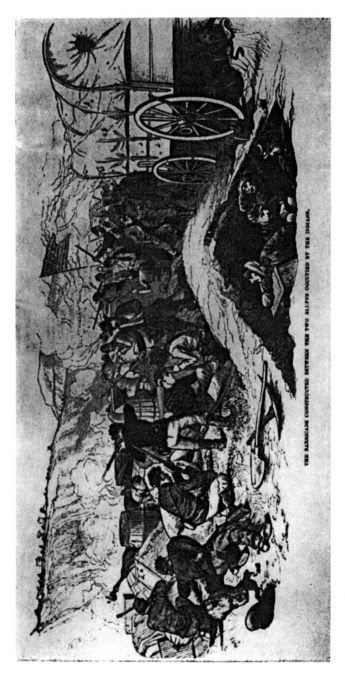

THE BARRICADE CONSTRUCTED BETWEEN THE TWO BLUFFS OCCUPIED BY THE INDIANS.

This drawing of Thornburg's besieged men appeared in *Frank Leslie's Illustrated Newspaper* on November 8, 1879. *Photo Courtesy of Denver Public Western Collection.*

Marker on top of Thornburg ambush 20 miles from Meeker.
Photo Courtesy of Denver Public Library Western Collection.

Five chiefs of the Uncompahgre band. Ouray in center. *Photo Courtesy Walker Art Studios.*

group arrived at Douglass' camp on Plateau Creek. A squaw of Perune who was guarding Josephine Meeker saw the men approaching and made quite a commotion trying to hide the white girl from view. Her actions attracted the attention of the party, and Josephine, also curious about the squaw's maneuvers, stood up and peeked out of the tepee. There she saw Adams, the first white man she had seen since the massacre. He dismounted and asked who she was. He then told her that he had come to release her and the other captives and that she should be ready to leave in the afternoon, if possible.[5]

At the upper end of the camp Adams found thirty or forty Indians boisterously talking in a tepee. He went inside and told them the purpose of his visit. They told him to wait until Douglass returned and talk with him. The chief arrived about an hour later, and Adams explained his mission. Douglass invited the agent and his party into the tepee where a long discussion took place from eleven o'clock that morning until four or five in the afternoon.[6]

At first the Utes refused to release the prisoners in spite of Ouray's orders. Some of the Indians spoke in a very hostile manner and proposed that they kill the intruding white men and continue on their way. Sapowanero put a quick end to this kind of talk by telling them that Ouray was already very angry at what had occurred at the White River Agency and would take personal action against any Ute who continued hostilities. Though excited and elated by their recent victory, they were afraid of Ouray.[7] Finally Douglass agreed to release the women and children, whom he had held captive for twenty-three days, provided that Adams would ride on to White River and stop General Merritt's troops from moving against the Indians.

Adams accepted this offer and the conference was concluded. He asked Douglass to have Mrs. Price and Mrs. Meeker brought up from the brush along the river where they had been hidden upon the arrival of the white men. He arranged for all three women to sleep in the same tent for the night. Then, after providing saddles and horses for the captives to leave on the next day, he rode with Douglass to the main Indian encampment.

On the following morning the other members of the rescue

party departed with the women and children for the Uncompahgre Agency, where they stayed at Ouray's home on the outskirts of present Montrose. Ouray and Chipeta treated the former captives with hospitality. In commenting about it Josephine Meeker wrote:

> We found carpets on the floors, curtains at the windows, lamps on the tables, stoves in the rooms, and fires burning. We were given the whole house to ourselves.[8]

Josephine's brother, Ralph Meeker, met them here. He found them to be poorly dressed and in a highly nervous condition from their long ordeal.[9] A few days later he took them to Alamosa where they caught a train for Greeley.

Meanwhile, after leaving the captives, Adams and Douglass proceeded to Captain Jack's camp, arriving there about eleven o'clock that night. Adams sat up all night listening to the Utes' version of the Thornburg fight, which they wanted him to pass on to the officials in Washington.[10]

At daybreak the tired agent started for Merritt's quarters on White River. Several Indians accompanied him, and this number gradually increased to twenty-five as he rode along. They were afraid to go with Adams into the soldiers' camp but awaited his return in order to learn what General Merritt intended to do. The Utes were eager for peace.

After the consultation with General Merritt, Adams returned with the Indians to Plateau Creek to see if the Utes had kept their promise. He also had another conference with them at this time and, since they all desired peace, he concluded that those engaged in the recent atrocities could be easily picked out through an investigating committee. Officials of the Department of Interior had come to the same conclusion.

A special commission was, therefore, appointed by the Secretary of the Interior and the Secretary of War to investigate the uprising. This commission was composed of Major General Edward Hatch, Charles Adams, Ouray, and First Lieutenant Gustavus Valois, who served as recorder and legal advisor.[11] This commission met at the Uncompahgre Agency on November 12, 1879. They heard the testimony of Douglass, Johnson,

So-wa-wick, Mrs. S. F. Price, Mrs. A. D. Meeker; Joseph W. Brady, who was a miller at the Los Pinos Agency; Yanco and Washington, who were Uncompahgre Utes; Josephine Meeker; Henry Jim, a White River Ute who was a former interpreter for Agent Meeker; and Captain Jack, leader of the attack on Thornburg.

General Hatch told the Indians that the attack on Thornburg was a fair fight and nothing would be done to those who participated in it. However, he went on to say that the Utes who had taken part in the murder of unarmed men at the White River Agency would be tried and punished if found guilty.[12]

The three captive women named twelve White River Utes who had taken part in the massacre. Ouray objected to taking the testimony of women, which was against Indian custom. The commission tried to get some of the Utes to corroborate the testimony of the women, but they all refused to truthfully answer any question which might incriminate themselves or others of their tribe.

Ouray defended his people for refusing to testify correctly. He said that all of the Northern or White River Utes had been directly or indirectly engaged in the massacre, and a man couldn't be expected or compelled to testify against himself.

Adams and General Hatch finally asked Ouray to have the twelve men named by the women brought in for trial. Ouray agreed to do so on the condition that they be tried in Washington rather than in Colorado.

In a moment of bitterness, Ouray went on to say, "The Colorado people are all our enemies and to give our men up to be tried in this state would be as if we gave them up, knowing that they would be hung instantly. . . . You three [referring to Hatch, Adams, and Valois] are all my enemies. I am one against three. You hate me. . . . I have not one friend among you. You will not give me justice, and that is why I want to go to Washington where I will, at least, have one friend."[13]

Jack, Antelope, and Colorow freely confessed to starting the fight against Thornburg when told that participants in the ambush would not be punished. They, at the request of Ouray, attempted to bring in the twelve men whom the three women had accused of killing Meeker and his employees, but none would come except Douglass. Douglass admitted that he was the leader of the insurrection at the agency. He was later imprisoned at Fort Leavenworth for a time and then liberated.[14]

It was brought out at the investigation that the coming of troops on to the reservation was the immediate cause of the uprising. Josephine Meeker testified that during her captivity Douglass said to her, ". . . if the soldiers had not come and threatened the Indians . . . the agent and the employees would not have been killed."[15]

The testimony revealed that the women had been moderately well treated. Susan, sister of Ouray, who had married a White River Ute, was particularly hospitable to the captives.[16]

After it became evident that the commission could not determine who the guilty Indians were, it was agreed that a party of Ute leaders should be taken to Washington, D. C., to testify before an investigating committee of the United States House of Representatives. So, on January 15, 1880, eleven Utes in charge of Charles Adams[17] and Otto Mears left for the national capitol with eleven Utes. Other witnesses including Josephine Meeker, Captain Payne, and Lieutenant Cherry.[18]

The result of this congressional investigation added nothing of importance to the findings of the special commission. So, with the exception of Douglass, the perpetrators of the Meeker massacre remained unpunished.

While in Washington during the investigation, Ouray and Chipeta visited Carl Schurz, Secretary of the Interior, at his home. In his private memoirs Schurz wrote:

> Ouray and Chipeta often visited me at my home and always conducted themselves with perfect propriety. They observed the various belongings of the drawing room with keen but decorous interest and were especially attracted by a large crystal chandelier suspended from the ceiling. They wished to know where such a chandelier could be bought and what it would cost. . . . Ouray was by far the brightest Indian I have ever met.[19]

After realizing the futility of ascertaining the identities of the guilty Indians, the government turned to a more important problem—namely, the transfer of the Northern or White River Utes to another agency outside of Colorado.

FOOTNOTES

[1]Secretary of the Interior Carl Schurz to Commissioner of Indian Affairs, October 11, 1879, Bureau of Indian Affairs, Letters Received 1879, Colorado I 2131.

[2]Frank Hall, *History of Colorado*, Vol. 2, pp. 503-504.

[3]*Ibid.*

[4]Contrary to the popular legend, Chipeta did not help in the rescue.

[5]Elizabeth Agnes Spiva, *The Utes in Colorado—1863-1880,* Master's Thesis, 1929, Western State College, p. 119. Manuscript in possession of Western History Dept. of the Denver Public Library.

[6]*Ibid.,* p. 120.

[7]Hall, *op cit.,* p. 504.

[8]*Ibid.*

[9]Marshall D. Moody, "The Meeker Massacre," *Colorado Magazine,* April, 1953, p. 102.

[10]Spiva, *op. cit.,* p. 123.

[11]Moody, *op. cit.,* p. 102.

[12]Sidney Jocknick, *Early Days on the Western Slope of Colorado,* p. 196.

[13]Ouray was referring to Carl Schurz, Secretary of the Interior.

[14]Jocknick, *op. cit.,* p. 200.

[15]Moody, *op. cit.,* p. 102.

[16]See Mrs. Price's account in Appendix.

[17]Adams later was appointed minister from the United States to Bolivia. He lost his life in a fire at the Gunnry Hotel in Denver August, 1895, soon after his return to the United States.

[18]U. S. Congress, 46th Cong., 2 sess., 1879-1880. "House Miscellaneous Document 38" contains the testimony given by these individuals.

[19]Albert B. Reager and Wallace Stark, "Chipeta, Queen of the Utes and Her Equally Illustrious Husband Noted Chief Ouray," *Utah Historical Quarterly,* July, 1933, p. 106.

TREATY OF 1880

For some time settlers of northwestern Colorado had been trying to get the government to move the White River Utes off the rich mineral and agricultural lands in the White River area. The Meeker massacre and Thornburg ambush so incensed the people of Colorado and the nation that it brought the entire matter to a head.

The question was discussed with the Ute delegation who came to Washington to testify before the congressional committee concerning the outbreak. Chief Ouray was at first opposed to removing the White River Utes, and the government did not want to act against his wishes, since he had been of invaluable help in putting down the uprising and rescuing the captives.

However, Ouray was finally persuaded to sign an agreement dated March 6, 1880, whereby not only the three White River but also the Uncompahgre band and the three Southern Ute bands were all to be placed on new reservations.

According to this Treaty of 1880, the three White River bands were to be moved completely out of Colorado and placed on the Uintah Reservation in northeastern Utah.

The Uncompahgre Utes were to be reassigned to a more limited reservation than formerly on agricultural lands along the Grand (Colorado) River near the mouth of the Gunnison River in Colorado. The treaty provided, however, that if there were not a sufficient quantity of agricultural land to go around in this area, then the Uncompahgre band was to be located upon other unoccupied agricultural lands as may be found in that vicinity and in the Territory of Utah.

A reservation for the three bands of Southern Utes was to be established upon the unoccupied agricultural lands on the La Plata River in Colorado, and if there was not suficient such lands on the La Plata and its vicinity in Colorado, then upon unoccupied agricultural lands on the La Plata and its vicinity in the state of New Mexico.[1]

Provision was made for allotments of 160 acres of agricultural land and an additional quantity of grazing land not to exceed this amount to each head of a family. Allotments of eighty acres of agricultural land with an additional quantity of grazing land not more than eighty acres were also to be made to each single Ute over eighteen who was not the head of a family, to each orphan child under eighteen, and to each Ute then living or born prior to the making of these allotments not otherwise provided for. A commission was to be appointed to make these allotments and to select the lands that the Utes were to occupy.

The Department of the Interior estimated that there were 3000 heads of families and 1000 youths over eighteen who would be eligible for allotments.[2]

In consideration for their concessions, the Utes were to receive, in addition to the annuities and benefits already provided in the Treaty of 1873, enough money from the government to produce an income of $50,000 a year to be distributed per capita to them forever.

The treaty refused any pay to the White River Utes so long as any of the participants in the Meeker massacre remained at large, and it stipulated that annual pension payments be made to dependents and victims of the massacre for twenty years from money that would otherwise go to the White River Utes.

Congress approved this agreement on June 15, 1880, but before it could go into effect, it was necessary to get the consent of three-fourths of the Utes.[3] President Grant appointed a commission of five men to go to the reservation and get the required number of signatures. Members of this commission were Chairman Manypenny of Ohio, A. B. Meachem of Washington, D. C., J. J. Russell of Iowa, Bowman of Kentucky, and Otto Mears of Colorado.[4]

After arriving in Western Colorado, this commission held a council with the Indians in the Uncompahgre Valley. Most of the Utes refused to sign the agreement, and it looked as if the treaty were doomed.

In an effort to induce the Southern Utes to sign it, Ouray, accompanied by his wife Chipeta, Chipeta's brother John McCook, and a few other attendants, left the Uncompahgre Agency on August 14, 1880, and started for the Southern Ute Agency at Ignacio. The little group arrived there three days later.

The great chief's arrival was unheralded and even generally unknown for several hours until Will Burns, one of the interpreters at the agency, by chance obtained the information from one of the Southern Utes. Burns immediately started looking for Ouray's tepee and finally found it a few hundred yards north of the agency buildings. Upon entering he found Ouray lying upon some blankets and clothed only in breech clout, leggings and moccasins.[5] This was unusual for Ouray, since he usually dressed in more civilized attire.

Noticing that the Indian was restless and in apparent pain, Burns asked him what was the matter. Ouray replied that he had not been feeling well since leaving the Uncompahgre Agency. The interpreter then asked the chief if he wanted a doctor but received no answer.

Burns, nevertheless, went to the agency headquarters and reported what he had seen to Colonel Page, the agent, who, with the agency physician, went right away to Ouray's camp. Ouray's stomach was badly swollen, and he seemed to be rapidly growing worse. The doctor diagnosed the case as an acute attack of kidney trouble—probably Braight's Disease—and he told the agent that Ouray was in a very critical condition. Page sent a courier to get Dr. Hopson of Animas City to consult with the agency physician. A messenger was also sent to the Uncompahgre Agency.[6]

Dr. Hopson visited Ouray twice, the last time being on Sun-

day, August 22nd. On Sunday evening Dr. Lacy of the Uncompahgre Agency arrived after a hurried trip. While the three
doctors tried to treat Ouray, his medicine men were holding
incantations and pounding his abdomen with their fists and
bucking their heads against his chest to drive out the evil spirit.

From Saturday until Tuesday (August 24, 1880), when he
died, Ouray lingered in a comatose state from which he was
aroused only at long intervals. Late Monday evening it became evident that Ouray could not live many hours, and Dr.
Hopson returned to Animas City. On Tuesday morning at
eleven o'clock an Indian arrived at the agency building and
asked to see Dr. Lacy, who accompanied him back to Ouray's
tepee. When nearly there another Indian stepped out of the
tepee and silently motioned them back. Ouray was dead.

At the time of his death there were nearly a thousand Indians camped in the vicinity of his camp. Within ten minutes
after he died the Indians had moved more than a mile away because of their superstitious fear of the dead.

Ouray's attendants sewed his body up in new blankets and
buffalo robes, tied cords and ropes around it, and slung it
across his saddle horse.

Nathan Price, a Southern Ute, told the small group that his
father, Chief Suvata, was buried on the rocky mesa two miles
south of Ignacio and suggested that this would be a good place
to bury Ouray.[7] So, accompanied by Chipeta, McCook, Buckskin Charley, who was a famous Southern Ute chief, and four
other Utes, Ouray was taken about two miles south of Ignacio,
and his body was placed in a natural cave on the mesa. His saddle was laid beside him and the cave was then filled with rocks.
Five horses were killed near the grave as a burial sacrifice.[8]

After Ouray's death, Chipeta made Carl Schurz, Secretary of
the Interior, a present of the buckskin suit that her husband
had worn when he and she last visited the Secretary in his
Washington home.[9]

Ouray's unexpected death appeared to be the final blow to
any hope of persuading three-fourths of the Utes to sign the
Treaty of 1880. Otto Mears, however, saved the day by private-
ly paying two dollars in cash to every Ute that he could per-

suade to sign it. By September 11, 1880, he had the necessary number of signatures.

When Manypenny, chairman of the commission, learned about Mears' strategy, he refused to endorse the treaty on the grounds that Mears was guilty of bribery. He filed charges against Mears with the Secretary of Interior, Carl Schurz.[10]

That fall James A. Garfield was elected President, and Kirkwood of Iowa was appointed Secretary of the Interior to replace Carl Schurz.

In 1881 Mears was ordered to Washington to stand trial. The investigation was held in the office of the Secretary of Interior. In the presence of the two Colorado seators—Henry M. Teller and N. P. Hill—Kirkwood asked Mears if he had given the Utes money to sign the treaty.

Mears replied that he had paid them two dollars each since the Indians claimed that the two dollars in cash was worth more to them than the government's promise of fifty thousand dollars per year, which they would probably never get.

"Was the money you paid them your own, or was it paid by the government?" Kirkwood asked.

"I paid it out of my own pocket."

"How much did it cost you?'

"Twenty-eight hundred dollars."

"Send me a bill for it," Kirkwood said, "and I will see to it that the government reimburses you. You did a good job, and I am grateful."[11]

After getting three-fourths of the Utes to sign the treaty, the commission's next task was to establish the exact locations of the respective reservations before moving the Utes to them.

The Southern Utes were left in southwestern Colorado on their old reservation strip, which is fifteen miles wide and 110 miles long.

The treaty specified that the White River Utes should be placed on the Uintah Reservation in northeastern Utah; so there was no problem there.

However, the commission was divided among itself as to the location of the new reservation for the Uncompahgre or Tabeguache band. Meacham and Manypenny believed that the treaty was very specific in its stipulation that this band should be placed on the Grand (now called the Colorado) River near its junction with the Gunnison at the present site of Grand Junction.

The exact words of the disputed phrasing were "The Uncompahgre Utes agree to remove and settle upon agricultural lands on Grand River near the mouth of the Gunnison River in Colorado, if a sufficient quantity of agricultural land shall be found there; if not, then upon such other unoccupied agricultural lands as may be found in that vicinity and in the Territory of Utah."

Otto Mears, sharing with most Coloradoans the desire to get the Uncompahgre Utes out of the state so that the region could be opened for white settlement, interpreted this phrasing differently from Meacham and Manypenny and argued that it gave the commission an alternative, if the majority so desired, of placing the band on a reservation in the Territory of Utah. This was definitely a very liberal interpretation of the treaty.

Mears was supported in this view by Russell and Bowman, which gave them a majority of three to two.

On one occasion when the argument between the commissioners was at white heat, Bowman lost his temper and knocked Meacham down. As a result, Bowman was forced to resign, which placed the board in a deadlock of two to two concerning the issue.

The Secretary of Interior was sympathetic with Mears' viewpoint, and he appointed Judge T. A. McMorris of Colorado to replace Bowman, which broke the deadlock in favor of removal of the Uncompahgre Utes to Utah.

In examining the Utah country for a new reservation for the Uncompahgre Utes, Mears and his cohorts decided to establish it southeast of the Uintah Reservation where the Duchesne and White Rivers enter the Green River.

So, as a result of the Treaty of 1880, both the White River Utes and the Uncompahgre Utes were to be moved out of Western Colorado which they had inhabited for centuries.

While the commission was deciding upon the future destiny of the Utes, an unfortunate incident occurred on the Uncompahgre Reservation in Western Colorado between the Indians and a party of freighters who were passing through.

On September 29, 1880, just a year after the Meeker massacre, a son of Chief Shavano by the name of Johnson was shot and killed by A. D. Jackson, who was in charge of a freighting party. The Utes were drunk and had been annoying the white men. After Johnson was shot, the Indians rode away. The freighters did not believe that the Ute was seriously wounded, but he died that night.[12]

The next afternoon about four o'clock a Ute chief, accompanied by two white employees of the agency, stopped the wagon train, which was on its way to the mines. They said that an Indian had been killed, and they wanted the murderer.

While they were talking, about thirty Indians approached and surrounded the wagons. They kept the drivers covered with their rifles until Major William H. Beery, the agent, arrived with sixteen soldiers and arrested the freighters.

The trespassers were taken to the agency where they were guarded through the night by two soldiers and ten Utes. Several times during the night the Indians tried to take the prisoners by force.

Next morning Jackson confessed the shooting. The other freighters were then disarmed and allowed to go on their way. A small force of soldiers went along to guard the newcomers to a place on the Saguache road beyond reach of the angry Indians.

Three of the agency employees and a Ute started for Gunnison with Jackson who was to be put on trial. They had progressed about three miles when a group of Indians suddenly appeared and overpowered the guard.

The prisoner was taken to the edge of a bluff, and one of the Utes shot the young white man in the side. Then, they pushed his body over the cliff into a gulch, where it was discovered three weeks later by J. F. Howard, the agency farmer.

FOOTNOTES
[1]*Senate Documents*, Vol. I, "Indian Affairs, Laws, and Treaties," Document No. 452, pp. 181, 182, 183.

[2]Helen M. Searcy, "Otto Mears and the Utes," *Pioneers of the San Juan*, Vol. I, p. 25.

[3]*Senate Documents, op. cit.*, p. 186.

[4]Searcy, *op. cit.*, p. 25.

[5]*La Plata Miner*, September 4, 1880, p. 1. Newspaper in possession of the Western History Department of the Denver Public Library.

[6]*Ibid.*

[7]Mrs. C. W. Wiegel, "The Reburial of Chief Ouray," *Colorado Magazine*, Oct., 1928, p. 169.

[8]S. F. Stacker, "Ouray and the Utes," *Colorado Magazine*, April, 1950, p. 136.

[9]Albert Reagan and Wallace Stark, "Chipeta, Queen of the Utes and her Equally Illustrious Husband, Noted Chief Ouray," *Utah Historical Quarterly*, July 1933, p. 106.

[10]Searcy, *op. cit.*, p. 26.

[11]*Ibid.*, p. 27.

[12]Sidney Jocknick, *Early Days on the Western Slope of Colorado*, pp. 211-215.

EXODUS OF THE UTES

Otto Mears went to Salt Lake City and made arrangements to have accommodations and provisions ready for the Uncompahgre and White River Utes upon their arrival at their adjoining reservations in northeastern Utah. Preparations for their removal took many months. Government surveys were made to establish boundary lines, bridges were built, and buildings constructed.

Just prior to their departure, General R. S. MacKenzie, commander of the troops at Fort Crawford, assembled the White River and Uncompahgre bands near his headquarters, which was at the bend of the Uncompahgre River just east of where the town of Olathe now stands. The general had a force of nine companies of cavalry and nine of infantry within a radius of five miles.

The Utes did not want to leave their old domain and made all kinds of excuses for delay. They pleaded for more time to gather their stock. They said that they wanted to go to the Yampa River on a last hunt to kill sufficient game for the coming winter. Denied this, they demanded one more trip to Cow Creek and the Cimarron.[1]

MacKenzie had already given the Indians an extension of time, but he told them that he would give them ten more days in which to attend to these matters and be prepared to leave.

Colorow's band was camped between two bluffs a short distance away from MacKenzie's headquarters. Soldiers were stationed on these bluffs to keep Colorow and his followers under continual observation.

It was fortunate that this was done because someone had smuggled whiskey to the Indians, and they were in a reckless mood. After a week of watching during which nothing happened, the sentinels caught sight of a thick cloud of dust, accompanied by a loud barking of dogs. Cloud after cloud of dust arose as the drunken Utes, all riding in a bunch, began their charge on MacKenzie's camp.

Soldiers on the bluffs began blowing bugles and shooting rockets to sound the alarm. The codes and signals warned MacKenzie so that when Colorow and his men came galloping into view around a bend of the river, they were met by four companies of cavalry in battle formation.[2]

Amazed at this unexpected preparedness against their attempted surprise attack, the Utes instantly slackened their pace, engaged in a brief parley, and then beat a hasty retreat back to their own camp.

That night General MacKenzie sent for Mears and McMorris, the only two commissioners in the area, and told them that he was anxious to move the Indians right away before there was any more trouble. The commissioners signed the paper for removal, and the Utes were informed that they must be ready to start for their new reservations in two hours. MacKenzie emphasized his order by placing six pieces of artillery on a hill overlooking the Ute camp.

When the time limit was up, the Utes began their long trek to northeastern Utah. A few days previously[3] Agent Berry had issued them sufficient rations at the Uncompahgre Agency to last them throughout the journey.

They were taken down the Uncompahgre River to the Gunnison which they followed to the Grand, now called the Colorado River.[4] Large boats were used to ferry the Indians and their property across the Colorado near the present site of Grand Junction. These boats remained for many years, and western immigrants and early settlers made use of them to cross the big river.

On September 1, 1881, the last band made their exodus from Western Colorado, and they arrived at their destination on September 13th.[5]

A short time after their arrival, Otto Mears visited the new reservations to inspect supplies. While he was there, Cojoe, a Ute chief, tried to kill him, claiming that it was because of Mears that the Uncompahgre Utes had to leave Colorado.

The commission which was appointed to select and remove the Utes to their new reservations continued its supervision over the Indians at the new agency until March 13, 1883, when the commission was abolished.

Otto Mears, who played such an important role in removing the Uncompahgre and White River Utes from Western Colorado, was a small Russian Jew, who was born May 3, 1840, in Kurland, Russia. His father, who was born in England, died when Otto was a year old. His mother, a Russian girl, also died when Otto was a child, and the orphan boy went to live with his mother's brother, who had a family of ten boys and two girls. Otto had trouble with the other boys and didn't mix well with any of the members of his uncle's family; so when he was a little over nine years old, he was sent to England to live with a relative of his father, who, in turn, sent him on across the ocean to another relative in New York City.

A year later when he was ten, the New York relative passed him on to another relative in California, where Otto sold newspapers on the streets of San Francisco. Here the years passed while Mears worked at various and sundry jobs, including one prospecting trip to Nevada in search for gold after it was discovered at Wabuska in 1859.

After returning to San Francisco he took out naturalization papers, and when Abraham Lincoln ran for president, Mears voted for him. When the Civil War broke out, Mears enlisted in the First Regiment of California Volunteers Company in the spring of 1861. During the war he served under Kit Carson in fighting the Navajos. He was discharged in 1864. Upon leaving the Army he went to Santa Fe and worked there for a time in the mercantile business. A year later he moved to Conejos in the San Luis Valley of Colorado and established a general merchandise store.

Noticing that there was no gristmill in the region, he built one. There was not enough wheat in the area to keep his mill running; so he went to Saguache at the upper end of the Valley to farm and raise wheat for his gristmill. The government was buying flour at Fort Garland, and Mears intended to sell the flour that he milled to the government. However, the price of flour took a nosedive; so instead of hauling his wheat down to the gristmill at Conejos as planned, he tried to take it north over Poncha Pass. The road was so rough that he upset his wagons, which were full of loose wheat.

William Gilpin, who later became territorial governor of Colorado, happened along on horseback. Seeing Mears' predicament, he suggested that Mears build a toll road, saying that some day there would be thousands of people coming into the San Luis Valley. This incident is what started Mears building toll roads for which he is remembered today.

He completed the road over Poncha Pass in 1867. His next road was built from Saguache to Lake City in 1871. After other roads in the San Juan were constructed by him, he became known as "The Pathfinder of the San Juan." The construction of these toll roads and railroads in southwestern Colorado brought him even greater fame than did his dealings with the Ute Indians.

He died on June 24, 1931, at 91 years of age in Pasadena, California. According to his wishes, his ashes were scattered on Engineer Mountain above Animas Fork in the San Juan country. A memorial tablet in his honor was placed in the solid rock of the cliff at the edge of Bear Creek Falls along the Million Dollar Highway between Ouray and Silverton.[6]

FOOTNOTES

[1]Sidney Jocknick, *Early Days on the Western Slope of Colorado*, p. 222.

[2]*Ibid.*, p. 24.

[3]August 27, 1881.

⁴In 1921 the name of the "Grand River" was changed to the "Colorado River."

⁵Jocknick, *op. cit.,* p. 226.

⁶Helen M. Searcy, "Otto Mears and the Utes," *Pioneers of the San Juna,* Vol. I, pp. 15-21. Most of Helen Searcy's article was dictated by Otto Mears in April, 1926, at his home in Pasadena, California.

TRADING WITH THE INDIANS

After the Uncompahgre and White River Utes were removed from Colorado, they drifted back into the northwestern part of the state every fall around early October to hunt and trade. They claimed that when they consented to move to their new reservations they reserved the right to hunt on their old domain. They came in bunches from fifteen to twenty, bringing their papooses, wives, horses, dogs and tepees. While in this area, they traded at the Hugus and Company store in Meeker and at C. P. Hill's trading post at the present site of Rangely.

The Hugus and Company store was Meeker's first store, and it was located in the first of the old adobe barracks to be sold at auction in the fall of 1883. N. Major, the manager, bought the building for fifty dollars and moved his goods into it from his trading post in Powell Park about four and one-half miles down the White River. He had an ample waist line, and whenever Major and the portly Colorow met, they would compare waist lines.

One January while taking inventory the clerks found a lot of straw hats which they had been unable to sell. Meeker was a cattle country at this time, and no self-respecting cowboy or cattleman in those early years would be seen wearing such a dudish article as a straw hat.

The ingenious manager of the store proceeded to give each business man in town one of the straw hats with the request that he be sure to wear it the next time the Utes showed up. A few days later the Indians arrived. It was a cold wintry day, but as a favor to the store manager, whenever the business men ventured outdoors, they wore their straw hats.

The Utes were very much impressed at seeing so many of these strange looking hats, and decided that they were another peculiar fad of the white man. Desiring to get on the band wagon, the Indians bought every straw hat left in the store, paying one dollar each for them whereas the regular price was only twenty-five cents. They also purchased a colored ribbon with each hat to tie under their chins in order to help hold the hats on.

Then, a little later the Utes rode off in a snowstorm, and every one of them was proudly wearing a straw hat.[1]

C. P. Hill's trading post at Rangely was started in a tent in 1882. Hill freighted in groceries, dry goods, bullets, and guns from Rawlins, Wyoming, until 1884 when he built a wagon road over Douglas Pass to the newly established town of Grand Junction.

One day Hill left the store without locking the door. When he returned, a big Ute was standing on a chair and taking something from the top shelf. Hill pushed the Indian off the chair and began hitting him with his fists, breaking a finger. The thief was bruised up considerably but did not fight back. The Ute and his companions disappeared for a few days, and when they returned, they ordered Hill to pack up and leave. Hill refused to comply with their request, and the Indians went away. Several days later they came back and told Hill that it was all right for him to stay.[2]

Trading with the Indians was very tedious work. They would usually get their quarters, half dollars and dollars changed into nickels and buy their staples by the nickle's worth, since a nickel was one of the few coins the value of which they actually understood. Hill and his wife often sold eight or ten small sacks of sugar to the same buyer with a nickel's worth of sugar in each sack.

For the most part the Utes paid for their supplies with home-tanned buckskin. After it was weighed, Hill would give them cash for it with which they bought their supplies and equipment. They didn't understand the meaning of credit. When they had no money, they didn't buy anything with the promise to pay for it in the future. Instead, they would beg for the commodities which they desired.[3]

Hill usually kept plenty of bullets on hand during the fall when the Indians came into the region to hunt. One time when his supply was low, he heard that the Utes were on their way, which was earlier than usual. So, Hill saddled his horse and rode to Grand Junction to obtain enough bullets to get him by until his freight wagons arrived.

FOOTNOTES

[1]Ed Saltmarch Account, C.W.A. Interviews, 1933-34, Rio Blanco County, pp. 173-174. In possession of the State Historical Society of Colorado.

[2]Mrs. C. P. Hill, "Rangely and C. P. Hill's Trading Post," C.W.A. Interviews, 1933-34, Rio Blanco County, pp. 86-88. In possession of the State Historical Society of Colorado.

[3]*Ibid.*

THE UTE WAR OF 1887

The game was very plentiful in northwestern Colorado and very scarce on the Ute reservations in Utah. Consequently, it was not unusual that the Utes came on to their old hunting grounds every fall to get enough meat to last them through the winter.

These wandering small bands made great depradations upon the game, sometimes killing thousands of elk and deer. They used what meat they could, dried some for the future, and utilized the hides for tepees, clothing, and trading. While the men hunted, the squaws often went up into the high valleys to fish and gather wild berries. The country was only sparsely populated with white settlers at this time, and the Utes would often be in the region for weeks killing game before anyone knew of their presence.

They kept coming each year in increasing numbers, and in 1887 they brought with them about 200 horses and 150 sheep. State game laws were in effect by this time, and Joe Burgott had been appointed the first game warden of northwestern Colorado.

Burgott was determined to enforce the game laws even where the Indians were concerned; so when a group of Utes were reported to be killing deer in great numbers on the North Fork about half a mile above its junction with Sand Wash Creek in what is now Moffat County, he gathered a posse and started out with a warrant to serve on them.[1]

Upon reaching the Ute camp Burgott read the warrant to the Indians, which they did not understand. Then, the game warden proceeded to arrest a young Ute with the intention of bringing him to Meeker for trial, but the Indian broke away and ran. "Limpy" Watson, one of the deputies, took a shot at the fleeing man and wounded him. Being outnumbered, the posse rode away.

About this same time Sheriff Jim Kendall and Jack Ward rode up to another Ute camp in order to arrest a Ute who was accused of stealing horses. Again the Indians resisted, and no arrest was made.[2]

Another man carried news to Glenwood Springs that he had been shot at by Utes at the head of Flag Creek.

All of these minor encounters were greatly exaggerated, and word spread throughout northwestern Colorado that the Utes were on the warpath, killing and burning everything in their path.

The mayor of Meeker sent a telegram to Governor Alva Adams asking him to send troops immediately in order to prevent another massacre.[3] Adams called out the Colorado National Guard. The Aspen Company arrived in Meeker first, followed by more state militia, who were accompanied by a staff of officers from generals to quartermasters.

The commanding officer of the Aspen Company sent out orders for all settlers in the vicinity of Meeker to come into town. Nearly everyone complied with his request and barricaded themselves each night in the large adobe barracks, and guards were stationed at strategic points. The war was expected to last about three months.[4]

Cattlemen and cowboys congregated at Meeker from all over the country before the Colorado National Guard arrived. Seventy-two volunteer cowmen under the command of Sheriff Jim Kendall set out from Meeker around August 20, 1887, in pursuit of the Indians.[5]

In spite of the panic, Mike Drum, an old Irishman, continued carrying the mail each day from Meeker to Rangely, and the mail stage did not cancel any of its regular runs from Rawlins, Wyoming, to Meeker. A. G. Wallihan drove a wagon from Lay, which was just west of Craig, to Glenwood Springs. En route he stopped at Meeker where he learned of the Indian scare. He was told that it was not safe to venture out of town. However, he continued on to Glenwood and returned to Craig without even seeing an Indian.

While the excited whites quickly prepared themselves for war, the frightened, well-meaning Utes were hurrying back to their reservation in Utah, not understanding what the commotion was all about. In their haste they left much of their livestock behind them.

Sheriff Kendall and his seventy-two volunteers chased the Utes from the North Fork of Sand Wash Creek in present Moffat County to the head of Coal Creek near Cross Mountain. From here their trail led to the head of Wolf Creek, which flowed into White River about thirty miles west of Meeker. The pursuing cowmen had occasional feasts off the sheep and goats that the Indians left behind on their camp grounds.

On the fourth night the posse realized that the Utes were headed for their reservation. The Indians had plenty of horses and changed mounts every day while their pursuers rode the same horses which were badly in need of feed and rest.

The sheriff, believing that the Colorado National Guard had arrived in Meeker by this time, sent a note by one of the cowboys to the commanding officer suggesting that he proceed at once to the mouth of Wolf Creek with one hundred men to head off the Utes.

The troops arrived at the mouth of Wolf Creek just in time to see the rear guard of the Indians fleeing down White River. Several of the officers galloped on ahead to ask them to surrender, but they refused to do so.

On the following day the posse reached White River. The men were running low on provisions, and they were hungry and tired. Several of them rode up to a bunch of cattle and shot a big steer for supper. While they were eating, a soldier rode in on his way back to Meeker to report how the war was progressing.[*]

After supper the posse saddled their horses and overtook the soldiers farther down the river. The tracks of the Utes were fresher than they had ever been since the pursuit started.

Although it was getting late, the sheriff called for volunteers to ride on to Rangely that night. About forty cowboys and twenty-five or thirty members of the Naional Guard from Leadville and Aspen volunteered to go. The others were to follow the next day.

The retreating Utes came in to Rangely that evening thoroughly exhausted. They did not expect their pursuers to reach Rangely that day; so they turned their horses out to graze, keeping a few close by.[7]

While they were making camp, scouts unexpectedly appeared and told them that a large band of cowboys and soldiers were just a short way behind. The Indians hastily packed the few horses which were handy and started west. They rode some ten miles down White River and made camp late that night.

The volunteer group reached Rangely shortly after the Utes had left. The newcomers fed all the hay that they could get to their tired horses and obtained food from the settlers and from Hill's trading post. They rounded up the horses that the Indians had left behind and crowded them into a willow-woven corral until it would hold no more. Then many more of the Indian ponies were herded against a drift fence leading to the corral.[8]

A small guard was detailed to look after the several hundred horses that had been corraled. However, this little force was assaulted by settlers, visitors, and horse thieves who got away with all but a few of them. These were turned over to General George Crook for disposal to their rightful owners.[9]

At daybreak the volunteer group started out, hoping to reach the Utes and have it out with them before they reached the Utah line.

The posse arrived at the Ute camp about six or seven o'clock that morning. It was situated in a large crescent bottom covered with willow patches. The White River was on one side and rim rocks on the other. Most of the Indians were in the rim rocks awaiting the white men.

When the Utes saw the regulation uniform of the soldiers, they sent a messenger with a white rag to arrange for a council.[10]

A hot-headed cowboy jerked up his rifle and shot at the Ute as he advanced. The messenger ducked behind a rock, and the shooting began.

Several Ute horsemen were seen galloping through the willows. Six members of the posse gave chase. The Indians disappeared over the bluffs with the white men in hot pursuit. When they neared the bluffs, they found them to be full of hidden warriors, who began shooting at the over-zealous pursuers.

Too late, they found that they had been led into a trap. The six riders whirled their horses around and galloped away from the bluffs. Two men were hit by the deadly fire, and a third had his horse shot out from under him.

The remaining three safely reached the other members of the posse. It was everybody for himself as the posse charged the Utes and drove them back from rock to rock. Toward evening the Indians were all in full retreat, leaving behind more of their horses. Soldiers and cowboys who had lost their horses picked mounts from the captured Indian ponies. The posse was just getting ready to return to Rangely when the rest of the cowboys and National Guard who had been left behind rode up. They helped care for the three wounded men.

The Indian fighters returned to Rangely that night, where they found several pack horses loaded with grub. This furnished the volunteer group with their first meal in twenty-four hours. More men and pack trains arrived the next day, making over 200 men in camp.

Two white men died as a result of the fray[11] and were buried with full military honors. Two others were wounded, and six horses were killed. No one knew how many Utes were killed, for nearly all the fighting was done under cover of junipers and rocks. The Indians carried their dead and injured along with them. Some authorities claim that Colorow was wounded in this battle and died a year or two afterward from the effects of it.[12]

This fiasco, commonly referred to as the Ute War of 1887, cost the state more than $75,000.[13]

FOOTNOTES

[1]Thomas Baker, "Ute War of 1887," C.W.A. Interviews, 1933-34, Rio Blanco County, p. 82. In possession of the State Historical Society of Colorado.

[2]Ibid.

[3]H. A. Wildhack's Account, C.W.A. Interviews, 1933-34, Rio Blanco County, p. 100. In possession of the State Historical Society of Colorado.

[4]Baker, op. cit., p. 82.

[5]James Goulding, "Reminiscences of an Old Timer on the Ute War," Meeker Herald, Feb. 15, 1934. Article reproduced in C.W.A. Interviews, Rio Blanco County, 1933-34, p. 127.

[6]Ibid.

[7]Mrs. C. P. Hill, "Rangely and C. P. Hill's Trading Post," C.W.A. Interviews, 1933-34, Rio Blanco County, pp. 86-88.

[8]Ibid.

[9]"Twenty Years After," Meeker Herald, May 16, 1908. Article reproduced in C.W.A. Interviews, 1933-34, Rio Blanco County, p. 207. In possession of the State Historical Society of Colorado.

[10]Gouldng, op. cit.

[11]Sgt. Folsom of the Aspen National Guard and Jack Ward, a cowboy.

[12]S. C. Patterson, C.W.A. Interviews, 1933-34, Rio Blanco County, p. 74. In possession of the State Historical Society of Colorado.

[13]Meeker Herald, Oct. 15, 1887.

UTE WAR OF 1897

The phony War of 1887 did not stop the Utes from coming back into northwestern Colorado each fall on their regular hunting expeditions. Friction between the settlers and the Indians continued to grow year after year until it finally culminated in another ludicrous but tragic encounter known to old-timers as the "Ute War of 1897." This put an end to the Utes' annual hunting trips into Colorado.

Excerpts from the *Craig Courier* give an on-the-scene background leading up to the so-called Ute War of 1897:[1]

> Nov. 14, 1891—"Game Warden Taylor goes to the western end of county (now known as Moffat County. At this time Moffat County was a part of Routt County.) to warn the Indians about killing game."
>
> September 23, 1892—"If the Ute hunters come to Colorado as they did last year, there will be trouble."
>
> Nov. 4, 1892—"At present there are said to be some Utes within 75 miles of Craig who are slaughtering deer, and there is talk among the settlers of organizing a company to drive them away."
>
> Oct. 27, 1893—"J. S. Hoy writes, 'For the past week the streets of Vernal in the Uintah country, Utah, have been almost crowded at times with Utes on their way into Colorado for their annual destruction of game.' "

Dec. 1, 1893—"The Oscar Wilde game wardens are afraid to go after the Indians."

Oct. 5, 1894—"We'll gamble that in less than three weeks the Utes will be enjoying their usual sport killing Routt County game. Mr. Collicotte (the game warden), can you see the point?"

Oct. 12, 1895—"The Indians are known to be within forty miles of Craig at the present time, and they have already secured many hides. It is not known whether or not the Utes have permission to leave the reservation, but, permit or no permit, this wholesale slaughter of game should be stopped."

Oct. 19, 1895—"The White River Utes may have treaty rights to hunt in Colorado, but they should be subject to state laws regarding game."

Nov. 16, 1895—"The Indians have been bolder in their depredations on game in Routt County, and it seems that they are presuming that the western portion of the county owes them a living. . . . A gentleman who has just returned from Brown's Park states that he saw one Ute who had a four horse load of deer hides last week."

June 6, 1896—"The U. S. Supreme Court has decided that the Indians are amendable to state laws when off the reservation."[2]

Dec. 5, 1896—"Deputy returns from lower country stating that the Utes with forty horses loaded with deer hides beat him across the state line."

For a number of years there had been considerable pressure put on the game wardens of Routt County to arrest Ute hunters and discourage them from making their yearly hunting trips. However, the appointment of game wardens was largely political, and they had no stomach for arresting uncivilized Indians. The citizens of the county asked for the appointment of a local man who was familiar with the problem and who would not be afraid to prosecute the Utes.

In 1896 this plea was granted by the appointment of a choir singer from Craig. However, he waited for two months after the Indians had completed their hunting and returned to their reservation before even going into the western part of the county.[3]

The arrival of a big sheep outfit early that winter took the minds of the citizenry off the Utes for a time. After the last sheep was driven out, the people again turned their attention to the Indian problem, determined to bring the matter to a head the next fall.

G. W. Wilcox, another local man, replaced the choir singer as warden with the definite purpose of prosecuting the Utes and scaring them out of the country.

As fall approached, settlers began to watch anxiously for the Indians. In October Wilcox received reports that a group of Utes were camped on the Snake River near Cross Mountain about forty-five miles west of Craig.

Wilcox deputized ten or eleven cowboys and headed for the camp. Upon arriving on October 24, 1897, they found four old men and a large number of squaws.[4] The young bucks were out hunting. The posse decided to arrest the four old men before the hunters returned. Apparently there was plenty of evidence that the game laws had been broken.

The Indians did not understand what the warden and his deputies wanted, and they refused to cooperate. The old Utes were lifted on horses, but they would slip off on the opposite sides. Protesting squaws and dogs tugged at the game wardens.[5]

Finally, several members of the posse lifted one Indian on his horse and held him while Al Shaw, a deputy, tried to tie him on. Shaw was bending over to tie a rope when a squaw ran over with a butcher knife and cut the ropes that bound the old man to the horse. At the same time one of the Ute bucks grabbed a rifle and hit Shaw over the head with the stock. The hammer of the gun hit the deputy behind the ear and knocked him out. The shock of the impact however, tripped the hammer and the rifle went off, the bullet hitting a squaw.[6]

When the gun went off, the squaw holding the butcher knife started after Miles Overholtz, a young cowboy, who took to his heels. As she gained on him, someone yelled, "Look out, Miles. She's about to catch you."

Overholtz whirled around and shot his pursuer in the stomach.

These incidents caused the startled posse to start shooting.

Amos Bennett, a noted hunter and tourist guide, became so excited that he pumped the cartridges out of his rifle without firing a shot. Someone else apparently got Indian fever also because Al Shaw's gun was also found pumped dry even though Shaw was unconscious during most of the gunplay.

Others in the posse were more effective in their shooting. When the firing ceased, four bucks and two squaws lay on the ground.[7] Two of the bucks were dead.

Fearing reprisals from the Indians when they returned from the day's hunt, the posse rode away. Some of them went to E. B. "Longhorn" Thompson's isolated ranch in Brown's Park and moved the women and children to Vaughn's ranch for safety. Others rode to Craig for help. Sheriff Charles Neiman hastened to the rescue with a strong force of men from Steamboat, Hayden, and Craig. Captain Wright of Fort Duchesne, headquarters of the Ute reservation in Utah, also started out with his troops to the scene of the trouble. He passed many Utes coming down the north side of the Yampa River on their way back to the reservation. Some of their horses were packed while others had poles attached to the horses' sides with loaded baskets swinging from the poles.[8]

On the day following the killings, Jack White, locally famous bronco buster and gunman, Tom Armstrong, and Gabel set out for Lily Park just west of Cross Mountain to warn the families of John W. Lowell and Henry Goodwin. As the three riders neared the north end of Cross Mountain, they were fired upon by several Indians who had not as yet left the country. White and Armstrong were unhorsed by this volley, and several bullets came close enough to tear through their clothes. They ran to Cross Mountain and hid, returning to Vaughn's ranch that night.[9]

Gabel galloped ahead toward "Longhorn" Thompson's ranch with bullet holes in his clothes and in the cantle of his saddle. He loped up to the deserted Thompson ranch where there was an outlaw horse in the pasture. Ordinarily Gabel couldn't have ridden this bronco, but believing that the Indians were after him, he caught the outlaw and rode him bucking and galloping to the Bassett ranch in Brown's Park in two hours.

The next day—which was Monday—a party of about twelve Indians set fire to the hay stacks and stables at Thompson's ranch.

On Tuesday Wilcox and his posse left Vaughn's ranch for Lily Park and returned with the Lowell and Goodwin families, making a total of about ten women and two men who had been assembled by the posse at this ranch for protection. The next Sunday the posse and settlers returned to their respective homes after eating nearly all of Vaughn's winter provisions.[10]

During this Indian scare a hundred and twenty other settlers from the troubled area congregated at the village of Lay, eighteen miles west of Craig, for two weeks, fearfully waiting for the Utes to return from their reservation and make a revenge attack. However, nothing occurred; so they gradually drifted back to their various ranches.

The governor appointed Judge David C. Beaman of Pueblo, Senator C. E. Noble of Colorado Springs, and Joshua Walbridge of Steamboat Springs to investigate the shooting of the Indians. The federal government appointed Elisha Reynolds from the Crow Agency to accompany the state committee on its investigation, and take separate testimony.[11]

On December 7th testimony was taken in Hartzell's jewelry store in Craig concerning the trouble, and on the next day the commissioners went with Wilcox to the scene of the killing. Then, the investigators went to Meeker, Rifle, and Price, Utah, for further testimony. At Price they heard the Indians' version of what happened. The investigation lasted well into the winter, and Wilcox and his deputies were cleared.

The Indian fighters who participated in this Ute War of 1897 had little to be proud of, but they did put a permanent stop to the Utes' annual hunting trips into Colorado.

FOOTNOTES

[1]These excerpts have been reproduced in C.W.A. Interviews, 1933-34, Moffat County, pp. 180-182. In possession of the State Historical Society of Colorado.

[2]Ibid., pp. 192-195.

[3]Ibid., pp. 262-263.

Ute camp on reservation near Ignacio—1890. Photo by H. S. Poley. Courtesy of Denver Public Library Western Collection.

Group of Utes—1894. Photo by H. S. Poley. Courtesy of Denver Public Library Western Collection.

Ute war party—1899. Photo by *H. S. Poley*. *Courtesy Denver Public Library Western Collection.*

U. S. government school. Teachers' and farmers' buildings—Towaoc—1908. *Photo by H. S. Poley. Courtesy of Denver Public Library Western Collection.*

Remains of an old hunting shelter built by the Utes near Cedaredge. These are occasionally found, but this is in better condition than most.
Photo Courtesy Walker Art Studios.

Buckskin Charlie and wife. *A W. H. Jackson photo by Courtesy of State Historical Society of Colorado.*

Ouray and Ignacio. *Photo Courtesy State Historical Society of Colorado.*

Chipeta and Ouray. This picture was taken in Washington, D. C., in 1878. *Photo Courtesy State Historical Society of Colorado.*

[4]*Craig Courier*, Dec. 4, 1897. Article reproduced in C.W.A. Interviews, 1933-34, Moffat County, p. 194. In possession of the State Historical Society of Colorado.

[5]*Craig Courier*, Nov. 6, 1897. Article reproduced in C.W.A. Interviews, 1933-34, Moffat County, p. 192.

[6]E. V. Houghey, "Troubles Between Indians and Game Wardens," C.W.A. Interviews, 1933-34, Moffat County, pp. 211-214. In possession of the State Historical Society of Colorado.

[7]*Craig Courier*, Nov. 6, 1897. Article reproduced in C.W.A. Interviews, 1933-34, Moffat County, p. 192.

[8]Account of Bob Bryant, C.W.A. Interviews, 1933-34, Moffat County, pp. 244-251.

[9]Account of Carey Baker, C.W.A. Interviews, 1933-34, Moffat County, pp. 215-219.

[10]Captain Wright's Version, C.W.A. Interviews, 1933-34, Moffat County, p. 194.

[11]*Craig Courier*, Dec. 11, 1897.

LAST DAYS OF CHIPETA

About a year after Ouray's death in 1880, Chipeta was moved
to the new reservation in northern Utah with the other members of her band. Except for a report in a Denver newspaper
on April 1, 1883, that she had remarried a White River Ute
named Toomuchagut at the Ouray Agency in Utah,[1] her activities for the next thirty-five years were little known.

When Chipeta first moved to Utah, the federal government
promised to build a house for her which would be as well constructed and furnished as her home on the Uncompahgre. Instead, she was given a two-room house on White River that was
never plastered or furnished.[2] She used the house very little,
if at all, living in a tepee like most of her people.

In 1916 it was called to the attention of the Indian Commissioner that Chipeta was getting old[3] and that she had been
sadly neglected by the government for the past thirty-five years
since she had left Colorado.[4]

Cato Sells, the Commissioner of Indian Affairs, decided that
the government had not shown the proper appreciation for her
many services and great distinction as the celebrated wife of
Chief Ouray. Desiring to do something for her while there was
still time, the Commissioner looked her up.

She was found living with a small group of nomadic Utes who
ran a thousand sheep and some thirty cattle. During the summer these Indians pastured their livestock at the head of Bitter

Creek near the Book Cliffs in Utah. Each winter they moved their sheep and cattle to a lower elevation in the neighborhood of Dragon, Utah.[5]

The Indian Commissioner asked Chipeta if there was anything that she would like to have the government do for her.

Through an interpreter she replied, "No, I expect to die very soon."

When Chipeta refused help, Cato Sells discussed the matter with the reservation agent, suggesting that perhaps furniture would be an appropriate gift.

The agent explained that Chipeta was an Indian of the old school. She wore a blanket, painted her face, spoke very little English, and preferred to eat and sleep on the ground. During Ouray's lifetime she had lived in a house with furniture, but she had been without such conveniences for so long that she would have no use for them.

The agent said that at various times during her life on the reservation in Utah she had been presented with gifts from white admirers. Almost invariably the gifts had been of such a nature that Chipeta had not known how to make use of them.

Once she had been given some fifty and one hundred dollar bills, but, not realizing their value, she had passed this green paper on to friends. At another time she had been donated a trunk filled with beautiful silk. Chipeta had no need for such finery and gave most of it away. A valuable set of China which had been presented to her was found unused in an old cellar at her summer camp on Bitter Creek, since she much preferred enamel-ware to China-ware.

The agent suggested that a gaily colored shawl would be an appreciated gift. Sells then authorized the agent to spend twenty-five dollars for a shawl. The agent wrote back that the type of gaudy shawl which Chipeta would much prefer was only worth twelve dollars or less.

Since twenty-five dollars had been authorized, Sells decided that the agent should get two highly colored shawls for her during the year. A shawl was then purchased for twelve dollars at the agency's trading store and sent to the Indian Com-

missioner who, in turn, shipped it back to Chipeta along with
a letter of appreciation for her services.

In a short time Sells received the following reply, written
with the agent's help:

Mr. Cato Sells
Indian Commissioner
Washington, D. C.
My friend,
Your beautiful shawl received and was appreciated very
much. In token of shawl received am sending you a saddle
blanket, also a picture of myself.

I am in good health considering my age and hope to live
much longer to show my friendship and appreciation to all the
kind white people. I am also glad that there is no more trouble
between the Indians and white people, and hope that this state
of affairs exists through the rest of my life.

Under separate cover you will find the saddle blanket and
hope that same is appreciated as much as the shawl was.

With best wishes I am always
Your friend,
*her mark   CHIPETA
Witness:
(Signed) T. M. McKee, P.M.[6]

As Chipeta grew older, she gradually became totally blind.
She was operated on in Grand Junction without success. After
she became blind, her relatives stretched a cord from her tepee
out into the brush, which she could follow to obtain privacy.

On August 17, 1924, at her summer headquarters on Bitter
Creek she died of chronic gastritis at the age of eighty-one. Her
relatives buried her in a shallow grave in a little sand wash.[7]

Some time later Albert Reagan searched for the grave while
in the Bitter Creek country on government business. Finding
it in such an exposed place where the body would be washed
away within a few years, the white man advised John McCook,
Chipeta's brother, that she be reinterred in a more permanent
location.[8]

By 1925 Chipeta's death had become generally known to the
whites. When the citizens of Montrose heard of it, a Commun-

ity Committee was organized to try to have her body brought to Montrose and placed in a memorial mausoleum on her old home site.[9]

McCook gave his consent to have Chipeta's remains removed to Montrose, and the matter was taken up with the Indian Agent, F. A. Gross, who made arrangements for transfer of the body.

On March 3, 1925, C. E. Adams, editor of the Montrose newspaper, received a letter from the agent informing him that Chipeta's body had been exhumed and was ready for shipment. The mausoleum was still incomplete, and Gross wrote Adams that it should be hurried since it would make a bad impression on McCook and other Indians accompanying the body if the remains were put in an undertaking establishment to await completion of the vault.[10]

By return mail Adams wrote:

F. A. Gross, Supt.
Fort Duchesne, Utah
Dear Sir:
    Men at work on tomb. Weather fierce, but we will have it ready.
    Wire when you start or when ready. We want to make the Indians feel we are in earnest and thereby inspire them to make a diligent search for enough of Ouray's remains to make a tomb for him (also).
    Better wire.

                                    C. E. Adams
                                    Montrose, Colorado.

The spring was stormy, making the concrete difficult to pour, and there was danger of it freezing and cracking. Nevertheless, the work progressed rapidly. On March 7th Adams sent a telegram to the Duchesne Agency:

Wire immediately approximate dimensions of Chipeta's box.[11]

The body of Chipeta arrived at Montrose on March 15, 1925. It was accompanied by Hugh Owens, agricultural agent of the Indian service at Fort Duchesne; Rev. M. J. Hersey, a minister who represented the agent and who had received Chipeta

into the Episcopal Church twenty-seven years before; John Mc-
Cook, and another Ute by the name of Yagah.[12]

At 2:30 that afternoon the queen of the Utes was taken to the
Ouray Memorial Park and reburied with an elaborate ceremony before 5,000 people.

The Ouray Memorial Park is a historic shrine on the highway
just south of Montrose. It is now owned and maintained by the
State Historical Society. In addition to Chipeta's tomb, the
park contains a cement tepee built over the spring on Ouray's
old farm. The adobe brick building where Ouray and Chipeta
used to live stands a short distance west of the tepee. It was
originally situated one hundred yards north of its present location. This is all that remains of the Ute buildings in this locality. North of the building is Chipeta's cement tomb, and beside
it is the grave of her brother John McCook, who died in 1937
and was buried there.

On July 15, 1956, the Ute Indian museum was dedicated at
the Ouray Memorial Park. It was built by the State Historical
Society of Colorado and contains relics and other objects of Ute
history.

FOOTNOTES

[1]*The Denver Republican*, April 1, 1883, p. 8.

[2]Albert Reagan and Wallace Stark, "Chipeta, Queen of the Utes
and Her Equally Illustrious Husband, Noted Chief Ouray," *Utah
Historical Quarterly*, July, 1933, p. 106.

[3]73 years old.

[4]Notes on Chipeta by J. Monaghan, C.W.A. Interviews, 1933-34,
Moffat County, p. 63. In possession of the State Historical Society
of Colorado.

[5]*Ibid.*, pp. 63-68.

[6]*Ibid.*

[7]*Denver Post*, August 18, 1924, p. 1.

[8]Reagan and Stark, *op. cit.*, p. 108.

[9]Mrs. C. W. Wiegel, "The Reburial of Chief Ouray," *Colorado
Magazine*, Oct., 1928, pp. 165-166.

[10]Monaghan, *op. cit.*, p. 67.

[11]*Ibid.*, p. 68.

[12]Reagan and Stark, *op. cit.*, p. 108.

REBURIAL OF CHIEF OURAY

After Chipeta was reburied, the Community Committee of Montrose tried to obtain the remains of Ouray for reinterment beside Chipeta. Chipeta's brother, John McCook, was sent to Ignacio to get the permission of the Southern Utes to remove Ouray's body from its secret resting place.

McCook failed in his mission, but his visit did cause the white residents of Ignacio and the Southern Utes under the leadership of L. M. Wyatt and E. E. McKean, Indian Superintendent, to remove Ouray's remains to the Indian cemetery across the river from the Ignacio Agency.

Four old Utes who had helped in the original burial supervised the removal and acted as pall bearers at the second ceremony. These were Buckskin Charley, Joseph Price, McCook, and Naneese. The ceremony lasted for four days during which time the Indians performed many of their sacred rites. It was concluded by a Christian service.[1]

This reburial of the Utes' most celebrated chieftain was attended by the largest group of whites and Indians ever to assemble on the Southern Ute Reservation.

The authenticity of Ouray's remains was established in affidavits by Buckskin Charley, Joseph Price, John McCook, and Naneese. They were among the six men and one woman who had buried Ouray forty-five years before.

Buckskin Charley's affidavit reads as follows:

After he [Ouray] died, we wrapped the body in new blankets and buffalo robes and then tied cords and ropes around it and placed it on a horse. After putting the body on a horse, Nathan Price, a Southern Ute, told us that his father, Chief Suvata, was buried in the rocks about two miles south of Ignacio, and this would be a good place to bury Ouray, placing the two chiefs together. This I agreed to, and so we took the body of Chief Ouray and buried it in the rocky cavern below Ignacio in the same grave from which I helped to remove his bones a short time ago. There were six men and one woman who accompanied us to this . . . resting place. The one woman was Chipeta, the wife of Chief Ouray. . . .[²]

Although Ouray had joined the Methodist Church about two years before his death, some arguments arose between the Catholic and Protestant Utes as to which section of the cemetery he should be buried in. The Indian cemetery was divided by a fence, and it was customary to bury the Catholics on one side and the Protestants on the other. The Catholics wanted the great chieftain to lie on their portion of the cemetery, and the Protestant Indians, of course, wanted his remains buried on their side. So, in order to satisfy both factions, the dividing fence was removed, and Ouray's grave was dug half in the Protestant graveyard and half in the Catholic graveyard.

After the initial enthusiasm was over, the grave was neglected for a time. The gravestone leaned and cracked, and weeds flourished. About 1951 a group of public spirited young Utes cleared off the weeds and straightened the stone.

When Buckskin Charley, famous chief of the Mouache band of Southern Utes, died on May 9, 1936, he was buried beside Ouray. Severo, best known chief of the Capote band of Southern Utes, lies nearby in the Protestant cemetery. He died on March 24, 1913.

Ignacio, most famous chief of the Weeminuche band, which became known as the Ute Mountain Utes, died on December 9, 1913, and was buried in some unknown spot on the Ute Mountain Reservation near Navajo Springs, four miles south of Towaoc. Much later efforts were made to find his body in order to place it near the graves of the three renowned chiefs, but by this time all those familiar with the location of his remains were dead.

The superintendent of the Consolidated Ute Agency supervised a P.W.A. project for the erection of a monument in memory of these four distinguished chiefs. The monument when completed in 1939 was eight feet square at the base, five feet square at the top, and eighteen feet high.[3] It stands in the Ute Memorial Park on the east bank of the Los Pinos River near the Ignacio agency. Busts of Ouray, Severo, Ignacio, and Buckskin Charley are on the sides of the large memorial.[4]

FOOTNOTES

[1]Mrs. C. W. Wiegel, "The Reburial of Chief Ouray," *The Colorado Magazine*, Oct., 1928, p. 167.

[2]*Ibid.*, p. 169.

[3]"Monument to Four Ute Chiefs is Dedicated," *The Durango Herald-Democrat*, September 25, 1939.

[4]S. F. Stacher, "Ouray and the Utes," *Colorado Magazine*, April, 1950, p. 140.

SOUTHERN UTE CHIEFS

Only a mere fraction of the great Ute confederacy still remains in Western Colorado. The Treaty of 1880, which removed from Colorado the Northern and Uncompahgre Utes, left the three Southern Ute bands just where they were situated before the agreement was entered into. The reservation, created by the treaty, is a strip of land approximately fifteen miles wide and 110 miles long in the extreme southwestern portion of Colorado. This land is cut by deep and narrow canyons and crossed by streams which originate on the San Juan range and empty into the San Juan River just south of the New Mexico border. This narrow strip was continually trespassed on by miners, ranchers, stockmen, sawmill operators, and railroad crews.

At the time of the Treaty of 1880, the Southern Utes had three outstanding chiefs. They were Buckskin Charley, chief of the Mouache band; Severo, chief of the Capote band; and Ignacio, chief of the Weeminuche band. The total population of these bands numbered about 800.[1] The present population (1955) is 1220.

Buckskin Charley, or Charles Buck, was born around 1840 in the Cimarron county of southeastern Colorado. His Indian name was Yo-o-witz, meaning the Fox. His father was a Ute, and his mother an Apache. Both of his parents died before he reached the age of eleven.[2]

When a young man he participated in many battles against the plains Indians. In one engagement with the Comanches, Buckskin Charley was hit in the forehead by a pistol bullet, and he carried the scar for the rest of his life.

He was about five feet six inches tall, and he had a muscular, stocky build. He inherited his color from his Apache mother and was lighter complexioned than most Utes. He spoke broken English but understood all that was said to him in that language. He wore a drooping black mustache, which was quite a distinctive feature since mustaches were rare among Indians.[3] Even in his later years, he was as straight as a ramrod.

When he was about thirty years old, he became chief of the Mouache band. Long before land allotments were made to the Southern Utes, Buckskin Charley built a log cabin on the Los Pinos River and began to clear and farm the land which was later given to him as an allotment. He raised a large garden for his family and grain and hay for his sheep, cattle, and horses. He pastured his livestock on Mesa Mountain during the winter. It was largely due to his influence that so many members of his band began taking up farming at the turn of the century.[4]

Buckskin Charley served as a scout for a time with the United States Army in the Navajo country. While acting as scout he killed so many antelopes that the soldiers nicknamed him Buckskin Charley.

He was one of the six Indians who helped secretly bury Chief Ouray on August 24, 1880. He also helped remove Ouray's remains to the Ignacio Cemetery in 1925 and acted as one of the pallbearers at this ceremony.

During his lifetime he frequently went to Washington, D. C. on tribal matters and personally met seven United States presidents. A handsome plaque was presented to him in recognition of his service, and he seldom permitted himself to be photographed without it.[5]

The name of his first wife was Sally Buck, and they had three children. Buckskin Charley died in May, 1936, at the age of about ninety-five. He was buried beside Ouray at the Indian cemetery across the river from the agency.

Chief Severo was originally a member of the Mouache band

of Ute Indians, but after his marriage to a girl of the Capote band, he spent the rest of his life with the Capotes and eventually became their chief.

Like Buckskin Charley, Severo was born in the Cimarron country. One winter day when he was only a year old, the Cheyenne and Kiowa Indians raided the Mouache camp. Severo's mother fled with him on horseback across the icy Cimarron. The horse slipped, throwing his riders. The pursuing plains Indians thrust a lance into the baby's side as they passed, and Severo carried the scar until his death.

When Severo was a young man, he accumulated a number of cattle, horses, sheep, and goats. During the summer he grazed his livestock in the San Juan region of southern Colorado, and late each fall he moved them into New Mexico for the winter.[6]

It was due largely to Severo's influence that the members of the Capote band agreed in 1899 to accept allotments of land in severalty to farm rather than to continue their old nomadic way of life with lands held in common.

Severo died on March 24, 1913 at the age of sixty-seven. He was buried on the Protestant side of the Ute cemetery east of the Consolidated Ute Agency at Ignacio.

Chief Ignacio was born in 1828. He was not a chief by heredity but the son of a medicine man of the Weeminuche band. One time the medicine man failed to save the life of a prominent member of the band, and he was killed by the enraged family.

Ignacio, an overgrown boy of fourteen, happened along as his father was struck down. Grabbing his hunting knife, he jumped on the surprised assassins and stabbed a number of them before they realized what was going on. Then, taking cover, he shot from ambush with his bow and arrow most of the remaining members of the unfortunate family whenever the opportunity offered.

After killing twelve of the men who had murdered his father,[7] the boy returned to the band. His fellow tribesmen regarded him with awe, and when he became older, they chose him for their chief.

Ignacio was the tallest and largest of the Ute chieftains, and he maintained his straight, lithe figure throughout his eighty-five years. He stood six feet two inches tall in his moccasins and weighed 225 pounds.

Ignacio's Weeminuch band of Utes became known as the Ute Mountain Utes. Unlike the Mouache and Capote bands, who became known as the Southern Utes, the Ute Mountain Utes gave up their agricultural allotments around Ignacio for lands held in common in the western portion of the reservation, where they might continue their nomadic, uncivilized existence. Ignacio died here near the old Navajo Springs Agency which was located about four miles south of the present Towaoc Agency, and was buried by his people in some unknown spot in this area.

The headquarters of the Consolidated Ute Agency was named in his honor. The adjoining town of Ignacio was platted in 1910 when the whites purchased the land on which it stood from the Indians. It was incorporated July 7, 1913,[8] and has developed into a small farming, livestock, and trading center of about 500 people. It does a lively business in Indian articles. The Utes, who do not make jewelry or blankets, exchange sheep, buckskin, beadwork, and headdresses to the Navajos for jewelry and blankets, which are then traded to visitors at Ignacio for money or goods. For this reason the town has become a primary trading center for Navajo products.

On September 24, 1939, a large stone monument in memory of these three Southern Ute chiefs and Ouray was unveiled and officially dedicated in the Ute Memorial Park near the Ignacio Agency. There is a bronze plaque of each of the four chiefs on the monument.

FOOTNOTES

[1]Ralph Linton, *Acculturation in Seven American Indian Tribes,* p. 202.

[2]Isaac Cloud, a Ute who lived with Buckskin Charley for thirty-seven years, "Monument to Four Ute Chiefs is Dedicated," *Durango Herald-Democrat,* September 25, 1939. Article reproduced in Helen Sloan Daniels, *The Ute Indians of Southwestern Colorado,* pp. 86-88.

[3]Frank Hall, *History of Colorado*, Vol. 4, p. 64.

[4]Cloud, *op. cit.*

[5]*Pioneers of the San Juan Country*, Vol. 3, p. 128.

[6]Severo's biography as told by his son, "Monument to Four Ute Chiefs is Dedicated," *Durango Herald-Democrat*, Sept. 25, 1939. Article reproduced in Helen Sloan Daniels, *The Ute Indians of Southwestern Colorado*, pp. 89-90.

[7]Frank Hall, *op. cit.*, p. 64.

[8]*Colorado Magazine*, Sept. 1941, p. 187.

EARLY RELATIONS WITH THE SETTLERS

The Southern Ute Reservation in southewestern Colorado was so narrow that the whites and Indians came in daily contact with one another. Most of these relations were peaceful.

For example, one spring day H. C. Schroder, one of the first settlers in the San Juan Basin, discovered a large herd of Ute horses in his wheat field. He and a hired man hurried down to the corral where they bridled a couple of work horses and drove the Indian ponies out of the field. The rail fence around the field had been torn down by the Utes and rails flung in all directions.

Noticing a wisp of smoke in the distance, the two men rode over to it where they found Jim Hardy's camp. Hardy, a big, surly Indian, walked out of his tepee with a blanket over his shoulders. Schroder told the Ute to keep his horses out of fenced fields.

Hardy pointed in the direction of Schroder's cabin and asked if that was his camp. After being told that it was, the big Indian said, "Makem big eats. Me come quick."

Schroder and his employe rode back and prepared a big breakfast. Jim Hardy soon arrived with his squaw. Hardy walked in, but the squaw, afraid to enter the cabin, sat down on the woodpile.

The Ute slid his steak from the plate on to the bare boards of the table and pushed the knife and fork aside. Then, whipping out a sharp butcher knife from his belt, he proceeded to carve and devour big hunks of the juicy steak. At intervals he would issue slight grunts of satisfaction. After finishing his meal, he took a plateful of food out to the squaw.[1]

It was common in early-day Durango to buy freshly killed turkeys from the Utes, who would use most of the proceeds to buy whiskey. Sometimes the Indians also sold choke cherries or pinon nuts, and occasionally they just begged for money.[2]

For a time Charles Johnson, Sr., had the government contract for supplying flour and beef to the Southern Utes. It took about ten head of cattle a week. These cattle were driven to Ignacio and corraled. Then, one animal at a time was turned out. A group of Utes would give chase on horseback and rope it. When they finally killed and butchered the cow or steer, there was not a thing left. The Indians even caught and used the blood when the beef's throat was cut.

After the ten head were killed and cut up, the Indians tied the meat on their saddles or put it into old dirty sacks. Then, they would ride away amidst swarming flies and with the bloody quarters as likely as not rubbing against their horses' sides.[3]

In 1882 and 1883 Charles Johnson, Sr., opened up a little commissary on his ranch along the Dolores River at the present site of McPhee. The Southern Utes sold him lots of buckskin. Light hides weighing a pound and a half or less were worth $1.50, and heavier hides were worth about eighty cents. The Indians believed, however, that the more a hide weighed the more valuable it was; so Johnson had to pay accordingly to get the Utes to trade with him.[4]

The dime was the only piece of money that the Utes seemed to understand. If an Indian had a dollar, he would change it into dimes and then proceed to buy one dime's worth of supplies at a time. If, for example, he wanted sugar, he first bought a dime's worth and then another dime's worth, and so on until he finally got the amount he wanted.[5]

Indians delighted in getting the best of an exchange; so Johnson retarded his scales a few ounces so that he appeared to be giving his customers a little more than their dime's worth.

If any Indian happened to be around at mealtime, Mrs. Johnson would let them clean up whatever food the family left. Regardless of how much was left, the Utes invariably ate it all. They ate out of the vegetable dishes and platters, for they weren't familiar with the white man's custom of each person eating off plates. They ate their dessert first and the main course afterwards. Their favorite food was meat.

The Southern Utes had a race track near Johnson's ranch, and they spent a good deal of time there in their favorite sport. They occasionally competed against the cowboys and would bet their blankets on the outcome.[6]

Native tepees often surrounded the home of Timothy J. McCluer and his wife and two small children, who were among the first settlers in the present Durango region. It was a common occurrence for a group of Utes to unexpectedly arrive at meal time and squat down beside the table where the family was being served. Salt and sugar were the staples most enjoyed by the uninvited guests since neither of these commodities was included in their rations at that time. A teaspoon of salt made them content for an afternoon.

Chief Ignacio was particularly friendly to the McCluer family. He had just recently lost his first child—a little girl. After she died, he wore his hair bobbed as a symbol of mourning. As other children came into Ignacio's family, he named them after McCluer's sons and daughters.[7]

Robert Dwyer, who later became the first elected sheriff of La Plata County,[8] filed on 160 acres along the Animas River south of the present town of Durango and built a cabin. The Utes in the vicinity called him "Sorratz," meaning "Blue Pants."

One morning as he started to shut the door of his cabin, several Indians walked up and insisted on going inside. One Ute tried to push by him, asking for sugar and bacon. Dwyer had already fed them earlier in the day; so he told them that they couldn't go in.

The Indian kept right on trying to open the door; so Dwyer, losing his temper, struck the Ute, knocking him across the yard. The white man instantly regretted this hasty action, believing that he had got himself into trouble.

The Ute slowly picked himself up and looked at his assailant. Dwyer, expecting the redskin to attack him, was immensely surprised and relieved to see him advance with his hand outstretched. Dwyer shook the Ute's hand, and the Indians departed.

Early the next morning the same Indian that Dwyer had struck arrived with a pup which he gave to his assailant. It was a real Indian mongrel. Dwyer gave the Indian a big breakfast to show his gratitude for the peace offering.[9]

John Reid owned a large cattle ranch at the site where Ft. Lewis was later built twelve miles southwest of Durango. One afternoon during the spring roundup a group of cowboys were working a big herd of cattle at the ranch. Each cattleman's cows and calves were being respectively cut out of the herd and driven into a corral where the calves were branded.

The men were just changing bunches in the corral when a drunken cowboy rode into the corral. He dismounted to help brand but was so drunk that he merely got in the way.

Two Southern Ute Indians approached on horseback and watched the branding outside the corral fence. The drunken cowboy, who was in an ugly mood, suddenly whipped out his six-shooter and shot at them. The Indians then turned their horses and rode away.[10]

FOOTNOTES

[1]H. C. Schroder, "An Early San Juan Basin Story," C.W.A. Interviews, 1933-34, La Plata County, p. 15. In possession of the State Historical Society of Colorado.

[2]Helen Sloan Daniels, *Pioneers of the San Juan Country*, Vol. 3, p. 127.

[3]Interview with H. J. Porter, C.W.A. Interviews, 1933-34, Otero and Montezuma County, Vol. I, p. 356. In possession of the State Historical Society of Colorado.

[4]Ibid., p. 357.

[5]In Chapter XXIV Mrs. C. P. Hill writes about how the Northern Utes in trading at her husband's trading post at Rangely would get their quarters, half-dollars, and dollars changed into nickels, which was their chief medium of exchange. So, apparently, both nickels and dimes were used by the Utes in their trading.

[6]Account of Erastus Thomas, C.W.A. Interviews, 1933-34, Montezuma County, Vol. 2, p. 532.

[7]Lena S. Knapp, "Our Great Pacificator," *Pioneers of the San Juan*, Vol. 3, pp. 11-12.

[8]He was elected sheriff on October 2, 1877.

[9]Robert Dwyer, "Pioneer Sheriff," as related to Bridget Clark, *Pioneers of the San Juan*, Vol. 2, p. 43.

[10]Interview with Charles W. Pinkerton as related to Helen M. Searcy, *Ibid.*, p. 83.

THE MONUMENT CREEK KILLINGS

Relations between the Utes and the white settlers were not always so amicable.

In the spring of 1881 John Thurman was pasturing a large herd of horses on his and Dave Willis' ranch near Monument Creek a half-mile east of the Utah border in present Montezuma county.[1] One day Thurman discovered several Indians trying to catch some of the saddle horses, and he gave them a beating. The Utes left in an angry mood.[2] At the time of this incident, Dave Willis, co-owner of the ranch, was on his way to Chama, New Mexico, at the end of the railroad to get his family, who had been visiting in the east.[3]

Shortly after Thurman's altercation with the Utes, Dick May, who had a ranch near the present town of McPhee, started out for Thurman's place to buy some unbroken horses. Unbroken horses were then selling for fifty dollars a head while broken horses were worth about one hundred dollars.[4] May probably had from $600 to $1,000 in bills with him.[5] He was accompanied by Byron Smith, a visitor who was not well known in the region.

At about eleven o'clock that morning May and Smith met Erastus Thomas, Henry Goodman, the Quick brothers, and some other cowboys gathering cattle near the head of Yellow Jacket Canyon. Goodman had previously called Thomas out of the canyon to observe a group of passing Indians who seemed to be very angry about something. Goodman told May and Smith that the Utes were apparently on the prod, and he advised the two horse buyers to turn back. However, May and his companion decided to continue on, in spite of the warning.[6]

Pat and Mike O'Donnel had a camp at Willow Springs not far from Thurman's cabin, and on the next morning, which was May 1, 1881, one of their employees was sent over to borrow some baking powder. A gruesome sight met his eyes when he arrived. The cabin was burned to the ground. Two dead horses lay in front of the ruins. The body of Dick May, burned nearly past recognition, was found among the ashes. From 1500 to 2000 pounds of oats, stored in the cabin for winter horse feed, had fallen over the dead man's body during the fire, preventing it from being cremated. May's pocketbook was found on him. All of the paper bills had been destroyed by fire or stolen by the Indians, but some silver money still remained.

May was apparently killed right after breakfast. A lot of empty cartridges around his body showed that he had recognized his danger and had time to put up quite a fight. Apparently he had shot the two horses which lay nearby. One of them had Ray Sumner's brand on it, evidencing that his Indian rider had stolen him. Neither Byron Smith nor John Thurman was in sight.

The man who found the wreckage hastened back to the O'Donnel camp. Soon a group of men were on their way to Big Bend, located on the Dolores River two miles west of the present site of Dolores, to report the killing. On May 3rd a group of people from Big Bend[7] and Mancos rode up to Thurman's burned cabin to investigate the tragedy.

Thurman's body was finally found on the fourth day of the search on Cedar Point three quarters of a mile from the cabin. He had a plaited hackamore worth twenty or thirty dollars on his arm; so apparently he had been out to catch a horse when killed. The posse buried him right where they found him.

Erastus Thomas drove a big, half-broken team of mules to the burned cabin to haul May's body back to the Dolores River, where he was buried in the Johnson graveyard. He was the first white man to be buried on the Dolores.

Smith's body was never discovered. Some Indians said later that he ran down into a deep canyon at the time of the attack. They believed that he had been shot and probably died there.

When Dave Willis, co-owner of the ranch where the three men were killed, returned from Chama, New Mexico, with his family, he organized a posse from Big Bend and Mancos to follow the Utes.[8] Bill Dawson, Sheriff of Dolores County, got up a posse at Rico, and the two groups joined forces and took the trail of the Indians.[9] The posse followed the Utes to the south side of the Blue Mountains in Utah and on to the foot of the La Sal Mountains. Here the white men lost the trail. They scattered and finally picked up the tracks farther on. They led to the north side of the La Sal Mountains, where they finally overtook the Utes in a big sandy sagebrush wash.[10]

There the shooting started. Dave Willis, Thurman's partner, was shot from his horse right at the beginning of the fight. Sheriff Dawson of Rico then took charge of both posses.

About ten of his men jumped off their horses and crouched down in a sandy arroyo to escape the flying bullets. The sheriff, realizing that they were in a trap, sent Uncle Tim Jenkins, an old Indian fighter, to order them out. Jenkins only weighed about 110 pounds, but he was well versed in the ways of Indian warfare.

The men were scattered in the arroyo a hundred yards or so, and Uncle Tim rode up and down the gulch while the Utes shot at him from the rim rocks. He explained to the cornered men that they presented perfect targets, and he urged them to get out and join the rest of he posse before the Indians started to pick them off. However, they were paralyzed with fear, and not one of them dared to make a run for it. Finally, in order to save his own life, Jenkins left the doomed men to their fate. All of them were killed in the arroyo.[11]

In the battle Jordon Bean of the Dolores Valley was shot in the head but not killed. He hid in the oak brush that night, and he could hear the Utes beating around the brush looking for him. The wounded man was later hauled home in a wagon.

Josh Alderson, a member of the posse, became so excited

during the battle that he ran around saying that he had lost the barrel of his rifle.[12]

Those killed in the fray included H. M. Melvin, Dave Willis, Hard Tarter, Wiley Tarter, John B. Galloway, Jimmie Heaston, Tom Click, and two brothers by the name of Wilson. Jim Halls, Harg Eskridge, and Jordon Bean were injured.[13]

When news reached Mancos of the Indian fight, the residents built a stockade fort around the old log school house. The women and children were guarded in this fortress, and a company was formed to fight off the Utes in case of an attack. After the scare had subsided, the stockade was used for fire wood at the school house.

The following October Mrs. Dave Willis, accompanied by her brother Ray Weston, H. M. Barber, Dalton Reynolds, and Cal House went to the La Sal Mountains and brought back the remains of Dave Willis of Mancos and H. M. Melvin of the Dolores Valley. Willis was buried at Mancos, and Melvin was probably buried on the old Cal House ranch along the Dolores River.[14]

FOOTNOTES

[1]Mrs. A. W. Dillon, "Early History of Montezuma County," *Dolores Star*, Set. 4, 1908. Article reproduced in C.W.A. Interviews, Montezuma County, Vol. I, p. 125. In possession of State Historical Society of Colorado.

[2]Account of Fred H. Taylor, C.W.A. Interviews, Montezuma County, Vol. 2, pp. 445-446. In possession of State Historical Society of Colorado.

[3]From a letter to Martin Rush signed by Heigo Weston. Letters in possession of the Secretary of the Montezuma County Old Timers' Association. Reproduced in C.W.A. Interviews, Otero and Montezuma Counties, Vol. I, p. 183. In possession of State Historical Society of Colorado.

[4]Account of Erastus Thomas, C.W.A. Interviews, Otero and Montezuma Counties, Vol. 2, pp. 530-532. In possession of State Historical Society of Colorado.

[5]Account of Fred H. Taylor, C.W.A. Interviews, 1933-34, Otero and Montezuma County, Vol. 2, p. 446. In possession of State Historical Society of Colorado.

[6]Thomas, *op. cit.*

[7]At this time in May, 1881, there was no town where Dolores now stands, but there was a settlement known as the Big Bend where the Dolores River turns abruptly north, a short distance west of present Dolores. Big Bend was a supply center in a cattle country. There was a store and post office there as well as a log school building. Provisions were freighted in from Durango. When the Rio Grande and Southern Railroad was built along the Dolores River in 1892, a new town site was located and the town of Dolores was started some two miles up the river from Big Bend.

[8]Letter to Martin Rush from Heigo Weston, *op. cit.*, p. 183.

[9]Account of Fred H. Taylor, *op. cit.*, p. 446.

[10]*Ibid.*

[11]*Ibid.*, p. 447.

[12]Account of J. M. Rush, Sr., C.W.A. Interviews, Otero and Montezuma County, Vol. 2, p. 329. In possession of State Historical Society of Colorado.

[13]*Ibid.*, p. 328.

[14]Letter to Martin Rush by Heigo Weston, *op. cit.*, p. 184.

THE WHITE RIVER CANYON FIGHT

In 1879 Charles Johnson, Sr., of McPhee, Colorado, turned some cattle out to graze south of the Blue Mountains in Utah. During the next few years cattle from other outfits were pastured on this range also. However, after the Monument Creek killings and the La Sal Mountain battle in 1881, the cattlemen waited for several years until conditions quieted down before venturing into this no-man's land to work their cattle.

In the latter part of June, 1884, three cattle outfits, consisting of three wagons, twenty-one men, and a hundred saddle horses, started out for the Blue Mountain range from the Durango-Big Bend area to round up their cattle and brand the calves.[1] While on their way, one of the cowboys shot and killed a Ute who refused to give up a saddle horse which he had appropriated from a white man.

On July 3rd as the cattle outfits were riding past the point of a hill south of the Blue Mountains, a large group of angry Utes attacked. The Indians galloped into the string of saddle horses, split the bunch and stampeded them. The cowboys managed to get a few into an improvised corral before they all got away.

Fred Taylor, one of Johnson's cowhands, rode up to the corral to see if any of his horses were in it. He found a white horse named White Cloud, which was one of Taylor's favorites. The cowboy dismounted, and began taking a partition of the corral bars down to catch him. As he worked, he kept talking to the excited animal, telling him that the Indians wouldn't get him. Suddenly a bullet hit White Cloud in the middle of the forehead, scattering his brains all over Taylor and the corral.[2]

In the meantime, the Utes had set fire to two of the chuck wagons and pushed them off the trail into the brush.

The twenty-one cattlemen and cowboys were not prepared to fight Indians. While most of them had six-shooters, which were not very effective against the Utes' long-range rifles, the white men had only seven Winchesters.

A one-armed cowboy named Billy Wilson from the Texas Panhandle took charge of the disorganized cowmen. Wilson was an experienced Indian fighter, having engaged in many skirmishes with the Comanches. He had lost his arm in one of these fights. Within twenty minutes he could see that the Indians had won the day.

The Utes had the cattle outfits hemmed in at the point of a hill with all outgoing trails blocked. Billy Wilson led the retreat down the lower trail. The cowmen broke through the barricade and headed for home. A number of the cowboys had lost their horses and saddles and were forced to ride double behind some of the others on the way back.[3]

When the defeated white men returned and reported the attack, Captain Perine of Fort Lewis started out in pursuit of the hostile Utes with eighty soldiers and forty cowboys. They followed the Indians as far as White River Canyon close to the Colorado River.[4]

That morning before daybreak while the horses were being packed, Henry Goodman rode on ahead along the narrow trail to find out the location of the fleeing redskins. The Utes had a lot of goats with them, and Goodwin heard some of them bleating up in the rim rocks overlooking the narrow trail over which the soldiers and cowboys would have to pass.[5] The scout hastened back to warn the white men of the ambush. He told Captain Perine that the Indians were in such an impregnable position that they could hold off a hundred men apiece from behind the rocks where they were hidden.

The captain, after a discussion with the leaders of the expedition, assembled his forces and advised everyone to return home.

Jimmy Higgins, a cowboy whom everyone called "Rowdy," belittled the danger and volunteered to go up to the rim rocks where the Indians were if the government scout, Joe Wormington, would follow. Captain Perine protested such foolhardiness, but the two men started out, anyway, while everyone else watched.

It was barely daylight as they started up the hill toward the waiting Indians, Rowdy in the lead. They rode for quite a distance before dismounting and proceeding cautiously on foot.

When they got within easy shooting range, the Utes opened fire. Wormington, the scout, fell wounded, and as Rowdy began running back down the hill, he was hit.[6]

Mancos Jim, leader of the Indian band, and John Taylor, a negro who had married a Ute squaw and joined the tribe,[7] taunted the dying white men with such mockery as,

"Oh, my God, men, give me some water. My God, I'm suffering so."[8]

After the scout and cowboy were dead, the Indians stripped their bodies of clothing and took the saddles and bridles from their horses.

The soldiers and cowboys below watched the gruesome sight helplessly. Ted Carlyle, a big Englishman, was observing the tragedy through field glasses. While he was looking, a spent bullet unexpectedly fell between his feet. It so startled him that he turned a somersault and rolled down the hill. He was a huge man, and his ludicrous fall gave a touch of comedy to the drama being enacted above.

While most of the Indians' guns were of small calibre they had one buffalo gun, known as a 45-120, which some of the cowboys claimed had been in the possesssion of Dave Willis when he was killed in the La Sal Mountains three years before. The big gun would shoot a quarter of a mile, and about five seconds after each report a bullet would strike near the posse.

One cowboy tried to find one of its slugs, and while he was looking, a bullet landed near him. It caught him by surprise, and he fell and rolled unhurt over a rock to provide another brief moment of laughter for his tense comrades.

There was a pool of alkali rain water near where the posse was camped. Fred Taylor mixed most of this water with fifty pounds of flour to make bread and used what was left to make coffee. In three hours the pool was gone.

Realizing that it would be impossible to recover the bodies without seriously endangering other lives, the soldiers and cowboys returned home by way of the Blue Mountains. The Utes watched their withdrawal without trying to pursue them.

Years later some man happened across the skeletons of Wormington and "Rowdy" in the White River Canyon and buried them.

FOOTNOTES

[1]Account of Fred H. Taylor, C.W.A. Interviews, 1933-34, Otero and Montezuma Counties, Vol. 2, p. 452. In possession of State Historical Society of Colorado.

[2]Ibid.

[3]Bob McGraw, "Early Mancos History," notes taken by Minnie Rush in presence of Heigo Weston and J. M. Rush, Jr., C.W.A. Interviews, 1933-34, Otero and Montezuma Counties, Vol. 2, p. 471. In possession of State Historical Society of Colorado.

[4]Taylor, op. cit., p. 453.

[5]Account of Joanna Spalding Todd, C.W.A. Interviews, 1933-34, Otero and Montezuma Counties, Vol. 2, p. 512. In possession of State Historical Society of Colorado.

[6]Taylor, op. cit., p. 454.

[7]McGraw, op. cit., p. 471.

[8]Todd, op. cit., p. 513.

THE BEAVER CREEK MASSACRE

After the White River Canyon fight, participating cowboys from several different outfits agreed to kill the first Utes discovered off the reservation.[1] This hostility toward the Indians was aggravated by prevalent rumors that the red hunters were killing cattle and stealing horses on their expeditions into the Dolores River country. It was reported that the Utes were cutting out the loins from freshly killed beef animals and leaving the rest.[2] The Southern Utes were also being accused of exchanging their stolen horses for horses stolen by the White River Utes to help prevent recognition.

While the Utes may have occasionally killed a cow or stolen a horse, the reports of their misdeeds were, in all probability, highly exaggerated. The horse stealing for which they received the credit was done primarily by white rustlers.[3]

One pleasant June day in 1885 a group of cowboys happened across an Indian camp of a dozen or more Southern Utes on Beaver Creek several miles north of the Charles Johnson place, where the village of McPhee now stands. The Indians had written permission from their agent to hunt in that region, and they didn't realize how unwelcome they were. They had stopped at the Johnson store enroute to their camp on Beaver Creek. They were peaceable and minding their own business.[4]

The cowboys assumed that most of the Utes were out hunting so decided to stage their raid early the next morning—Satur-

day—when all the party was in camp. In the meantime, one of
the riders looked over the surrounding country to make certain
that no campers were about, since if any of the Utes escaped
the planned massacre, they would likely make a revenge attack
on any white persons that they might find in the vicinity.

When the cowboy returned, he reported that he had seen
only one tent in the neighborhood and that was occupied by a
group of surveyors who could look after themselves. The man
was wrong in this assumption, however, since the surveyors had
moved out the day before, and the Spalding family, consisting
of Mr. and Mrs. Spalding and their grown son and daughter,
had arrived and set up their tent at the same pleasant location.[5]

Next morning at daybreak the avenging cowboys opened fire
on the Ute camp from higher ground. One buck ran out of a
tepee holding up a baby to inform the assailants that there were
women and children in the camp.[6] The white men shot both
down in cold blood and proceeded to slaughter the remaining
nine or ten victims, who made no effort to defend themselves.

The Spaldings were awakened by the first shots. Mrs. Spalding called to her daughter, Joanna, and told her that apparently
someone was out deer hunting already. Then, volley after volley broke the morning stillness.

Joanna's twenty-seven-year-old brother grabbed the girl and
put her on a horse just as she was clad.

"Ride over to that cabin a mile and a half above here," he
ordered. "There must be an Indian fight going on, and you
must get out of here right away. We'll meet you later."[7]

He asked his mother to get on the other horse, but she refused, saying that she didn't want to make a target of herself.

When Joanna arrived at the cabin, she called out, and three
astonished cowboys appeared at the door. When they recovered
from their amazement, they invited her to come in.

In a few minutes Mrs. Spalding also rode up, and the two
women remained at the cabin until nine o'clock before returning to their tent. While they were at the cabin, the cowboys
who had staged the raid arrived. At that time Joanna met Sam
Todd, whom she married seven months later.

One Ute miraculously survived the massacre, and on his way

back to the reservation, he reported the event to another party of Utes whom he met in the Montezuma Valley.[8]

On Saturday evening of the same day that the Utes were murdered on Beaver Creek, the Genthner family, who lived seven miles from Big Bend near Totton's Lake, were preparing for bed. The three older children were already in bed upstairs, and the baby lay quietly in the downstairs bedroom, which his parents occupied. Mr. Genthner, who during the afternoon had walked all the way to Big Bend to get the mail, lay fully clothed on the big double bed, reading the weekly assortment of papers and letters. His wife, who was in her nightdress, sat nearby reading also.[9]

Noticing a flicker of light outside, Mrs. Genthner walked to the window to investigate.

"The house is on fire!" she exclaimed.

Genthner jumped from the bed, and grabbing a bucket of water near the wash basin, he flung open the door and rushed outside.

Mrs. Genthner heard the report of guns and looked out the door to discover her husband lying on the ground. As she rushed over to him, a bullet seared through her shoulder. She immediately suspected the presence of Indians, but none were in sight.

"I'm killed," Genthner gasped. "Go back into the house and look after the kids."

"I'm shot too," she told him.[10]

She ran back into the flaming house where the children lay asleep. The dog, which also had been shot, accompanied her inside where he fell dead on the floor. She awakened the youngsters and quickly explained what had happened. Then, holding the baby in her good arm and leading the next youngest child with the other hand she hurried out the back door, followed by the two older children. All of them were barefooted and dressed only in their night clothes.[11]

Their nearest neighbors were William Wooley and his son Doug. Wooley, a Mexican war veteran, was one of the first settlers in the Montezuma Valley, arriving there in 1881.[12] William was away at the time, and Doug, who had seen Indians about the place during the day, had taken his gun and gone out into the brush to sleep.

Mrs. Genthner luckily came upon him there in the brush sound asleep. She had her oldest boy slip up and move his gun out of reach before she awakened him.[13]

Doug Wooley told her to lie down so that if any Indians were around they would be less likely to see her. She complied for a while until she became chilled from the blood on her night-gown. Wooley then assisted her and the children to the Louis Simon ranch. When Mrs. Simon first saw the wounded lady, she fainted from fright.[14]

Doug Wooley warned the settlers along the Dolores River about the Indian outbreak, while the Simons took care of the Genthner family.

On the following day some men from Big Bend drove up to the Simon ranch in a wagon to take Mrs. Genthner and her children back with them. Another larger group rode to the Genthner ranch to bury the badly burned remains of the dead man.

Dr. Winters was summoned from Durango to treat the wounded shoulder of Mrs. Genthner. While awaiting his arrival Ben Drake, a veterinarian, came from Cross Canyon to render first aid treatment. At this time it was customary for the people on the Dolores to contribute five or ten dollars apiece in order to give Dr. Winters four hundred dollars a year to come to the Big Bend area whenever needed.

Meanwhile, frightened settlers buried their belongings and started for the Charles Johnson ranch at present McPhee. Johnson had a big stone barn with its windows high up along the sides. This barn was located in an open spot where no one could approach without being seen. It was not the first time that ranchers in the area gathered at the Johnson place to defend themselves against an expected attack.[15]

The Johnsons were not at home to greet the incoming pioneers. They were away for the day to attend the funeral of Ben Quick, the first man to be buried in the old cemetery near the present site of Dolores. Quick had been thrown from a horse that he was breaking. He tried to hold on to him and

Chipeta's and Ouray's home near present site of Montrose, Colorado, from 1875 to 1881. *Photo Courtesy of State Historical Society of Colorado.*

Chief Ouray's bones and coffin at the time of transfer from original grave. *Picture from S. F. Stacker, Ignacio, Colo., by Courtesy of State Historical Society of Colorado.*

Buckskin Charlie and John McCook, brother of Chipeta, holding bones of Chief Ouray at scene of Ouray's original grave after bones were dug up for reinterment in the Indian cemetery at Ignacio. *Photo by S. F. Stacker, Ignacio, Colorado, in the files of State Historical Society of Colorado.*

Buckskin Charlie—a leading chief of the Southern Utes who helped bury Chief Ouray in his secret grave. *Photo Courtesy State Historical Society of Colorado.*

Monk Shavano and Chipeta (standing by tree). This picture was taken by J. D. Nixon in Delta about 1912. The two were on their way to Ignaco to visit Buckskin Charlie. *Photo Courtesy of Mrs. Charlie Parker.*

Monk Shavano, son of old Chief Shavano; Jim McCook, son of Chipeta's brother John McCook; Yagah (accompanied Chipeta's body to Ouray Memorial Park), and his wife. This picture was taken by J. D. Nixon about 1912 in Delta. These Utes were enroute from their Ouray Agency in Utah to visit Buckskin Charlie at Ignacio.

Chipeta holding Jim McCook's baby. This picture was taken in Delta by J. D. Nixon about 1912. Chipeta and a group of Utes were enroute from the Ouray reservation in Utah to visit Buckskin Charlie at Ignacio.

John McCook, brother of Chipeta, standing beside concrete tepee at Ouray National Memorial Park near Montrose. *Photo Courtesy of Denver Public Library Western Collection.*

the bronco stepped on his hand. Blood poisoning set in, and although Dr. Winters was sent for, he arrived too late to save his life.

When the Johnsons returned home from the funeral, their yard was full of people cooking and making camp. Some of the women were in the basement of the big fourteen-room adobe brick house cooking tin after tin of biscuits in preparation for a siege.[16]

The neighbors remained there for the next two or three days, sleeping in the yard. No Indians appeared; so the settlers finally returned to their ranches.

When Mrs. Genthner had recovered sufficiently to travel, she went to Durango, where she was met by her brother. He took her and the children back to his home in California.

Doug Wooley, the hero of the day, was an unusual character. When his father William married his second wife, Doug left home and lived alone. He didn't like to associate with people, and if he saw anyone approaching, he would hide in the brush. He became more or less of a hermit.[17]

After the Genthner affair the Southern Utes were required to have passes whenever they went off the reservation. They were supposed to show these passes to anyone who asked to see them. One day two Indians passed by the Taylor ranch and proudly exhibited their passes.

One of the passes read, "This is a pretty good Indian. He's all right."

On the other pass was written, "This is a damned son of a bitch. Look out for him."[18]

The massacre of the Indians on Beaver Creek was a taboo subject in the early days. Fear of retaliation by the Utes, as well as fear of government action against the killers played an important part in keeping the subject out of conversations.[19] Also, none of the settlers, including the participants, was proud of the incident.

The Indian agent at Ignacio went up to the scene of the shooting with a company of soldiers. He threatened to prosecute the guilty cowboys, but nothing was done.[20]

The swollen, fly-blown bodies of the victims lay out on

Beaver Creek for a long time. Finally, when the Utes got up enough courage to visit the spot again, they buried the bleached bones of their people.[21]

FOOTNOTES

[1]Senator George E. West, "The Oldest Range Man," *Pioneers of the San Juan Country,* Vol. 2, p. 121.

[2]Account of Mrs. Mary Taylor, C.W.A. Interviews, 1933-34, Otero and Montezuma Counties, Vol. I, p. 101.

[3]Account of H. J. Porter, C.W.A. Interviews, 1933-34, Otero and Montezuma Counties, Vol. 2, p. 358. In possession of State Historical Society of Colorado.

[4]*Ibid.*

[5]Account of Joanna Spalding Todd, C.W.A. Interviews, Otero and Montezuma Counties, Vol. 2, p. 504.

[6]Account of Mrs. Mary Taylor, *op. cit.,* p. 101.

[7]Todd, *op. cit.,* p. 505.

[8]Reports differ as to the identity of this survivor. James Hammond of Dolores claims that the survivor was the night herder of the Indian horses (account of James Hammond, C.W.A. Interviews, Montezuma County, Vol. 2, p. 497). Mrs. Mary Taylor said that the survivor was a squaw (account of Mrs. Mary Taylor, C.W.A. Interviews, Montezuma County, Vol. I, p. 101).

[9]Account of Mrs. Lucy McConnell, C.W.A. Interviews, 1933-34, Otero and Montezuma Counties, Vol. 2, p. 306.

[10]*Ibid.*

[11]*Ibid.,* pp. 306-307.

[12]Frank Hall, *History of Colorado,* Vol. 4, p. 227.

[13]Account of Sarah Moore, C.W.A. Interviews, 1933-34, Otero and Montezuma Counties, Vol. 2, p. 322.

[14]*Ibid.,* p. 323.

[15]Account of Mrs. Howard Porter, C.W.A., Interviews, 1933-34. Otero and Montezuma Counties, Vol, I, p. 175.

[16]Account of Sarah Moore, *op. cit.,* p. 321.

[17]Account of Fred H. Taylor, C.W.A. Interviews, 1933-34, Otero and Montezuma Counties, Vol. 2, p. 458.

[18]Account of Mrs. Mary Alverda Estes Taylor, C.W.A. Interviews, 1933-34, Otero and Montezuma Counties, Vol. I, p. 102.

[19]Account of Mrs. Howard Porter, *op. cit.,* p. 175.

[20]Senator George E. West, "The Oldest Range Man," *Pioneers of the San Juan Country*, Vol. 2, pp. 121-122.

[21]Account of Mrs. Howard Porter, *op. cit.*, p. 175.

LIFE ON THE SOUTHERN UTE RESERVATION

The Treaty of 1880, which established the Southern Ute reservation boundaries in southwestern Colorado, did not result for a time in any change in their manner of life. The federal government continued to support them by issuing annuity goods and rations at regular periods. These consisted of flour, beef, sugar, coffee, soap, salt, baking powder, tinware, knives, forks, pots, kettles, coffee mills, washboards, blankets, coats, vests, trousers, overcoats, shoes, hats, caps, stockings, suspenders, canvas, shirts for the women, shawls, and combs. No household furniture was included in the issues.

Few Utes took up farming until the turn of the century. In 1891 there were only thirty-five farms of 160 acres each, and these were owned primarily by members of the Capote and Mouache bands. There were only three farmers at this time among the Weeminuche band. The government provided implements, wagons, harness, and seeds to the thirty-five farmers, but the Indians had to furnish their own horses. Most of the farmers lived in frame houses with shingle roofs and plank floors built for them by the government. They raised by irrigation oats, wheat, barley, hay and vegetables.[1]

Except for the thirty-five farmers, the Southern Utes dwelled in tepees and continued to live after the manner of their fathers. They hated work of all kinds and were habitually indolent except when engaged in hunting. There was so little game on the reservation that they did most of their hunting elsewhere.

The agency buildings were of both logs and rough lumber. There was a large issue house where rations were distributed, a warehouse, implement house, stable, hay loft, a council building, and houses for the agent and his eight white employees.

A police force made up of twelve Indians under the command of Chief Ignacio assisted the agent in maintaining discipline. The agent would notify Ignacio whenever a policeman was needed for any duty.[2]

There was a community meeting house at the agency where the agent occasionally met with the Indians to discuss matters of interest. The agent always brought an interpreter and secretary with him when attending these meetings. They were open to the public, and no Indian could speak more than once.

The production of buckskin was one handicraft at which the Utes excelled, and they also did some basketry and bead work. But, for the most part, the Indians merely lounged around, gambled, and drank whenever they could obtain liquor. By 1891 they had assimilated little, if any, of the white man's culture and beliefs, sticking stubbornly to the past traditions of their forefathers in all important respects.

Then, in 1895, Congress passed an act requiring the Secretary of the Interior to make allotments in severalty of farm land to the Southern Utes as written in the Treaty of 1880. Those Indians who did not elect to accept their individual allotments would be placed on certain lands in the western portion of the reservation, which were to be owned in common.[3]

Due to the influence of Buckskin Charley and Severo, members of the Capote and Mouache bands accepted their allotments, which were made in the fertile, eastern portion of the reservation near the Ignacio agency. Most members of the Weeminuche band, however, refused their allotments and withdrew to the semi-arid western portion of the reservation, where a sub-agency was established at Navajo Springs. Due to lack of sufficient water here, the sub-agency was shortly thereafter moved four miles north to its present location at Towaoc.

A lengthy period of land sales to white settlers followed the granting of allotments at Ignacio during which the Southern Utes were encouraged to part with much of their lands for cash or for inferior horses and trade goods.[4] However, through inheritance of the remaining lands which they held on to, almost all of the mature Utes at Ignacio have come into possession of farms and homes.[5] Today the Southern Ute Reservation around Ignacio consists of 5,291 acres of allotted land and 298,277 acres of tribal land held in common by the present 563 members of the tribe.[6]

The allotments around Ignacio refused by members of the Weeminuche band or Ute Mountain Tribe were returned to the Public Domain and opened for filing to white homesteaders in May, 1899.[7]

As a result of all this land manipulation, the two bands of Southern Utes have since the turn of the century owned individual farms scattered among the white holdings around the Consolidated Ute Agency at Ignacio, while the Weeminuche band, or Ute Mountain Utes, have lived for years a nomadic, solitary life on the Ute Mountain Reservation around the subagency at Towaoc, where all the land is held in common by the present 657 members of the tribe.

About 1920 a number of the Ute Mountain Tribe began filing on Public Domain land in the Allen Canyon area near Blanding and Monticello, Utah.[8] Today about 150 members of the tribe own 9,079 acres of allotted land in this region. The remaining 553,358 acres on the Ute Mountain Reservation are owned by the tribe and held in common.[9]

The Southern Ute family farm at Ignacio averages around forty acres. Alfalfa, wheat, and oats are the chief crops raised, and nearly all of the Ute farmers also have gardens.[10] Much of the hay and grain are fed to livestock rather than sold, although there are no large Indian-owned stock ranches at Ignacio. Hay and grain which the Southern Utes do not feed to their livestock are sold in the same markets as the products of their white neighbors.

Because of continual contact with the whites since around 1900, the Southern Utes made early adjustments to the white norms of conduct. Their farming activities also left them little time for observance of the old customs and caused them to rely on an individualistic economy, effectively destroying group solidarity.

This early trend at Ignacio toward adaptation to white civilization is well illustrated by a young Ute's account of a visit he had with his more conservative father:

"My father came to see me after the boy was born in the government hospital. He asked me, 'Did you go off alone and run after your baby was born?' I had to tell him I just took the day off resting around home. . . . He said that they always (ran) in the old days when a baby came. I'd do it just to please him, but the others would laugh at me. Besides, I have too much work on the ranch now, and that tires me out."[11]

For a long time now the Southern Utes at Ignacio have lived in frame or adobe houses during most of the year. These have floors, doors, windows, and heating arrangements.

There are no longer any medicine men among the Southern Utes. The old medicine men have died, and none of the younger men desired to take their place. This has been due partly to the growing appreciation for medical care and partly because none of the younger Utes desired to live a life of complete abstinence which was necessary to becoming a medicine man.

Yet, in spite of their many conformances to the white man's ways, the Southern Utes have retained some aboriginal standards which still make them a colorful, distinct people.

The Bear Dance and Sun Dance continue to be very popular occasions among them. An interesting innovation in the Bear Dance, however, is that while the modern Utes still dance the usual three days, they seldom dance all night as did their rugged ancestors. The same is true of the Ute Mountain Utes.

In respect to clothing, preference for the old customs is still seen. The older men, for example, wear long hair braids and the older women continue to wear long, full calico or velvet dresses, which are peculiarly Indian. While there still remain certain individualistic features in the dress of the younger generations, their fashions are closer to the white man's style than are the fashions among the Ute Mountain Tribe at Towaoc.

In 1926 the Southern Ute Tribe at Ignacio adopted a constitution and by-laws. The constitution provides for a council of six members, defines the council's jurisdiction, membership, and powers, and makes further provision for conducting all business concerning the tribe. One full-time policeman and a tribal judge are also elected to help maintain law and order. In addition to conducting court cases, the tribal judge may also perform marriage ceremonies among the Southern Utes. With the beginning of local self-government, the chief of the tribe has become merely an honorary office.[12]

Unlike the Southern Utes, the Ute Mountain Utes still continue a nomadic existence. Until 1931 when the ration system was stopped, they lived in idleness. After 1931 they started to raise a few sheep and cattle for a meager livelihood.[13]

Because of their different environment, the Ute Mountain Utes retained for a much longer period than the Southern Utes the traditions and mental outlook of their forefathers. Up until comparatively recent times, for example, they had no use for white doctors, depending almost entirely on the songs and antics of their medicine men to cure them. Today there are only two or three medicine men among the tribe.[14] While they are still very popular, the Ute Mountain Utes have gradually come to appreciate medical science as evidenced by 150 admissions to their hospital in 1953 and 280 in 1954. Likewise, in 1953 there were 4,817 visits to the Ute Mountain Health Center at Towaoc and 7,861 in 1954. All children are participating in the polio immunization program, and the tribal council has ordered the purchase of polio vaccine for pre-school children and expectant mothers.[15]

Until as late as 1950 the Ute Mountain Utes lived in tents, hogans, or wickiups, and did their cooking on small stoves over camp fires.

On June 6, 1940, the Ute Mountain Tribe adopted a constitution similar to the one adopted by the Southern Ute Tribe four years before. It provided for a council of seven members, including a representative from the Allen Canyon Utes in Utah. Two full-time policemen and a tribal judge are elected to maintain law and order.

In 1941 the school, hospital, and sub-agency at Towaoc were closed because of lack of water. In 1953 the Ute Mountain tribal council went to Washington and requested that the Towaoc Boarding School be reopened. Their request was granted, and in the fall of that year the school, hospital, and sub-agency were reopened. Adequate water was obtained through the purchase of some decrees from an irrigation company and by drilling wells.

Neither the Southern Utes nor the Ute Mountain Utes took readily to white schooling. At Towaoc, for example, a girl of fifteen after completing the first grade quit school to help her family herd sheep. Although attendance was supposed to be compulsory, it was impossible to enforce because the Indians, as a whole, would not cooperate. However, much improvement has been made in recent years.

The Towaoc Boarding School is an elementary school for grades one through six and is operated by the Montezuma Public School District. The buildings and utilities are furnished by the federal government. The district hires the teachers and the school has the same course of study as the other public schools of the state. The percentage of attendance as reported on the annual school report dated May, 1954, was about eighty-five percent.[16]

The Ute Vocational School at Ignacio is both a grade and high school. Percentage of attendance as reported on the annual school report dated May, 1954, was 85.8 per cent for those who live at home and 99.5 per cent for those who board at the school.[17] The federal government is contributing $72,000 this year for the improvement and expansion of the grade school at the nearby town of Ignacio so that the Southern Ute children now attending grade school at the Consoldiated Ute Agency may be transferred to it and go to school with the white children.

The Southern Utes and the Ute Mountain Utes have not been susceptible to the white man's religion. In 1940 there was a Roman Catholic mission and a Protestant mission at Towaoc. After the Towaoc sub-agency was closed in 1941, these missions were abandoned. When the sub-agency was reopened in 1953, a small Catholic church and a Protestant mission were again started.

In the town of Ignacio there were town churches but no missions at the adjoining Consolidated Ute Agency. The few Southern Utes who have become church goers attend the Catholic church.

To this day, however, very few Utes consider that they have been converted. At Towaoc a new cult, known as the peyote cult, has become a bulwark of faith against the encroachment of missionary influence. The peyote ceremony was introduced to the Utes around 1917 by Sam Loganberry or Cactus Pete, as he was sometimes called.

The tepee where the ceremony occurs faces the east in accordance with the ancient Ute concept that the patient may rise with the sun. A big bowl containing the peyote is placed on a half-moon mound, made out of the tepee floor. This mound represents to the Utes an old source of supernatural power.

The participants sit in a circle around the mound, and the leader of the ceremony conducts the chanting and praying, which is accompanied by two drummers, who also sit in the circle.

After an hour or so of chanting and praying, the peyote bowl is passed from one person to another, each taking out some of the narcotic and eating it. After the bowl has made the circle, it is again placed on the mound, and the worship is resumed. It is again interrupted by the water boy, who brings water to to the group after which the peyote is once more passed around. Then the chanting and praying is continued for another hour or so when the peyote bowl again makes the rounds. This ceremony usually begins each Saturday evening and continues until Sunday noon at which time it is concluded with a feast.[18] The peyote narcotic is quite potent, and before the service ends, most of the participants are in an exuberant mood.

The peyote cult combines many of the older Ute traditions, the ceremony resembling in some respects the old Ghost Dance.[19] It also has a certain touch of Christianity, which makes it a powerful competitor of the Christian Church.

At Ignacio the peyote cult did not take hold as it did at Towaoc. This may be partly due to the five-dollar or more grocery bill required of each participant for the peyote drug, which never did appeal to the money-minded native farming population.

Both tribes have had difficulty in accepting the white man's marriage standards. Until their constitutions were adopted in 1936 and 1940, most of the Utes got married "The Indian way" by mutual consent without benefit of clergy or civil law. Sexual promiscuity and separations were frequent until middle age, and there was no stigma to illegitimate births, which were fairly common.

The difficulty of divorce proceedings, as well as the three-dollar marriage fee to the tribal judge or justice of the peace, caused many of the Utes to continue the custom of marrying the Indian way even though their constitutions made it illegal.

One unsuspecting Indian paid the local judge the usual three-dollar fee for getting married the white man's way. A short time later when he appeared to get a divorce, he offered to pay six dollars, believing that if he doubled the original price a divorce could be speedily obtained.[20]

With the passing of the years, however, members of the two Ute tribes have gradually adjusted themselves to the white man's standards of morality so that the percentage of shifting family alliances is today perhaps no greater among the Utes than among the whites.[21]

Today all members of the two tribes are self-supporting, and their income is derived from two main sources—unearned income in the form of per capita distribution of tribal income from oil and gas leases, and earned income from farming, the production of livestock, and employment. The per capita income from unearned sources for members of the Southern Ute Tribe for 1954 was $3,250 and for members of the Ute Mountain Tribe it was $1,200.[22]

In 1939 the Utes on both the Utah and Colorado reservations brought suit against the government for payment on 4,404,000 acres of surface and sub-surface land and 787,000 acres of subsurface only, the latter including the territory embraced within the Rangely Oil Field.[23]

This suit arose out of the government's failure to comply properly with its commitments under the Treaty of 1880,

whereby it was agreed that the Utes receive a certain payment
for their reservation lands in Western Colorado. Some payments were made to the Utes for lands sold or taken into the
Forest Service, but there still remained more than 4,000,000
acres for which the government had refused payment.[24]

In 1947 the District Court at Grand Junction awarded the
2600 Utes in northeastern Utah and southwestern Colorado
$31,938,473.43. This suit was upheld by the United States
Court of Claims in 1950.[25]

Ernest L. Wilkinson and other attorneys who worked on the
case for the Utes were given a gross award of $2,800,000 for
their services. In addition to this sum, the Indians paid out of
their own tribal funds expenses amounting to $434,250.11.[26]
Three other suits are still pending.

The Southern Utes' share in the award money won thus far
after deduction of attorney fees was more than $5,000,000,
while the Ute Mountain Utes share was around $7,000,000. In
the distribution of this money each man, woman, and child of
the two tribes was given $500 in cash, which he could spend in
any way he desired, and $3,000 in credit, which must be used
for some constructive purpose, such as building homes or pur-
chasing livestock, pickups, farm or household equipment.[27]

Both tribes are in the process of conducting rehabilitation
programs. The basis of these programs is the Family Plan by
which each member of a family pools his $3,000 credit author-
ization for the purchase of things beneficial as agreed upon by
the family and approved by the agency staff and tribal com-
mittees.[28]

In connection with this rehabilitation program, efforts are
being made by the two tribes to improve their tribal lands.
For example, the Ute Mountain Tribe has purchased some
good summer pasture to be used in connection with their semi-
arid spring and winter ranges. The tribal council has also
recently bought some water from an irrigation company to
bring to their water-starved land, and it has authorized the is-
suance of a permit to the U. S. Geological Survey for a mineral
mapping of the Ute Mountain Reservation for the Atomic
Energy Commission. This project is estimated to take four

years to finish and will add to the tribe's knowledge about the resources on the reservation.[29] Also, many members of the tribe are getting rid of some of their horses to make more range for cattle and sheep.

It is still too early to accurately estimate the effects of the rehabilitation program, but a lot of activity is taking place.

While some of the Utes spent most of their $500 cash awards on whiskey, other families pooled their resources to buy new cars and other worthwhile commodities.

New homes, equipped with all the most modern conveniences, are springing up on the two reservations. Some of the Towaoc Utes, who until this program was started always have lived in tents, hogans, or wickiups, claim that the government is trying to make white men out of them. However, the rehabilitation director is trying to overcome this resentment by telling them that a man's race is told by what he feels in his heart and not in what type of dwelling he lives.

In October, 1953, a group of Ignacio Utes, garbed in a curious mixture of modern and ancient dress, made a three-day tour of Denver looking for ideas on how to spend their money for the construction of one hundred modern homes on the Southern Ute Reservation. The party, accompanied by three members of the tribal council, visited various types of Denver homes from the $45,000 bracket down to the $10,000 class.

"This kitchen is nice," remarked one of the group as she examined the electric range of a new kitchen. "We must all learn to cook with electricity. We want to get the best possible types of homes within our means so that our children may have better places to live than we did. I believe that a new day has dawned for my people."[30]

FOOTNOTES

[1]Frank Hall, *History of Colorado*, Vol. 4, p. 62.

[2]*Ibid.*, p. 66.

[3]Compilation of Material Relating to the Indians of the U. S., etc., inducting Certain Laws and Treaties Affecting Such Indians by Subcommittee on Indian Affairs of the Committee on Public Lands, House of Representatives, June 13, 1950.

[4]Ralph Linton, *Acculturation in Seven American Indian Tribes*, p. 181.

[5]*Ibid.*, p. 187.

[6]*Consolidated Ute Agency Annual Report*, 1954-1955.

[7]Hans Aspaas, a pioneer of Ignacio area who was one of above-mentioned homesteaders, personal interview, May 11, 1955.

[8]Robert L. Bennett, present superintendent of the Consolidated Ute Agency, personal interview, May 12, 1955.

[9]Consolidated Ute Agency Annual Report, 1954-1955.

[10]D. H. Watson, former superintendent of the Consolidated Ute Agency, "Consolidated Ute Agency in Colorado," Feb. 8, 1936. Original manuscript reproduced in Helen Daniels Sloan, *The Ute Indians of Southwestern Colorado*, pp. 70-71.

[11]Linton, *op. cit.*, p. 197.

[12]Sunshine Smith, a member of the Southern Ute Tribal Council, personal interview, May 11, 1955.

[13]Linton, *op. cit.*, p. 185.

[14]Harriett Why, member of the Ute Mountain Tribe, personal interview, May 12, 1955.

[15]*Consolidated Ute Agency Annual Report*, 1954-1955.

[16]*Consolidated Ute Agency Annual Report*, 1954-1955.

[17]*Ibid.*

[18]William Ashbaugh, an employee at the Towaoc Agency, personal interview, May 12, 1955.

[19]Sunshine Smith, personal interview, May 11, 1955.

[20]Lindon, *op. cit.*, p. 199.

[21]Sunshine Smith, personal interview, May 11, 1955.

[22]*Consolidated Ute Agency Annual Report*, 1954-1955.

[23]E. O. Fuller, (member of the Indian Dept.), letter written to Mrs. Wright Springer of the State Historical Society, Jan. 1951.

[24]S. F. Stacker, *The Colorado Magazine*, April, 1950, p. 140.

[25]Fuller, *op. cit.*

[26]*Ibid.*

[27]Robert B. White, (Ute Mountain Rehabilitation Director,) personal interview, May 12, 1955.

[28]*Ibid.*

[29]*Consolidated Ute Agency's Annual Report*, 1954-1955.

[30]*Denver Post*, Oct. 24, 1953.

THE UINTAH AND OURAY RESERVATION

On October 3, 1861, President Abraham Lincoln signed an executive order which created the Uintah Reservation. This reservation consisted originally of 2,487,474 acres of land in northeastern Utah.[1] Six years later in 1867 various bands of Indians at the Spanish Forks Reservation, located three miles west of the town of Spanish Forks, Utah, were transferred to the Uintah Reservation. These Indians were members of various Utah tribes, but after being placed on their new reservation, they became known as the Uintah Band, receiving their name from that of the reservation. This band, whose members were not Utes, should not be confused with the Uintah Band of Utes in northwestern Colorado.[2]

The first permanent agency to be established on the Uintah Reservation was at Whiterocks on Christmas day, 1868.[3] This agency was later moved seventeen miles south to Fort Duchesne, the present agency.

In September, 1881, the White River Bands of Utes, consisting of the old Yampa River Band, the Grand River Band, and the Uintah Band, were moved to the Uintah Reservation. The Uncompahgre Band of Utes was transferred at the same time to a reservation which joined the Uintah Reservation on the south and east. This became known as the Uncompahgre Reservation when it was created by executive order on January 5, 1882.[4] An agency was established at Ouray, Utah, ten miles south of Fort

Duchesne—the Uintah agency. The two agencies were later consolidated at Fort Duchesne, and the two reservations became known as the Uintah and Ouray Reservation.[5]

Congress passed an act on January 7, 1897, making individual allotments of land to members of the Uncompahgre Band not only on the Uncompahgre Reservation but also on the Uintah Reservation or elsewhere in the state of Utah.[6]

Five years later on May 27, 1902, Congress passed another act authorizing allotments of land in severalty to the White River and Uintah bands.[7]

As a result of these two acts, 77,000 acres of irrigated land and 19,000 acres of unirrigated land were made to individuals in the three bands (the White River Band, the Uncompahgre Band, and the Uintah Band). Of the 77,000 acres of irrigated land, the Utes sold 23,000 acres and leased 30,000 acres to non-Indians (whites). Of the 24,000 acres remaining to the individual Indians, the Utes are farming only about 7,000 acres, which leaves approximately 17,000 acres idle.[8] Alfalfa is the chief crop raised by the few Ute farmers.

As indicated by the above figures, the Ute Indians do not like to farm. However, the raising of sheep and particularly cattle is more in their line. In 1952 the sheep population on the reservation was 6,775. In 1953 the Indians had about 4,490 head of beef cattle.[9]

Permits to run livestock on the tribal grazing land must be obtained from the Tribal Busines Committee, which is the governing body of the Indians on the Uintah and Ouray Reservation. While the sheepmen usually tend their own flocks, most of the cattlemen are organized into associations which hire riders to herd the cattle for the members.

In 1905 the government quit alloting land to members of the Ute tribe and opened up the Uintah and Ouray Reservation for homesteading to white people, excluding land already allotted to the Indians and 274,000 acres which was set aside as a grazing and timber reserve for the Indians.[10] As a result of this homesteading and the large amount of land sold and leased by the Utes, the reservation is overrun by non-Indians.

Also, in 1905 the federal government. withdrew 1,110,000

acres from the reservation to create the Uintah Forest Reserve. Many years later in 1933 the Utes received some $1,100 each in payment for this land.[11]

It was not until 1945 that 236,000 acres of land which had not been homesteaded by white people was restored to the reservation.[12]

When the Taylor Grazing Act went into effect in 1933 certain lands amounting to 429,000 acres on the old Uncompahgre Reservation were placed in the Public Domain. The reason for this action was based on the grounds that the Indians had not been using this land and had failed to file non-use permits. The tribe took the matter to court and finally in 1948 won it back.[13]

The 1800 members of the Ute tribe on the reservation adopted in 1937 the Indian's Reorganization Act and in the following year they obtained a charter.[14] A constitution and by-laws was adopted by the tribe on January 19, 1937, which provided for a Tribal Business Committee of six, two from each of the three bands (Uintah, White River, and Uncompahgre bands). Members of this governing body are elected by secret ballot of the qualified voters for a four-year term.[15]

After becoming incorporated the tribe borrowed a limited amount of money from the federal government on June 10, 1940, under a revolving loan plan. The tribe loaned this sum to its members, and it materially helped the Ute cattle and sheep producers during the period of 1942 to 1950.

Like the Southern Utes and the Ute Mountain Utes in southwestern Colorado, the Utes in Utah have retained some of their old culture and customs throughout the years.

The Bear Dance and Sun Dance are still popular annual events. The Bear Dance takes place each spring at Fort Duchesne. By paying an admission of twenty-five cents white people may watch the performance. Since the dance is ladies' choice, squaws often ask some of the white men spectators to participate in the occasion with them. The Sun Dance, a religious ceremony designed to cure or avert physical infirmities, is usually held at Whiterocks in June.

Nine out of thirteen of the adult full bloods on the Uintah and Ouray Reservation belong to the peyote cult, which, as described in the preceding chapter, combines some of the Utes' ancient ceremonies and beliefs with certain aspects of Christianity. Most of the Indians who go to church belong to the Episcopal Church. The Episcopal missions were the first to be established on the reservation. Chipeta, it will be recalled, joined this church in 1898.

While the younger generations wear modern clothing, minor individualistic features peculiarly Indian occasionally appear, such as their flair for bright colors. The older Indians show a definite preference for the old style of dress, such as hair braids, shawls, and long full dresses.

By 1939 most of the Utes were living in frame houses, but there were a few who still insisted upon tepees. A survey conducted as late as 1951 by the planning division of the Ute tribe revealed that most of the Utes were living in log cabins and two-room frame houses.[16]

With the exception of beadwork for the tourist trade the Utes gradually abandoned their native crafts. With the sudden rise of income during the past few years, even this craft has been neglected. A recreational program started by the tribe in October, 1953, has been encouraging a revival of the old Indian arts and crafts.

Few Utes would submit to medical attention before 1930, but in 1939 there were 561 patients in the reservation hospital, indicating a gradual increase in appreciation for medical science.

The reservation hospital has been closed, but a clinic is in operation at Fort Duchesn. Ute patients are now sent to the hospitals of nearby cities and towns, which the government feels is less expensive than maintaining a hospital on the reservation. Permanently disabled Utes are sent to Indian service hospitals in other jurisdictions.

The Ute tribe has no compulsory health laws. However, the tribe's lawyer is at this writing drawing up an ordinance of sanitation requirements comparable to those of the surrounding white settlements.[17]

Until the late 1940's when oil was found on the reservation, the Utes' standard of living was quite low. In 1939, for example, their annual per capita income was only about $187.

In 1951 their income from gas and oil bonuses, rentals, leases, and royalties was further enhanced by initial payment of the money from the Judgment Fund. The Judgment Fund consists of the $32,000,000 which the Ute Indians in Colorado and Utah won in a suit against the federal government for failing to live up to its obligation under the Treaty of 1880. The Utes on the Uintah and Ouray Reservation were awarded $17,000,000 as their share of this money.

In distributing money from the Judgment Fund the Ute Tribe in Utah worked out a three year short-range experimental program from August 21, 1951 to August 21, 1954. This was approved by the United States Congress. It authorized an initial payment of $1,000 to each of the 1700 enrolled Utes on the Uintah and Ouray Reservation. This was followed by a per capita payment of $545 in 1952 and $500 in 1953. Payments during 1954 were authorized as $300 on July 1st from interest on the fund and $300 on August 27th from principal.

From August 21, 1951 to August 21, 1954 each Ute on the Uintah and Ouray Reservation received $4,135 in unearned income from the Judgment Fund and from oil and and gas interests.[18] Consequently, an average Indian family of four received some $16,540 during the period. This amount does not include wages or other earned income from farming and the production of cattle and sheep.[19]

Many of the Utes had difficulty in adjusting themselves to their newly found wealth and did not spend the money wisely. They had little resistance to sale pressure, and it was not uncommon to see as many as three brand new automobiles parked beside a two-room shack. New refrigerators, electric washing machines, and other similar equipment were often found on the porches or yards of Indians who had no electricity in their homes. In short, high pressure salesmen had a field day at the Indians' expense.

A goodly portion of the income was also used for gambling and the purchase of liquor, which, as a whole, the Utes have not as yet learned how to handle. Until 1954 it was illegal to sell liquor to Indians in the state of Utah. However, with their newly purchased automobiles it was no problem for the Utes to drive over the state line into Colorado to obtain whiskey.

This unaccustomed access to liquor plus the ability to purchase high-powered automobiles, which were also new to the Indians, caused a great increase in law violations on the reservation. For example, during the last four months of 1952 there were 151 law violations. More than eighty percent of these related to the consumption of liquor and the breaking of traffic regulations.[20]

Due to these law and order problems a recreational program was started by the tribe in October, 1953, and this has been successful in materially reducing law violations. The program includes a revival of Indian arts and crafts, promotion of community activities, initiating hobbies, and the encouragement of competition in sports and home landscape contests. A recreational director was hired by the tribe at a salary of $4,205 per year.

Some outstanding accomplishments resulted from the three-year short range program. Culturally speaking, the mixed bloods, who will be discussed later, profited the most since they have shown greater ability to adapt themselves to modern conditions than have the full bloods.

In the educational field, the chief objective of the tribe during the program was to transfer all Ute children from the bureau-operated Indian school on the reservation to public schools in the area. Through a gradual process this objective was obtained by June 30, 1952. The Indian school was closed at this time, and the Ute boys and girls of school age have been attending the public schools of Uintah and Duchesne Counties.

This wholesale transfer of Ute children to public schools has created problems for both the Indian families and the public school officials. The background of the Indian child is quite different from that of the white child, and many of the Ute pupils do not have homes with sufficient lighting, heating and space conducive to proper study.

The teachers also have had to make major adjustments. Many of them were unprepared to teach non-English speaking children. Furthermore, additional buses and classrooms have had to be provided on short notice to take care of the influx of Indian pupils.

Due to lack of definite jurisdiction between the tribe and the state over delinquent Indian children, attendance enforcement has been difficult.

However, the Ute parents and the public school officials are cooperating to iron out these various problems wisely and efficiently.

During the 1953-54 school year 93 per cent of the 547 eligible Ute children were enrolled in some school with an average daily attendance of about 86 per cent. The average daily attendance of the non-Indian children was about 93 per cent.

In May, 1953, eighteen Ute boys and girls graduated from high school. Seven of these entered institutions of higher learning.

During the three-year period a credit program was worked out by the tribe. The tribe was advanced $1,545,000 from the Judgment Fund for this program, and an additional $250,000 was advanced in August, 1954.

The credit division is administered by a committee of five Indians. For loans of more than $5,000 but less than $10,000 approval of the Tribal Business Committee and the superintendent (agent) must also be obtained. Loans exceeding $10,-000 must be approved by the area office.

Thirty-four per cent of the loans was used for the purchase of livestock, twenty-two per cent for permanent improvements, and twelve per cent for buying machinery. The balance was spent for such miscellaneous items as education, buying seeds, etc.

At the start of the three-year program on August 21, 1951, most of the Utes were living in log cabins and two-room frame houses. The majority of the Indians had no desire to improve their living conditions, believing that modern homes were needless luxuries. Besides, they did not want to live like white people.[21]

As an inducement to improve their homes, five welfare modern houses were constructed at Whiterocks for aged Utes. Upon seeing first-hand how comfortable and convenient these five homes were, the Indians soon began sending in requests for similar houses.

To help out with the housing program the Tribal Business Committee appropriated $450,000 for home building. This money was turned over to the credit division to be loaned out in accordance with credit requirements.

The Business Committee also provided the Utes with substantial discounts in their purchase of building material. For example, 1,350,000 feet of timber was cut by the tribe during the three-year period for use in building modern homes on the reservation. This lumber was sold to the Indians at cost. The tribe also offered an electric wiring subsidy up to $125 and a well drilling subsidy under which the tribe paid one-half of the drilling costs up to $250.

As a result of this housing project, thirty-seven new homes were constructed, twenty-two purchased, and thirteen remodeled. Also, during the same period from August 21, 1951 to August 21, 1954, fifty-five wells were drilled, and approximately 91 per cent of the Ute homes had electricity by 1954.

The three-year experimental program proved a good training ground for the tribe in launching a long-range program. The method and procedure by which this will be carried out was approved by the tribe on October 14, 1953. A planning board, composed of representatives from five reservation communities, make recommendations. The agency and tribal employees serve as consultants and advisers.[22]

It was provided in the long-range program that $500 from the Judgment Fund be given outright in 1956 to each Ute. In addition, $4,000 will be given to each member of a family after it has outlined a family program for spending the money beneficially. These family programs must receive the aid and approval of the planning board and the agency tribal employees.[23] This long-range program applies only to the full blood Utes.

Of the 1800 Indians now living on the Uintah and Ouray Reservation, 1300 are known as full blood Utes and 500 as mixed blood Utes. The mixed bloods are, for the most part, descendants of the original Indians placed on the reservation from Spanish Forks, Utah, in 1867. These Indians seldom mar ried into the Ute tribe but united with non-Indians and mixed blood persons of other tribes.[24] The mixed bloods, which also includes persons who have one-half or more non-Indian blood, kept to their own group and had little, if any, social contact with the full blood Utes. These Indians have, as a whole, been more progressive than the full bloods in adjusting themselves to modern conditions.

For these reasons on March 31, 1954, the Ute tribe at a general council meeting decided by a vote of 108 to 6 to separate the two groups and move the mixed bloods off the reservation.

Congress approved the tribe's request and in August, 1954, passed an act providing for the partition of all the reservation assets between the two groups and removal of the mixed bloods from federal supervision by 1961. A complete appraisal of all assets of the reservation is being made, and when this is done, the mixed bloods will be given their proportionate share. In 1961 their share of the reservation lands will go on the tax rolls.

The federal government hopes that within the next fifteen years the full blood Utes will also have advanced sufficiently to likewise be withdrawn from federal supervision and be absorbed in the nation's economy as self-sufficient citizens.

FOOTNOTES

[1]Mrs. Adelyn Logan, (Asst. Manager of Realty Division of the Uintah and Ouray Reservation), personal interview, May, 1956.

[2]The Uintah Band in northwestern Colorado made up one of the seven bands of the original Ute tribe.

[3]Miles Mildred Dillman, *Early History of Duchesne County*, p. 81.

[4]The Uncompahgre Reservation consisted originally of 1,933,440 acres of land.

[5]The Uintah and Ouray Reservation lies within parts of Duchesne and Uintah Counties in northeastern Utah about 150 miles east of Salt Lake City.

[6]The Uintah and White River Bands of Utes V. The U. S. of America, Court of Claims of the U. S. No. 47569, pp. 15-16.

[7]*Ibid.*, p. 17.

[8]Reginald O. Curry, (manager of the Uintah and Ouray Reservation), personal interview, May, 1956. Irrigation reports show that

in 1951 the total acreage farmed by the Indians was 7,439 acres. This dropped to 7,020 in 1952 and increased to 9,656 in 1953.

[9]Reginald D. Curry, *Three Year Report* (Aug. 21, 1951 to Aug. 21, 1954) to Commissioner of Indian Affairs, pp. 37-38.

[10]Court of Claims of the U. S. No. 47569, *op. cit.,* p. 19.

[11]Curry, *op. cit.,* p. 5

[12]Logan, *op. cit.*

[13]Curry, personal interview, May, 1956.

[14]Corporate Charter of the Ute Indian Tribe of the Uintah and Ouray Reservation, Utah. Ratified Aug. 10, 1938.

[15]Constitution and By-laws of the Ute Indian Tribe of the Uintah and Ouray Reservation, Utah. Approved Jan. 19, 1937.

[16]Curry, *op. cit.,* p. 60.

[17]Comparison of the health of the Utes with the health of the people of Utah and of the United States from 1951 to 1954 shows the following. The infant mortality among the Utes was proportionately more than four times that of the citizens of Utah. Death from heart trouble was less than half that of the average for the population of the United States. Tuberculosis took a toll of nine Utes during the three-year period, which proportionately is more than eight times that of the United States.

[18]Curry, *op. cit.,* p. 70.

[19]The total per capita payments during this three-year period from local gas and oil bonuses, rentals, leases ,and royalties amounted to $2,640,964. This, together with payment of interest on the Judgment Fund of $2,365,805 and the payment of $2,224,000 of principal on the Judgment Fund made a grand total of $7,230,769.

[20]Curry, *op. cit.,* pp. 14-16.

[21]*Ibid.,* pp. 60-61.

[22]*Ibid.,* p. 70.

[23]Curry, personal interview, May, 1956.

[24]Curry, *op. cit.,* pp. 73-76.

APPENDIX I

TREATY NEGOTIATED WITH THE UTES FOR
SAN LUIS VALLEY IN 1868[1]

ARTICLES of a treaty and agreement made and entered into at Washington, D. C., on the second of March, 1868, by and between Nathaniel G. Taylor, Commissioner of Indian Affairs; Alexander C. Hunt, Governor of Colorado Territory and ex officio Superintendent of Indian Affairs, and Kit Carson, duly authorized to represent the United States, of the one part, and the representatives of the Tabewatch (Tabeguache), Mouache, Capote, Weeminuche, Grand River and Uintah bands of Ute Indians (whose names are hereto subscribed), duly authorized and empowered to act for the body of the people of said bands, of the other part, witness:

Article 2. The United States agree that the following district of country, to-wit: Commencing at that point on the southern boundary line of the Territory of Colorado where the meridian of longitude 107 degrees west of Greenwich crosses the same, running thence north with said meridian to a point fifteen miles due north of where said meridian intersects the 40th parallel of north latitude; thence due west to the western boundary line of said Territory; thence south with said western boundary line of said Territory to the southern boundary line of said Territory; thence east with said southern boundary line to the place of beginning, shall be, and the same is hereby, set apart for the absolute and undisturbed use and occupation of the Indians herein named and for such other

friendly tribes or individual Indians as from time to time they may
be willing, with the consent of the United States, to admit among
them; and the United States now solemnly agree that no persons,
except those herein authorized so to do, and except such officers,
agents, and employees of the Government as may be authorized to
enter upon Indian reservations in discharge of duties enjoined by
law, shall ever be permitted to pass over, settle upon, or reside in
the Territory described in this article except as herein otherwise
provided.

Article 3. It is further agreed by the Indians, parties hereto,
that henceforth they will and do hereby relinquish all claims and
rights in and to any portion of the United States or Territories,
except such as are embraced in the limits defined in the preceding
article.

Article 4. The United States agree to establish two agencies on
the reservation provided for in article 2, one for the Grand River,
Yampa and Uintah bands, on White River, and the other for the
Tabewatch, Mouache, Weeminuche and Capote bands, on Los Pinos
Creek on the reservation, and at its own proper expense to construct
at each of said agencies a warehouse or storeroom for the use of the
agent in storing goods belonging to the Indians, to cost not exceeding fifteen hundred dollars; an agency building for the residence of
the agent, to cost not exceeding three thousand dollars, and four
other buildings for a carpenter, farmer, blacksmith and miller,
each to cost not exceeding two thousand dollars; also a school house
or mission building, so soon as a sufficient number of children can
be induced by the agent to attend school, which shall not cost exceeding five thousand dollars.

The United States agree, further, to cause to be erected on said
reservation, and near to each agency herein authorized respectively,
a good waterpower sawmill, with a grist mill and a shingle mill attached, the same to cost not exceeding eight thousand dollars each;
provided, the same shall not be erected until such time as the Secretary of the Interior may think it necessary to the wants of the
Indians.

Article 5. The United States agree that the agents for said Indians, in the future, shall make their homes at the agency buildings; that they shall reside among the Indians, and keep an office
open at all times for the purpose of prompt and diligent inquiry
into such matters of complaint by and against the Indians as may be

presented for investigation under the provisions of their treaty stipulations, as also for the faithful discharge of other duties enjoined on them by law. In all cases of depredation on person or property they shall cause the evidence to be taken in writing and forwarded, together with their findings, to the Commissioner of Indian Affairs, whose decision, subject to the revision of the Secretary of the Interior, shall be binding on the parties to this treaty.

Article 6. If bad men among the whites or among other people, subject to the authority of the United States, shall commit any wrong upon the person or property of the Indians, the United States will, upon proof made to the agent and forwarded to the Commissioner of Indian affairs at Washington, proceed at once to cause the offender to be arrested and punished according to the laws of the United States, and also reimburse the injured person for the loss sustained.

If bad men among the Indians shall commit a wrong or depredation upon the person or property of any one, white, black or Indian, subject to the authority of the United States and at peace therewith, the tribes herein named solemnly agree that they will, on proof made to their agent and notice to him, deliver up the wrongdoer to the United States, to be tried and punished according to its laws, and in case they wilfully refuse so to do, the person injured shall be reimbursed for his loss from the annuities or other moneys due, or to become due to them, under this or other treaties made with the United States.

Article 7. If any individual belonging to said tribe of Indians or legally incorporated with them, being the head of a family, shall desire to commence farming, he shall have the privilege to select, in the presence and with the assistance of the agent then in charge, by metes and bounds, a tract of land within said reservation not exceeding one hundred and sixty acres in extent, which tract, when so selected, certified and recorded in the land book, as herein directed, shall cease to be held in common, but the same may be occupied and held in exclusive possession of the person selecting it and his family so long as he or they may continue to cultivate it. Any person over eighteen years of age, not being the head of a family, may, in like manner, select and cause to be certified to him or her for purposes of cultivation, a quantity of land not exceeding eighty acres in extent, and thereupon be entitled to the exclusive possession of the same as above directed.

For each tract of land so selected a certificate containing a description thereof and in the name of the person selecting it, with a certificate endorsed thereon that the same has been recorded, shall be delivered to the party entitled to it, by the agent, after the same shall have been recorded by him in a book to be kept in his office, subject to inspection, which said book shall be known as the "Ute Land Book."

The President may at any time order a survey of the reservation; and when so surveyed Congress shall provide for protecting the rights of such Indian settlers in their improvements, and may fix the character of the title held by each.

The United States may pass such laws on the subject of alienation and descent of property, and on all subjects connected with the government of the Indians on said reservation and the internal policies thereof, as may be thought proper.

Article 8. In order to insure the civilization of the bands entering into this treaty, the necessity of education is admitted, especially by such of them as are or may be engaged in either pastoral, agricultural or other peaceful pursuits of civilized life on said reservation, and they therefore pledge themselves to induce their children, male or female, between the ages of seven and eighteen years, to attend school; and it is hereby made the duty of the agent for said Indians to see that this stipulation is complied with to the greatest possible extent; and the United States agree that for every thirty children between said ages who can be induced to attend school a house shall be provided, and a teacher competent to teach the elementary branches of an English education shall be furnished, who will reside among said Indians, and faithfully discharge his or her duties as teacher, the provisions of this article to continue for not less than twenty years.

Article 9. When the head of a family or lodge shall have selected lands, and received his certificate as above described, and the agent shall be satisfied that he intends in good faith, to commence cultivating the soil for a living, he shall be entitled to receive seeds and agricultural implements for the first year not exceeding in value one hundred dollars, and for each succeeding year he shall continue to farm, for a period of three years or more, he shall be entitled to receive seeds and implements as aforesaid, not exceeding in value fifty dollars; and it is further stipulated that such persons as commence farming shall receive instructions from the farmer herein provided for; and it is further stipulated that an additional black-smith to the one provided for in the treaty of October 7th, 1863, referred to in article 1 of this treaty, shall be provided with such iron, steel and other material as may be needed for the Uintah, Yampa and Grand River agency, known as the White River agency.

Article 10. At any time after ten years from the making of this treaty, the United States shall have the privilege of withdrawing the farmers, blacksmiths, carpenters and millers herein, and in the treaty of October 7th, 1863, referred to in article 1 of this treaty, provided for, but in case of such withdrawal, an additional sum thereafter of ten thousand dollars per annum shall be devoted to the education of said Indians, and the Commissioner of Indian Affairs shall, upon careful inquiry into their condition, make such rules and regulations, subject to the approval of the Secretary of the Interior, for the expenditure of said sum as will best promote the educational and moral improvement of said Indians.

Article 11. That a sum, sufficient in the discretion of Congress, for the absolute wants of said Indians, but not to exceed thirty thousand dollars per annum, for thirty years, shall be expended, under the direction of the Secretary of the Interior, for clothing, blankets and such other articles of utility as he may think proper and necessary upon full official reports of the condition and wants of said Indians.

Article 12. That an additional sum, sufficient in the discretion of Congress (but not to exceed thirty thousand dollars per annum), to supply the wants of said Indians for food, shall be annually expended under the direction of the Secretary of the Interior, in supplying said Indians with beef, mutton, wheat, flour, beans and potatoes, until such time as said Indians shall be found to be capable of sustaining themselves.

Article 13. That for the purpose of inducing said Indians to adopt habits of civilized life and become self-sustaining, the sum of forty-five thousand dollars, for the first year, shall be expended, under the direction of the Secretary of the Interior, in providing each lodge or head of a family in said confederated bands with one gentle American cow, as distinguished from the ordinary or Mexican or Texas breed, and five head of sheep.

Article 14. The said confederated bands agree that whensoever, in the opinion of the President of the United States, the public interest may require it, that all roads, highways and railroads, authorized by law, shall have the right of way through the reservations herein designated.

Article 15. The United States hereby agree to furnish the Indians the teachers, carpenters, millers, farmers and blacksmiths, as herein contemplated, and that such appropriations shall be made from time to time, on the estimates of the Secretary of the Interior, as will be sufficient to employ such persons.

Article 16. No treaty for the cession of any portion or part of the reservation herein described, which may be held in common, shall be of any validity or force as against the said Indians, unless executed and signed by at least three-fourths of all the adult male Indians occupying or interested in the same; and no cession by the tribe shall be understood or construed in such manner as to deprive, without his consent, any individual member of the tribe of his right to any tract of land selected by him, as provided in article 1 of this treaty.

Article 17. All appropriations now made, or to be hereafter made, as well as goods and stock due these Indians under existing treaties, shall apply as if this treaty had not been made, and be divided proportionately among the seven bands named in this treaty, as also shall all annuities and allowances hereafter to be made; provided, that if any chief of either of the confederated bands make war against the people of the United States or in any manner violate this treaty in any essential part, said chief shall forfeit his position as chief and all rights to any of the benefits of this treaty; but further provided, any Indian of any of these confederated bands who shall remain at peace and abide by the terms of this treaty in all its essentials shall be entitled to its benefits and provisions, notwithstanding his particular chief and band may have forfeited their rights thereto.

FOOTNOTE

[1]*Senate Documents,* Volume II, p. 990.

APPENDIX II

TREATY NEGOTIATED WITH THE UTES—1873[1]

ARTICLES of convention, made and entered into at the Los Pinos agency for the Ute Indians, on the 13th day of September, 1873, by and between Felix R. Brunot, commissioner in behalf of the United States, and the chiefs, head men and men of the Uncompahgre, Tabequache (Tabeguache), Mouache, Capote, Weeminuche, Yampa, Grand River and Uintah bands of Ute Indians, witnesseth:

Article 1. The Confederated band of the Ute Nation hereby relinquish to the United States all right, title and claim, and interest in and to the following described portion of the reservation heretofore conveyed to them by the United States, viz.: Beginning at a point on the eastern boundary of said reservation, fifteen miles due north of the southern boundary of the Territory of Colorado, and running thence west on a line parallel to the said southern boundary to a point on said line twenty miles due east of the western boundary of Colorado Territory; thence north by a line parallel with the western boundary to a point ten miles north of the point where said line intersects the 38th parallel of north latitude; thence east to the eastern boundary of the Ute reservation, and thence south along said boundary to place of the beginning; provided, that if any part of the Uncompahgre Park shall be found to extend south of the north line of said described property, the same is not intended to be included therein, and is hereby reserved and retained as a portion of the Ute reservation.

Article 2. The United States shall permit the Ute Indians to hunt upon said lands so long as the game lasts and the Indians are at peace with the white people.

Article 3. The United States agrees to set apart and hold as a perpetual trust for the Ute Indians a sum of money, or its equivalent in bonds, which shall be sufficient to produce the sum of twenty-five thousand dollars ($25,000) per annum, which sum of twenty-five thousand dollars ($25,000) per annum shall be disbursed or invested at the discretion of the President, or as he may direct, for the use and benefit of the Ute Indians, annually forever.

Article 4. The United States agrees, so soon as the President may deem it necessary or expedient, to erect proper buildings and establish an agency for the Weeminuche, Mouache and Capote bands of Ute Indians at some suitable point to be hereafter selected, on the southern part of the Ute reservation.

Article 5. All the provisions of the treaty of 1868, not altered by this agreement, shall continue in force, and the following words from article 2 of said treaty, viz.:

"The United States now solemnly agrees that no persons, except those herein authorized to enter upon Indian reservations in discharge of duties enjoined by law, shall ever be permitted to pass over, settle upon or reside in the territory described in this article, except as herein otherwise provide," are hereby expressly reaffirmed, except so far as they applied to the country herein relinquished.

Artcle 6. In consideration of the services of Ouray, head chief of the Ute Nation, he shall receive a salary of one thousand dollars ($1,000.00) per annum for the term of ten years, or so long as he shall remain head chief of the Utes, and at peace with the people of the United States.

Article 7. This agreement is subject to ratification or rejection by the Congress of the United States and of the President.

FOOTNOTE
[1]*Senate Documents*, Volume I, p. 151.

APPENDIX III

THIRD TREATY WITH THE UTES—1880[1]

THE CHIEFS and head men of the confederated bands of the Utes now present in Washington hereby promise and agree to procure the surrender to the United States, for trial and punishment, if found guilty, of those members of their nation, not yet in the custody of the United States, who were implicated in the murder of United States Indian Agent N. C. Meeker, and the murder of and outrages upon the employees of the White River Agency on the twenty-ninth day of September, eighteen hundred and seventy-nine, and in case they do not themselves succeed in apprehending the said parties, presumably guilty of the above mentioned crime, that they will not in any manner obstruct, but faithfully aid, any officers of the United States, directed by the proper authorities, to apprehend such presumably guilty parties.

The said chiefs and head men of the confederated bands of Utes also agree and promise to use their best endeavors with their people to procure their consent to cede to the United States all the territory of the present Ute reservation in Colorado, except as hereinafter provided for their settlement.

The Southern Utes agree to remove to and settle upon the unoccupied agricultural lands on the La Plata River, in Colorado; and if there should not be a sufficiency of such lands on the La Plata River and its vicinity in Colorado, then upon such unoccupied agricultural lands as may be found in that vicinity and in the Territory of Utah.

The Uncompahgre Utes agree to remove to and settle upon agricultural lands on Grand River, near the mouth of Gunnison River, in Colorado, if a sufficient quanity of agricultural land shall be found there; if not, then upon such other unoccupied agricultural lands as may be found in that vicinity and in the Territory of Utah.

The White River Utes agree to remove to and settle upon agricultural lands on the Uintah reservation in Utah.

Allotments in severalty of said lands shall be made as follows:

To each head of a family one quarter of a section, with an additional quantity of grazing land not exceeding one-quarter of a section.

To each single person over eighteen years of age one-eighth of a section, with an additional quantity of grazing land not exceeding one-eighth of a section.

To each orphan child under eighteen years of age one-eighth of a section, with an additional quantity of grazing land not exceeding one-eighth of a section; and to each other person, under eighteen years of age, now living, or who may be born prior to said allotments, one-eighth of a section, with a like quantity of grazing land.

All allotments to be made with the advice of the commission hereinafter provided, upon the selection of the Indians, heads of families selecting for their minor children, and the agents making the allotment for each orphan child.

The said chiefs and head men of the confederated bands of Utes further promise that they will not obstruct or in any wise interfere with travel upon any of the highways now open or hereafter to be opened by lawful authority in or upon any of the lands to be set apart for their use by virtue of this agreement.

The said chiefs and head men of the confederated bands of Utes promise to obtain the consent of their people to the cession of the territory of their reservation as above on the following express conditions:

First: That the Government of the United States cause the lands so set apart to be properly surveyed and to be divided among the said Indians in severalty in the proportion hereinbefore mentioned, and to issue patents in fee simple to them respectively therefor, so soon as the necessary laws are passed by Congress. The title to be acquired by the Indians shall not be subject to alienation, lease, or incumbrance, either by voluntary conveyance of the grantee or by the judgment, order or decree of any court, or subject to taxation

of any character, but shall be and remain inalienable and not subject to taxation for the period of twenty-five years, and until such
time thereafter as the President of the United States may see fit to
remove the restriction which shall be incorporaed in the patents
when issued, and any contract made prior to the removal of such
restriction shall be void.

Second: That so soon as the consent of the several tribes of the
Ute Nation shall have been obtained to the provisions of this
agreement, the President of the United States shall cause to be
distributed among them in cash the sum of sixty thousand dollars of
annuities now due and provided for, and so much more as Congress
may appropriate for that purpose; and that a commission shall be
sent to superintend the removal and settlement of the Utes, and to
see that they are well provided with agricultural and pastoral lands
sufficient for their future support, and upon such settlement being
duly effected that they are furnished with horses, wagons, agricultural implements, and stock cattle sufficient for their reasonable
wants, and also such saw and grist mills as may be necessary to
enable them to commence farming operations, and that the money
to be appropriated by Congress for that purpose shall be appor-
tioned among the different bands of Utes in the following manner:
One-third to those who settle on the La Plata River and vicinity,
and one-sixth to those settling on the Uintah reservation.

Third: That in consideration of the cession of territory to be
made by the said confederated bands of the Ute Nation, the United
States, in addition to the annuities and sums for provisions and
clothing stipulated and provided for in existing treaties and laws,
agrees to set apart and hold, as a perpetual trust for the said Ute
Indians, a sum of money or its equivalent in bonds of the United
States, which shall be sufficient to produce the sum of fifty thousand
dollars per annum, which sum of fifty thousand dollars shall be
distributed per capita to them annually forever.

Fourth: That as soon as the President of the United States may
deem it necessary or expedient, the agencies for the Uncompahgre
and Southern Utes be removed to and established at suitable points,
to be hereafter selected, upon the lands to be set apart, and to aid
in the support of said Utes until such time as they shall be able to
support themselves, and that in the meantime the United States
Government will establish and maintain schools in the settlements

of the Utes, and make all necessary provision for the education of their children.

Fifth: All provisions of the treaty of March second, eighteen hundred and sixty-eight, and the act of Congress approved April twenty-ninth, eighteen hundred and seventy-four, not altered by this agreement, shall continue in force, and the following words from article three of said act, namely, "The United States agrees to set apart and hold, as a perpetual trust for the Ute Indians, a sum of money or its equivalent in bonds, which shall be sufficient to produce the sum of twenty-five thousand dollars per annum which sum of twenty-five thousand dollars per annum shall be disbursed or invested at the discretion of the President, or as he may direct, for the use and benefit of the Ute Indians forever," are hereby expressly reaffirmed.

Sixth: That the commissioners above mentioned shall ascertain what improvements have been made by any member or members of the Ute Nation upon any part of the reservation in Colorado to be ceded to the United States as above, and that payment in cash shall be made to the individuals having made and owning such improvements upon a fair and liberal valuation of the same by the said commission, taking into consideration the labor bestowed upon the land.

Done at the city of Washington this sixth day of March, Anno Domini eighteen hundred and eighty.

FOOTNOTE

[1]*Senate Documents*, Volume I, pp. 181, 182, 183.

APPENDIX IV

THORNBURG AMBUSH AND RESCUE

(Extract from an article entitled, "Three Indian Campaigns," by General Wesley Merritt, U. S. A., published in *Harper's New Monthly Magazine,* 1889. From files of J. L. Riland of Meeker.)

On the 1st of October, 1879, the garrison at Fort Russell, Wyoming Territory, was startled by the receipt of telegrams recounting a disaster that had overtaken the command of Major Thornburg, who was known to be marching to the relief of the white inhabitants of the Ute Indian Agency. In this command, which had been attacked by the Utes, was part of the garrison of Fort Russell.

"Major Thornburg is killed; Captain Payne and two other officers, including the surgeon of the command, are wounded. The command is surrounded and constantly pressed by the hostiles; fifty men are killed and wounded, and all the horses are killed."

These were the fragments of news which dribbled through the wires, all too slowly for the impatient comrades of the small beleagured force in the wilds of Colorado.

"You will proceed with all available troops in your command to the rescue of Payne and his sorely pressed command," said the dispatch from the comanding general of the department to the officer in command at Fort Russell. Officers were assembled and the orders for preparation given. No need to insist on haste; the dead, wounded, and beleagured were kith and kin to those going to the rescue, endeared by hundreds of associations which make men stick closer than brothers. Each officer went about his work with the coolness and precision of the usual preparation for a routine service, though there were decision and promptitude which told of the serious work ahead.

In four hours from the time the news first reached Fort Russell all the troops of cavalry, with their horses and equipments, for which there was transportation by rail, were on the cars, and running as fast as steam could carry them toward Rawlins, a point two hundred miles distant on the Union Pacific Railroad, from which the march was to commence across the country to the scene of disaster.

By daylight on the following morning (October 2nd) a force of about two hundred cavalry and less than one hundred and fifty infantry had collected at Rawlins station. The move to the relief of Payne and his command must be made as soon as sufficient force was collected. Payne had reported he was sorely pressed by the Indians on every side, and had many wounded, among the rest the medical officer. His supplies were sufficient to last for five days from the 29th of September. The way to the scene of the disaster was long, and succor must arrive in three days of the time still left for the troops at Rawlins. Other troops were being hurried forward, but they could not reach the railroad starting point for a day or two at least. Rumors were current that the Southern Utes had broken out, which would increase greatly the strength of the hostiles. The greater their strength, the less time remained for saving the shattered and maimed command. Even then the Ute Indians on the war-path had been largely augmented by the malcontents from kindred bands, and were making every effort to destroy the weak remnant of Thornburg's command.

In anticipation of the fewness of the available cavalry for the rescue, and with knowledge that no infantry unassisted could make the march in time to be of service, light wagons, with as good teams as the country could afford, had been ordered collected from the country around Rawlins, in which to transport the infantry. This was all done, and the supplies of every kind transferred to wagons and pack trains, so that the command marched out from Rawlins at eleven o'clock on the morning of October 2nd. There was a distance of 170 miles to be traversed before the fate of the besieged command could be determined.

The march was a cause for calculation and judgment. A single dash of fifty or even seventy-five miles can be made by horses as racing men say, on a breath, but at the end of this greatest distance still a hundred more miles were left to be accomplished. Too much haste at first, wearing out the horses, would leave the command afoot and helpless. Would the command reach its destination in time **was** one absorbing thought in the mind of every officer and trooper in the column.

It is difficult for one who has never marched on the plains to form a conception of the tedium and seeming slowness of the progress. The cavalry command scouting after Indians will see the landmarks, apparently a few miles off, made so by the clear atmosphere of the plains, stand out as though one could walk to them in a few hours, remain during the days of marching in the same places and with the same appearance. Were it not that nearer objects conveyed the fact of distance gained, one might easily imagine that he was journeying in a land where the efforts of motion were nullified by the sorcerer's art, and progress was impossible. And if this is so when a usual march is being made, who can tell the exasperation at the want of apparent progress on the road the rate of travel of which means life or death to those whom it is one's duty to save! At the end of the first ten hours from the start the relieving column had accomplished about forty-five miles. Everything was brought up, and the command was still in good condition. Here a halt was made till dawn of day, at break of which the onward march was resumed.

Let us now, while still marching forward, recall, as was done by everyone in the rescuing column hundreds of times, what had occurred to Thornburg's command. Ten days before the news of his disaster reached Fort Russell, Major Thornburg left Rawlins station with a force of calvary and infantry to protect the agency and its white inhabitants from the Indians they were there to feed and instruct. The Indians had grown restless under the efforts of the agent to teach them farming and the other industries of the whites, and the agent became anxious for the safety of his family and himself.

Thornburg moved leisurely through the country, making convenient camps after usual marches, without molestation, and not until the sixth day were any Indians seen. In the camp, after it was established on this day, several Ute Indians of prominence visited

Major Thornburg in the afternoon, talked freely and pleasantly with him and his officers, and departed about nightfall, apparently in a most friendly mood. This was more than a hundred miles from the agency. After this Thornburg pursued his march without incident.

On the morning of the 29th of September, while his command was separated by a short distance, he came on the Utes in a strong force near a pass in the mountains which bounded their reservation. Their attitude was extremely hostile. While incredulous of their intent to fight, he took the precaution to deploy the part of the command with him, at the same time by signs trying to open communication with the Indians. His overtures were met by a volley from the Indians, which was at once replied to by the troops, the skirmish line being slowly withdrawn to connect with the rest of the command and to protect the wagons.

In battle, Indians always send warriors to the flanks and to the rear of the force with which they fight. It has thence passed into a proverb that "there is no rear" in an Indian engagement. The Utes pursued these tactics with Thornburg's command, in the meantime violently engaging his skirmishers in front. While concentrating his command, and when a few hundred yards from the wagons, Thornburg was killed. The command was united at the wagons, and, surrounded by the hostiles, hurried measures were taken for defence, the fighting on each side being continued with desperation. The wagons were formed in an irregular circle, and the contents, together with the dead animals which had fallen near by, were used in constructing a sort of defensive work. Within this ghastly protection the wounded men were conveyed, and soon, with the implements in the wagons, a circular rifle-pit was constructed. And now a new danger threatened. A high wind arose soon after the commencement of the attack, and the Indians fired the dry grass and brush to the windward of the wagons, and taking advantage of the smoke and fire, made a furious attack in the hope of burning the defenders out. This was a terrible danger, but with coolness and courage the troops combated the flames, and it was not long before their fury was expended.

Later in the day the Utes made a violent onslaught on the breastworks, but being repulsed, settled down to watch their prey in the hope that starvation or lack of water would finish the work. During the night the means of defence were strengthened, and water was obtained by force from the stream near by for the famishing wounded and suffering defenders. Couriers were also sent out into the darkness in different directions with the hope that the distressful condition of the command could be made known and relief hurried to them. The couriers succeeded in passing out, and carried the news that started the relief command from Fort Russell.

On the last day of September, and for four days in October, the command contended with the Indians, repulsing attacks made from time to time, answering shot with shot and taunt with taunt—for many of the Utes spoke English. Each night the defense works were strengthened, and each day defended against renewed attacks. A deep square pit was dug in the interior of the circle, in which the wounded were made comfortable, the medical officer, though wounded himshelf, dressing the wounds of those most needing attention. At night, also, armed parties sent out for water succeeded in bringing in a supply, though at times meeting resistance and fighting for what was obtained. In this way the time for five long days and nights was occupied, who can tell with what anxieties, gloomy forebodings, and doubting hopes!

In the meantime the rescuing force was losing no time. Without drawing rein, save for a needed rest at intervals to conserve strength for the whole of the work, the command pressed on wth unflagging energy, marching with advance-guard, and at times flankers, to prevent the possibility of ambuscade or surprise. The country was quiet, and no signs of Indians were discovered. A halt was made on the second night, after completion of little less than two-thirds of the whole distance to be accomplished. At daydawn the morning of the 4th of October the march was resumed. The unfinished distance must be completed by the following dawn. About one hundred miles had already been accomplished in twenty-three marching hours. More than seventy miles, to be marched over in daylight and darkness, in the next twenty-four hours, was before the command. This would require little less, if all went well, than twenty hours' constant marching!

In these days of rapid transit it is not easy for people to bring their ideas of travel down to the rate of march of a cavalry column. This, if long distances are marched, cannot safely exceed, including halts for rest, four miles per hour. A single horseman can do more than this, for he can regulate the rate according to the road, and he has not the dust and crowding of a mass of cavalry horses on narrow road to contend with. Besides, the single horseman provides himself with the best of horses, while the march of a cavalry column must be regulated to meet the abilities of the least enduring animal. All these elements entered into the calculation of the march of the rescuing force. It must make the march, and that, too, with undiminished numbers.

On this day's march several settlers were met by the command, fleeing for safety, and rumors of murders and depredations by the Indians were received from all quarters. At one point the head of the column was approached by an excited party asking medical assistance, who led the medical officer to a wagon in which a citizen was lying on an improvised bed, who was an unsightly mass of wounds, and had been left by the Indians for dead. His companion had been killed. When it was discovered that the wagon body in which he lay was nearly half full of loose cartridges, in which he had been trading with the Indians, sympathy for him was greatly diminished.

As night came on the difficulties of marching were much increased by the darkness and rough roads. From time to time halts had to be made, and staff officers sent to the rear to direct the column in the darkness and see that all kept well closed. After a seemingly interminable season of marching by the uncertain light of a waning moon, in which objects were dimly defined and always distorted, the hour indicated to the weary though watchful horsemen that they were approaching the scene of the conflict. No sound broke the stillness of the chilly night save the steady tramp of the horses and the rattle and jingle of the equipments of the men. The infantry part of the command, owing to the darkness and difficulties of travel, had fallen behind. A blackened heap of ashes on the highway, with fragments of iron and chains and pieces of harness and rubbish, marked where a train loaded with stores for the agency had been burnt, and further on the bodies of the slaughtered trainmen, with distorted features and staring eyes, told all too plainly of their short run for life—of the mercy they had pled for, and how their prayers had been answered by the merciless foe. These were not cheering omens. Had Payne and his men shared a like fate? No one had come to tell. But it would soon be known.

"It can't be far from here," said the guide, for the third time, as the command was brought to a halt, and every one strained eyes and ears for a sight of the surrounding country or a sound from the front. A bugler with his trumpet ready was close to hand to sound the call known as "Officers Call" in the cavalry, a certain sign of recognition, that there might be no collision with friends who, hearing the tramp of horses, might mistake the force for foes. Presently the guide satisfied himself that the command was near the place, and the clear notes of "the trumpet" awakened the echoes of the night.

Captain Payne in recounting the event says: "Believing it just possible for help to reach us next morning, I directed one of my trumpeters to be on the alert for the expected signal. And so it was; just as the first gray of the dawn appeared, our listening ears caught the sound of 'Officer's Call' breaking the silence of the morning, and filling the valley with the sweetest music we had ever heard. Joyously the reply rang out from our corral, and the men, rushing from their rifle-pits, made the welkin ring with their glad cheers!"

APPENDIX V

MRS. PRICE'S ACCOUNT OF MEEKER MASSACRE

(Full statement of Mrs. Shadrick Price—a victim of the Meeker Massacre—to the special commission appointed to investigate the Ute uprising. This statement was made in Denver on October 31, 1879).[1]

My name is Flora Ellen Price. I was born in Adams county, near Quincy, Illinois, and was married when I was twelve years old to Mr. Price. I was married in Wyoming, and moved to Nevada, where I saw much of the Shoshone Indians. I went from Nevada to Girard, Kansas, and thence to Greeley with my husband, and thence to White River, where he was employed as a farmer for the agency. At first the Indians were very kind. They came in to see us, and their squaws would pick up my children and make much of them. With the exception of Johnson and two or three other chiefs they didn't seem to be pleased with the agent. The trouble grew out of the plowing and the various improvements. My husband said the agency employees told him that the agent was shot at by some young Indians there, and the agent said so himself when they were talking it over in the room one evening. It was the general opinion also that he had been shot at by the Indians, but he did not want it to be known, on account of his family and because it would worry his wife. Besides, he was not entirely certain as to who fired and for what purpose.

The Indians were treated well as far as I know. The agency was kept in fine shape. Many improvements were made. A good table was set for the employees, and they were only charged $3.50 a week, which is much less than is charged at the other agencies, where it is $4 and $5. The best provisions were used and bought at Rawlins. Mr. Meeker refused to have any Indian blankets or Indian goods in the house so as to be free from all irregularities or charges of corruption. The Indians frequently ate at his private table, and the chiefs came and went when they pleased. They were treated kindly, but not allowed to take charge of the place, as they sometimes wanted to do.

The whole trouble, I think, was because the soldiers were coming in. They got very mad and on Saturday moved their tents across the river some distance and became uneasy and very anxious to know when the soldiers were coming in and if they were coming to the agency. I did not hear them make any threats against the agent. Douglass' boy shot himself accidentally in the foot, and Douglass remained at the river with several Indians. They ran up American flags on Sunday morning. On that day the Indians were all around the place. There were a good many of Jack's band who seemed to be very friendly, but still they were frightened a little about the soldiers coming in, and on Sunday night all had a big war dance about a quarter of a mile from the agency. There were a good many present, including the principal chiefs headed by Douglass. Just before daylight on Monday morning Douglass got up and made a big speech to the Utes. The massacre followed on that day. Between the time of the dance and the time of the massacre I heard that Jack said he would meet the soldiers and get them in the canyon where they would fight. Just before noon on Monday an Indian runner came in from where the Indians were on Milk Creek, and we supposed he brought some news to Douglass that they were fighting and perhaps had killed some Utes.

Douglass and several other Indians came in, and at dinner Douglass was very familiar, laughing and joking in such a manner one would not have thought anything was the matter with him, though he had previously taken his little boy from the school and said he was afraid of the soldiers but that he would bring him back that evening. He picked around the table, was laughing and joking with Mrs. Meeker, Josephine and me. He drank a little coffee and ate some bread and butter. Suddenly he turned around and went out doors. Mr. Price and Mr. Thompson and Frank Dresser were work-

ing on the building a few steps from the house. I saw him there
when I went out after my little girl. Douglass seemed to be in very
good spirits and was joking with the men. I had just returned and
began washing some clothes when the Indians fired. I saw, I should
judge, about twenty Utes around the houses. The firing party was
down at the barn, so Frank Dresser said. I saw the Ute, I did not
know his name, fire at Mr. Price and Mr. Thompson and Frank.
He was a White River Ute. I saw Mr. Thompson either running
with the purpose to escape or because he was shot.

I rushed in, took my baby and ran to my room. Frank Dresser
went to the boy's room, where he found the Indians had stolen all
their guns. He ran in after Mr. Price's gun and came out and shot
through the window Chief Johnson's brother, who died two days
afterwards. We ran to Josephine's room. In a few minutes after
twenty or thirty shots crashed through our two windows, we crawled
under the bed. The Indians were shooting all around. I could hear
reports of guns in all directions and glass falling from windows.
Josephine said the milk room is the safest place, and we ran there
as quickly as possible, and reached the milk room just as Frank
Dresser came in, and we all sat there quietly. My little boy was very
nervous. Mary (the other child) was quiet, and we remained there
all the afternoon till nearly sundown and until they set the buildings on fire. The shooting had ceased, and we began to see the
smoke curling through the cracks.

I said, "Josie, we have got to get out of here; you take Mary; I'll
take baby and we will try to escape in the sage brush across the
road."

She took Mary's hand and we went out, but first went to Mr.
Meeker's room. It was not disturbed. The doors were open and the
books were lying on the stand as he had left them. It was at first
thought we had better secrete ourselves in there, but I advised that
we had better try to escape then, as the Indians were busily engaged
in stealing the annuity goods. They had broken open the warehouse and were packing blankets on their ponies.

We started for the garden when Frank said, "Perhaps we can hide
in the sage brush and escape."

He ran through the gate in the field with Mr. Price's rifle. He
was near the field when I last saw him, and I did not suppose he was
hurt at all. Mrs. Meeker and I went inside the field through the
wire fence, and the Indians saw us and came toward us on the run,

firing as they ran. Some were on foot and some were on horseback
and they said, "Good squaw; come squaw; no shoot squaw."

We then came out as it was of no use to run, and gave ourselves
up. I hesitated to go with them at first, and told them they would
burn me or shoot me, but they said they would not harm us, and
then came up and took my hands and pulled me through an irrigat-
ing ditch. Then they took me to the river as fast as they could, one
on each side of me, to where the horses were, and then seated me
on a pile of poles. I asked them if I could go back to the agency and
get my money and clothes. They said no. I told them I was thirsty,
and a Ute who claimed to be an Uncompahgre—I don't know his
name—caught me by the shoulder and led me down to Douglass'
Spring, where he dipped up a pail of water and drank and then
gave it to me. We then went back and the Indian packed his effects
on a pony and spread a blanket on the saddle and told me to mount
my horse. My boy baby was with me and Mary was with Josephine.
She had taken the little girl from the first and carried my oldest
child, Mary, all through our captivity. We were in three separate
parties, but all in one company, not very far apart, through the
different journeys. I mounted the pony and the Indian took a seat
behind me. I held the baby in front of me and guided the animal.
About eight or ten Indians were in the company. Jim Johnson, a
White River Ute, rode out in the party with us. He did not say
anything to me only that he was going to take me to the Utes' squaw
camp, and he said the Utes "no hurt" me. I think he had a little
whisky in him.

The road over the large mountains was so steep it was all I could
do to sit on the horse. By this time it was quite dark. The Indian
that rode behind me pulled a watch out of his pocket and asked me
if I recognized it. I told him I thought I did but could tell better in
the morning. He took it from his neck and put the leather guard
around my neck and said it was my watch. I have worn the watch
ever since. It was Mr. Post's and belonged to his father; it was a
family relic. Mr. Post was chief clerk at the agency and had been
secretary of the Greeley colony, and was well known in Yonkers,
N. Y., where for many years he was postmaster and town clerk. This
Indian treated me tolerably well during the journey.

When we arrived at the camp that night a squaw came and took
my little boy from the horse and cried over him like a child. I
dismounted and sat down in Pursune's camp. I wasn't at all hungry,

and when they offered me coffee, cold meat and bread I could not eat. After a while Pursune's squaw got over her weeping, when they talked and laughed. All I could understand was when they repeated the soldiers' names and counted what number of men they had killed at the agency. They said they had killed nine. At first they said ten, and I told them differently, as I thought Frank had escaped. They asked me how many, and seemed to accept my statement as correct.

They spread some blankets for me to lie on, but I could not sleep. The moon shone very bright and everything looked ghastly. In the morning I went to Pursune's tent and sat by the fire. I was cold, for I had nothing to wear except a calico dress and shoes. I sat there weeping—I could not help it—with my little boy in my arms. The squaws came around and talked and looked at me and laughed and made fun of me. I didn't understand what they said, only occasionally a word. After a time some of the men came in and talked to the squaws and looked at me and laughed. The Uncompahgre Ute in whose charge I seemed to be went off after his horses and said at noon he would be back. He came about half-past twelve and brought two horses with him and said he was going to fight the soldiers. He put on his saddle, tied two blankets behind, put on his cartridge box, containing a good many cartridges, and rode off. He said he would send a squaw after me, and I should be moved from that camp and remain until he returned from fighting the soldiers. One of the squaws brought a blanket and gave it to me. I went along with her, and they told me then to go to work and bake some biscuits. I had them build a fire and bring water, and I baked some biscuits and made coffee and ate pretty heartily myself, the first I had eaten since I left the agency.

About an hour after supper an old squaw ordered me to go with her to another tent to sleep, so I went to Henry James' tent, where I sat down. They had no fire but soon made one and the squaws crowded around. Henry asked me a few questions. He said he told the Utes not to murder the people at the agency. He had been assisting the issuing clerk and acted as interpreter. He said they were friendly and he liked them very much. He said the Utes told him he was nothing but a little boy for refusing to kill the white men at the agency, but when they called him a boy, he said it was too much for him. He had no more to say after that. He asked me if I was going to stay all night in his tent. I said the squaw had brought me over there to sleep. He said, "All right; you stay here all night." So his squaw made me a very nice bed of about ten blankets. I went to bed and she tucked me in quite nicely. I slept well, got up, washed myself, combed my hair and felt pretty well. Henry's squaw cooked breakfast. She made bread and prepared some coffee and fried venison, and there was another squaw who brought in some fried potatoes.

I ate breakfast with my little boy in my arms, and presently Chief Johnson came in, looking very angry and troubled. He said, gruffly, "Hello, woman" and shook hands. He sat down and presently three more Utes came in. Johnson got out his pipe and they all had a smoke around, and they talked about the soldiers and their big battle.

Henry said to me, "You go now with Johnson to see your little girl, who is with Josephine." So I mounted the horse behind Chief Johnson and rode about five miles; when I came up to Douglass' camp I first saw Mrs. Meeker, and I went up to her, shook hands and kissed her, and felt very badly for her. She said, "Don't make any fuss."

Josephine and my little girl had been to a brook to get a drink. We sat down and had a nice talk until the squaws came and said I must go to Johnson's tent and the little girl to Pursune's. Miss Josie went down to Johnson's tent, where they put down Mrs. Meeker's comforter for me to sit on, and asked if I was hungry. I told them yes, and they went to work and cooked some dinner for me.

The next day we moved from that place to another camp. It was a very nice place, with grass two feet high, and a nice brook of clear, cold water flowing through it. The Indians had killed many soldiers, and were prancing around in their coats and hats, putting on airs and imitating soldiers and making fun of them while going through a burlesque drill, and making believe they were the greatest warriors in the West. They took a great fancy to my little child and wanted to keep him. They crept into the tent after him, and when they found they could not steal him, they offered three ponies for him. In the afternoon, about 2 o'clock, they cut a lot of sage brush, piled it up and spread over it the clothes they had stolen from the soldiers. Four of the Indians then began to dance around them and at intervals fell on their knees before them and thrust their knives into them and went through a mimic massacre of soldiers. Other Utes kept joining the party that was dancing until a ring was made as large as a good sized house. They would first run away, then turn and dance back the other way, yelling and howling like frescoed devils. They had war suits, fur caps with eagle feathers and they looked strangely hideous. They wanted Miss Josie and me to dance with them. We told them we could not: "We no sabe dance."

That afternoon Mrs. Meeker came over and we had an old-fashioned talk. She told us her troubles. They had threatened to stab her with knives, she said. Charlie, Chief Douglass' son-in-law, soon came around in a very bad humor, and as he could speak good English, we didn't dare to talk much after he appeared. Mrs. Meeker said she felt as though she might be killed any night; that they treated her very meanly. Josephine seemed down-hearted, though she was plucky. I tried to cheer her all I could. The Indians would not let us go alone any distance from the camp. They asked me if I had any money, and I told them I did not, as it was all burned. We asked them where the soldiers were, and they said they were down in that cellar, meaning the great canyon, where they had them hemmed in. They said the Indians would lay around on the mountains and kill the soldiers' horses. The soldiers would not appear at all in the daytime. At night they would slip out, only to be shot by the Indians. They threatened if I attempted to run away they would shoot me. Johnson put a gun to my forehead and told me he would kill me. I said, "Shoot away. I don't care if I die. Shoot if you want to."

He laughed then, and would say, "Brave squaw; good squaw; no scare."

They also said Josephine would very soon die, as she drank no coffee and ate very little. I told them it was the same at the agency, that she ate little and drank no coffee. They talked it over among themselves and said no more about it. They made fun of Mrs. Meeker, and said maybe the Utes will kill her. I said to them, "No, don't you kill my mother; I heap like her." "All right," they would say. "Pretty good mother; pretty good mother." Coho pointed his gun at me and threatened to kill me a good many times.

The Indians held considerable conversation with each other in regard to the massacre and tried to get information from us. They told stories of how the fight occurred and who were concerned in it. From all that I heard of their talk I think Antelope or Pauvitz shot the agent. Chief Johnson said he shot Thornburg in the forehead three times with the pistol, and then got off his pony and went to him and pounded him in the head and smashed his skull in. Then took some of his clothes off, but I did not see any of them worn in camp. The Indians Ebenezer, Douglass, Persune, Tim Johnson and Charley Johnson were at the agency massacre. Jack was not there. He was fighting the soldiers. Johnson's brother Iata was killed by Frank Dresser. Washington was on the ground. They all had guns and helped to shoot. Josephine said she saw an Indian named Creep there. I did not see any of the bodies at the agency. I only heard the firing toward the buildings where the men were working.

The Utes said they were going to kill all soldiers, and that the women should always live in the Utes' camp, excepting Mrs. Meeker. Douglass said she could go home by and by, when she would perhaps see Frank Dresser, who the Indians thought had escaped. They made me do more drudgery than they did Josephine. They made her cook and me carry water. They told me to saddle the pony, and I told them I did not know how. One day we left camp about three o'clock in the morning. We had no breakfast; only Josephine had roasted some meat on the coals in the morning. We rode all day in the thick dust without water. We reached Grand River about sundown where we camped in the sage brush. To the south the mountains were very high and the country was bleak and bare on the north. The Indians said they were going to take us to the agency. The next morning we went about five or six miles and camped in a grassy place where the horses could get enough to eat and remained there two days. We were camped very near a large mountain.

Johnson had field glasses, and all day with his field glass he was watching the soldiers and only came down to his supper. The Indians took turns watching during the night, and during the day they covered the hills and watched the soldiers through their glasses. Runners came in with foaming steeds constantly. At last news was received that the soldiers were on White River, moving south. At this Johnson was very angry. In the morning the ponies were uneasy, and they could not catch them. Johnson's young squaw did not get around to suit him, so he took a black snake whip, caught her by the hair and gave her a severe whipping. She cried and screamed. He then went to help his other squaw, Susan, Chief Ouray's sister, pack up. They put us on one horse and strapped my little girl in a blanket behind Josephine. I had my baby in front of me. Johnson was very mad and pointed his gun at each one of us. I told him to shoot me in the forehead. He said, "No good squaw; no scare." We started for another camping place south of the Grand River.

At last, one evening we heard that white men were coming from the Uncompahgre Agency of Chief Ouray to treat for our release. The next day the men came, and I told Johnson's wife that we wanted to wash some clothes. She gave us some matches and a couple of kettles and I went down to the creek to wash. While I was there Jim Johnson came with a couple of shirts for me to cleanse. He then went away, but soon came back again and said to me, "Don't you come to the camp, for we are going to have a big talk with all the Utes. Don't come until Coos comes after you." Coos is his young squaw.

Mrs. Meeker and I remained there in the brush all day, and dinner was sent to us by the squaws. Mrs. Meeker felt very much revived. You would not have thought she was the same woman. Captain Cline saw me in the brush and I held up my hands. He seemed to be looking at me, but presently he turned away as if the Indians were watching him. He did not let the Indians know he saw me. Presently a Ute came down and said to Mrs. Meeker, "Come mother; white man saw." So I took the clothes which I had washed under my arm and we walked joyfully to the tent. There we met General Adams, Captain Cline, Mr. Sherman, the Los Pinos agency clerk, and their party. They spoke to Mrs. Meeker first, they said, "How do you do?" with a deep and pathetic emphasis. They then shook hands with us till our hearts burned. One of the men said, "Can you give me a description of your captivity?" and we sat down and had a talk. The Utes all laughed at us. We did not have but a few minutes' conversation for fear it would not be good for us. Mrs. Meeker was talking with General Adams. He said she looked as if she were starved. He gave her a piece of cracker and some oysters. The Indians had already opened the cans, but, not knowing what they were, looked on with surprise, but they ate all the canned fruit and got away with some blankets.

In regard to my days of captivity I can only say the Indians were at times lively and joked with us, so that I was forced to laugh a good many times at their strange humor when I did not feel like it. It seemed to please them very much. They would say "Wano momets" (good woman). When Josephine came in they would say she was cross. She was very much grieved, and when her blood was up, she talked to them in a lively strain and made them treat Mrs. Meeker better. After Johnson and Mrs. Meeker had talked together about the agent, Mrs. Meeker came to Johnson's to stay. He treated her with great care. Previously she was not welcome. The meanest thing they did to the poor little woman was to frighten her with their knives and horrible grimaces and bad stories. They tried to scare us all out of our wits.

I think Douglass is the worst of the Indians. Jack is pretty mean also—mean enough for any purpose, no matter how bad. Johnson is the best. Johnson's wife was very kind. She treated me just like a mother, though sometimes when tired she would order me to get water. She treated my little girl very kindly, made moccasins for her, and grieved over her and my boy as if they were her own. She said the Utes had killed the child's papa. "Utes no good." She was for peace. She was Chief Ouray's sister, and Ouray was friendly to the whites and had sent messages to her to see that the whites were not abused, and should be returned soon.

The Indians laid all blame on Mr. Meeker. They said he brought the soldiers in and would have Jack, Pauvitz, Douglass and other chiefs, including Johnson, taken up for stealing and put in the calaboose. They said Meeker made great pictures of his being shot and had sent them to Washington. The Indians said they afterward found these pictures on Thornburg's body; that they had been sent by Meeker to inflame the soldiers, as the pictures represented the treatment the agency employes would receive from the Indians, and the soldiers must come to prevent it.

After we were released we stopped all night at Johnson's camp, and started early the next morning on ponies for the wagons, which had been left at the end of the road, about forty miles south toward the Uncompahgre river. General Adams had left us and gone to see the soldiers, so Captain Cline was in charge of the party and our escort to the wagons on the way back. The Indian escort, which had accompanied us for a time, left us, and Captain Cline grew suspicious. He was an old pioneer, had served in the army and had fought the Indians in New Mexico, and traveled over the Western Country so much that although a great friend of Ouray and his Indians, still he was suspicious of these savages and thought that while the escort had been with the White River Indians they had become corrupted. So when he saw that they had left us, he put spurs to his horse and pushed on ahead of the party to where the wagons were. He was afraid that they would cut the harness to pieces or do some mischief to prevent the captives from leaving immediately. This would keep them in the neighborhood, so that in case General Adams failed in stopping hostilities by a general pow-wow, they could recapture us and hold us as hostages for a further treaty.

Captain Cline reached the wagons in a short time, and as he suspected, found the Indians seated around the wagons in a body, with most of the blankets lying on the ground already divided among them. They had also got hold of the boxes of provisions and canned fruit which General Adams had brought for us. They had burst them open and were eating the contents. Captain Cline is personally acquainted with many of the Indians, and he completely astonished them. Jumping off his horse he threw the reins on the ground and rushing forward in great anger he shouted, "Chief Ouray shall hear of this and will settle with you."

He picked up an axe and began to split kindling wood to prepare for the captives. His object was to keep the axe in his hand and be master of the situation until the main party should arrive. He feared treachery, and, putting on a bold front, he made it pretty lively for the Indians. They fell back, got off the blankets, and gave up the canned fruit. Captain Cline threw the blankets on the wagon with what canned provisions there were left. Shortly after this occurrence we arrived with Mr. Sherman. We then traveled on to Chief Ouray's house.

Captain Cline was met by Ouray at the gate. The good chief looked at him a moment and said, "Captain, tell me how you found things when you reached the wagons."

The Captain was surprised, narrated the facts as I have stated. Ouray listened a moment and grimly smiling said, "Yes, you reached the wagons at such a time and you found Utes around the wagons eating fruit. I know all about it. Ouray not a fool. I had good and true Indians in the mountains around the wagons. They look down and see bad Indians, and then when wagons start safely the good Indians run back to Ouray on fast horses and tell Ouray, and Ouray make up his mind about it. Bad Ute can't fool Ouray."

The chief said this in broken English to the Captain, but when he spoke to Mr. Pollock, he conversed in eloquent and melodious Spanish, for he had been educated among the Spanish Mexicans of

Taos down on the border, and his words are always delivered with great fluency.

We were all treated well at Ouray's house. It had Brussels carpet, window curtains, stoves, good beds, glass windows, spittoons, rocking chairs, camp stools, mirrors and an elegantly carved bureau. We were received as old and long lost friends. Mrs. Ouray wept for our hardships, and her motherly face, dusky but beautiful with sweetness and compassion, was wet with tears. We left her crying. From this point we took the United States mail coaches with fleet horses and expert drivers. The journey over lofty mountains for three days and one night brought us out of the San Juan country to the swiftly flowing Rio Grande. The Indian Reservation was seventy miles behind us. Two ranges of mountains lay between us and that captivity of terror. We could not forget the noble Ouray and his true friends who lived there, yet it made our tired hearts beat rapturously when we saw the stam cars at Alamosa.

FOOTNOTE

[1]*The Greeley Tribune,* Nov. 19, 1879. A copy of this paper hangs in the Meeker Hotel at Meeker, Colorado.

BIBLIOGRAPHY

I BOOKS

Beckwith, Lieutenant E. G., *Reports of Explorations and Surveys,* Vol. II, "Reports of Explorations for a Route for the Pacific Railroad by Captain J. W. Gunnison," Beverly Tucker, Printer, Washington, D. C., 1855.

Bolton, Herbert E., *Pageant in the Wilderness,* Utah State Historical Society, Salt Lake City, 1950.

Carins, Mary Lyons, *The Pioneers,* The World Press, Inc., Denver, Colorado, 1946.

Carhart, Arthur H., *Colorado,* Coward-McCann, Inc., New York, 1932.

Colorado Writers Project of W.P.A., *Colorado,* Hastings House, New York, 1941, pp. 289-290.

Daniels, Helen Sloan, (compiler) *The Ute Indians of Southwestern Colorado,* Durango Public Library Museum Project, Durango, Colo., 1941.

Densmore, Frances, *Northern Ute Music,* Government Printing office, Washington, D. C., 1922, Smithsonian Institution, Bureau of American Ethnology, Bulletin 75.

Hafen, Leroy R. and Ann W., *Colorado,* The Old West Publishing Company, Denver, Colorado, 1949.

Hall, Frank, *History of the State of Colorado,* volumes II and IV. The Blakely Printing Company, Chicago, Ill., 1895.

Hanchett, Lafayettt, *The Old Sheriff and Other True Tales,* Mergent Press, New York, 1937.

Harris, W. R., *The Catholic Church in Utah* (1776-1909), Intermountain Catholic Press, Salt Lake City, 1909. (Escalante's journal.)

Huntington, D. B., *Vocabulary of the Utah and Sho-Sho-Ne or Snake Dialects with Indian Legends and Traditions,* Salt Lake City, Utah, 1872.

Ingersoll, Ernest, *Knocking Around the Rockies,* Harper & Brothers, New York, 1883.

Jocknick, Sidney, *Early Days on the Western Slope of Colorado,* The Carson-Harper Company, Denver, 1913.

Leckenby, Charles H., *The Tread of Pioneers,* The Steamboat Pilot Press, Steamboat Springs, Colorado, 1945.

Linton, Ralph, *Acculturation in Seven American Indian Tribes,* Chapter III, D. Appleton-Century Company, New York, 1940.

Sarah Platt Decker Chapter of the D.A.R. at Durango, Colorado, *Pioneers of the San Juan,* Volume I, The Out West Printing & Stationery Company, Colorado Springs, 1942.

Sarah Platt Decker Chapter of the D.A.R. at Durango, Colorado, *Pioneers of the San Juan,* Volume II, Durango Printing Company, Durango, Colorado, 1946.

Sarah Platt Decker Chapter of the D.A.R. at Durango, Colorado, *Pioneers of the San Juan,* Volume III, Durango Printing Company, Durango, Colorado, 1952.

II DOCUMENTS AND RECORDS OF THE
UNITED STATES GOVERNMENT

Bureau of Indian Affairs, Letters Received 1879, Colorado M 1862.

Commissioner of Indian Affairs, *Annual Reports,* 1879, XXXII.

Compilation of Material Relating to the Indians of the United States, etc., Including Certain Laws and Treaties Affecting Such Indians by Subcommittee on Indian Affairs of the Committee on Public Lands, House of Representatives, June 13, 1950.

Mansfield to Commissioner of Indian Affairs, October 18, 1879.

Bureau of Indian Affairs, Letters Received 1879, Colorado M 2096.

Meeker to Commissioner of Indian Affairs, July 15, 1879. Records of the Bureau of Indian Affairs, Letters Received 1879, Colorado M 1509. National Archives Record Group 75.

Meeker to Commissioner of Indian Affairs, September 8, 1879, Records of the Bureau of Indian Affairs, Letters Received 1879, Colorado M 1862.

Records of the Bureau of Indian Affairs, *Roster of Agency Employees,* 1879-80.

Report of the Board of Indian Commissioners, 1872, p. 109. Official document found among the unpublished papers of the Indian Bureau now housed in the National Archives Building.

"Reports of Explorations and Surveys . . . from the Mississippi River to the Pacific Ocean" . . . 1853-54, II, 12, Senate Ex. Doc. No. 78, 33rd Congress.

Secretary of the Interior Carl Schurz to Commissioner of Indian Affairs, October 11, 1879, Bureau of Indian Affairs, Letters Received 1879, Colorado I 2131.

Senate Documents, Volume I, "Indian Affairs, Laws, and Treaties," Document No. 452, pp. 181, 182, 183.

Senate Documents, Volume II, p. 990.

Senate Documents, No. 78, 33rd Congress, 2nd Session.

United States Congress, 46th Congress, 2nd Session, 1879-1880, "House Miscellaneous Document 38."

United States Statutes at Large, Volume 9, p. 984.

United States Statutes at Large, Volume 13, p. 673.

III INTERVIEWS

Ashbaugh, William (Towaoc), Employee at Ute Mountain Agency.

Aspaas, Hans (Ignacio), A pioneer of the Ignacio area.

Bennett, Robert L. (Ignacio), Present Superintendent of the Consolidated Ute Agency.

Curry, Reginald O., Manager of Uintah and Ouray Reservation.

Harriett Why (Towaoc), Member of the Ute Mountain Tribe.

La Plata County Interviews, Unpublished work of the C.W.A. workers for the State Historical Society, 1933-34. In possession of the State Historical Society of Colorado.

Moffat County Interviews, Unpublished work of the C.W.A. workers for the State Historical Society, 1933-34. In possession of the State Historical Society of Colorado.

Otero and Montezuma County Interviews, Unpublished works of C.W.A. workers for the State Historical Society, 1933-34. In possession of the State Historical Society of Colorado.

Rio Blanco County Interviews, Unpublished works of C.W.A. workers for the State Historical Society, 1933-34. In possession of the State Historical Society of Colorado.

Routt and Arapahoe County Interviews, Unpublished work of C.W.A. workers for the State Historical Society, 1933-34. In possession of the State Historical Society of Colorado.

Sunshine Smith (Ignacio), Member of the Southern Utes' Tribal Council.

White, Robert B. (Towaoc), Rehabilitation Director of the Ute Mountain Tribe.

IV MISCELLANEOUS

Borland, Lois (English instructor-director), "Historical Sketches of Early Gunnison" by Class of 1916 of Colorado State Normal School at Gunnison, Colorado, June 1, 1916. (Pamphlet)

Consolidated Ute Agency Annual Report (1954-1955). In possession of the Consolidated Ute Agency headquarters at Ignacio.

Culhume, Edward, "A History of LaPlata County," Master's Thesis, University of Colorado, 1934. In possession of Western History Department of the Denver Public Library.

Hartman, Alonzo (one of the pioneer employees at the Los Pinos Agency), "Memories and Experiences with the Utes in Colorado," An original manuscript. Reproduced on pages 5-15 in the master's thesis of John B. Lloyd entitled "The Uncompahgre Utes," Western State College, March 24, 1939. Thesis in possession of Western History Department of the Denver Public Library.

Letter by F. S. Dodge, Captain Ninth Cavalry, Commanding Officer of Company D at Fort Union, New Mexico, to Assistant Adjutant General, Fort Leavenworth, Missouri, concerning his attempted rescue of Major Thornburg's ambushed troops. Letter reproduced in Rio Blanco County Interviews, unpublished work of C.W.A. workers for the State Historical Society, 1933-1934, pp. 60-67.

Letters by E. O. Fuller (member of the Indian Department), Laramie, Wyoming, to Mrs. Agnes Wright Spring of the State Historical Society, February, 1951. Letter in possession of Wilson Rockwell.

Spiva, Elizabeth Agnes, "The Utes in Colorado (1863-1880)," Master's Thesis, Western State College, 1929. Thesis in possession of the Western History Department of the Denver Public Library.

V PERIODICALS AND NEWSPAPERS

Ayers, Mary C., "Howardsville in the San Juan," *The Colorado Magazine,* October, 1951.

Borland, Lois, "Sale of the San Juan," *The Colorado Magazine,* April, 1951.

Byers, Frank S., "The Utes," *Rocky Mountain News,* June 26, 1923.

Byers, William N., "History of the Ute Nation," *Rocky Mountain News,* April 16, 1880. See J. S. Randall Scrap Book, p. 13 for reproduction of article. Randall Scrap Book in possession of the State Historical Society of Colorado.

Colorado Magazine, Volume 18-19, 1941 (Place Names).

"Chipeta Marries Again," *The Denver Republican,* April 1, 1883, p. 8.

Covington, James Warren, "Federal Relations with the Colorado Utes," *The Colorado Magazine,* October, 1951.

Craig Courier, November 14, 1891; September 23, 1892; November 4, 1892; October 27, 1893; December 1, 1893; October 5, 1894 October 12, 1895; October 19, 1895; November 16, 1895; June 6, 1896; December 5, 1896; November 6, 1897; December 4, 1897. (These articles show development of trouble between Ute hunters and the white settlers of northwestern Colorado leading up to and including the Ute War of 1897).

Curry, Reginald O., *Thre Year Report* (Aug. 21, 1951 to Aug. 21, 1954) to Commissioner of Indian Affairs.

Dawson, Thomas F., "Major Thompson, Chief Ouray, and the Utes," *The Colorado Magazine*, May, 1930.

Dawson, Thomas F. and Skiff, F. J. V., "The Ute War: A History of the White River Massacre and the Privations of the Captive White Women among the Hostiles on Grand River," *Denver Tribune*, 1879.

"Death of Chief Ouray," *La Plata Miner*, September 4, 1880. Article in possession of the Western History Department of the Denver Public Library.

Dillon, Mrs. A. W., "Early History of Montezuma County," *Dolores Star*, September 4, 1908.

"Early History of the Utes to be Portrayed by Indians in Pageant of Progress," *Rocky Mountain News*, June 26, 1923.

Farley, Frank, "Meeker Massacre," *Rocky Mountain News*, July 7, 1929.

Goulding, James, "Reminiscences of an Old Timer on Ute War of 1887," *Meeker Herald*, February 15, 1934.

Hafen, Ann Woodbury, "Efforts to Recover the Stolen Son of Chief Ouray," *The Colorado Magazine*, March, 1939.

Hagie, C. E. (Former Professor of History at Western State College), "Gunnison in the Early Days," *The Colorado Magazine*, July, 1931.

Meeker Herald, October 15, 1887. (Ute War of 1887).

Middle Park Times, June 20, 1940. (The killing of Tabernash).

Merritt, General Wesley, "Three Indian Campaigns," *Harpers New Monthly Magazine*, 1889. (Article reproduced in Rio Blanco County Interviews, C.W.A. Workers, 1933-34, pp. 67-70. In possession of the State Historical Society).

"Monument to Four Ute Chiefs is Dedicated," *The Durango Herald Democrat*, September 25, 1939.

Moody, Marshall D. (Supervisor of Indian Records, National Archives, Washington), "The Meeker Massacre," *The Colorado Magazine*, April, 1953.

Mumey, Nolie, "John Williams Gunnison," *The Colorado Magazine*, January, 1954.

Reagan, Albert and Stark, Wallace, "Chipeta, Queen of the Utes and Her Equally Illustrious Husband, Noted Chief Ouray," *Utah Historical Quarterly*, July, 1933.

Stacher, S. F., "Ouray and the Utes," *The Colorado Magazine,* April, 1950.

"Twenty Years After," *Meeker Herald,* May 16, 1908.

Wiegel, Mrs. C. W., "The Reburial of Chief Ouray," *The Colorado Magazine,* October, 1928.

INDEX

CPSIA information can be obtained
at www.ICGtesting.com
Printed in the USA
FSOW01n2004080316
17818FS